The Cheating of America

Charles Lewis, Bill Allison,

and the Center for Public Integrity

WILLIAM MORROW / 75 YEARS OF PUBLISHING
An Imprint of HarperCollins*Publishers*

The Cheating of America

How Tax Avoidance and Evasion
by the Super Rich Are
Costing the Country Billions—and
What You Can Do About It

HarperCollins books may be purchased for educational, business, or sales promotional use. For information please write: Special Markets Department, HarperCollins Publishers Inc., 10 East 53rd Street, New York, NY 10022.

FIRST EDITION

Designed by Kate Nichols

Printed on acid-free paper

Library of Congress Cataloging-in-Publication Data
Lewis, Charles, 1953–
The cheating of America : how tax avoidance and evasion by the super rich
are costing the country billions, and what you can do about it / Charles Lewis,
Bill Allison and the Center for Public Integrity
p.   cm.
Includes bibliographical references and index.
ISBN 0-380-97682-X
1. Tax evasion—United States.   I. Allison, Bill.   II. Center for Public
Integrity.   III. Title.
HV6344.U6 L48   2001
336.2'06'0973—dc21   00-066206

01   02   03   04   05   WB/RRD   10   9   8   7   6   5   4   3   2

For my mother, Dorothy Cherry Lewis

—C.L.

For Dzeilana and Ismail

—B.A.

Where there is an income tax, the just man will pay more and the unjust less on the same income.

—PLATO

Anybody has a right to evade taxes if he can get away with it. No citizen has a moral obligation to assist in maintaining the government. If Congress insists on making stupid mistakes and passing foolish tax laws, millionaires should not be condemned if they take advantage of them.

—J. PIERPONT MORGAN

Contents

The Investigative Team

EXECUTIVE DIRECTOR
Charles Lewis

MANAGING DIRECTOR
Peter Eisner

PROJECT MANAGER
Bill Allison

SENIOR EDITORS
Alan Green
Bill Hogan

WRITERS
Erin Bartels
Paul Cuadros

Melanie Strong
Derrick Wetherell

RESEARCH EDITOR

Peter Newbatt Smith

RESEARCHERS

Neil Gordon
Adrianne Hari
Arfa Mahmoud
Myra Marcaurelle
Ann Parker
Daniel Suleiman
Vicki Velasquez
Amy Zader

THE CENTER FOR PUBLIC INTEGRITY

Mary Harrill
Hima Jain
Regina Russell

Preface

 On July 11, 1989, at the U.S. District Court in Manhattan, sixty-nine-year-old Leona Helmsley prepared for testimony in her highly publicized tax evasion trial. Helmsley and her eighty-year-old billionaire husband, Harry, who had been ruled medically unfit to stand trial for this much-anticipated courtroom drama, had for years presided over a real estate empire whose dozens of properties included the likes of the Helmsley Palace, a posh hotel advertised with a particularly memorable image: the bejeweled, impeccably coiffed Leona touting her establishment as "the only palace in the world where the queen stands guard." Now, in a much-ballyhooed turn of events, this self-proclaimed member of New York's ruling class was charged with forty-seven counts of tax evasion, extortion, mail fraud, and conspiracy. To the delight of many, who viewed Leona Helmsley as a tragically befitting metaphor of the "greed is good" 1980s, the real estate magnate had become vilified as a symbol of vicious avarice. In opening arguments, in fact, her own attorney had described her as a "tough bitch."

On this Tuesday in July, on the fourth day of testimony in a trial that would conclude at summer's end, the head housekeeper of Dunnellen Hall, the Helmsleys' twenty-eight-room, $11 million mansion in Greenwich, Connecticut, took the stand. And in one memorable exchange, Elizabeth Baum testified about a conversation with her former boss, Leona Helmsley, that would take its rightful place in the annals of New York legend. "I said, 'You must pay lots of taxes,'" Baum recalled. "She turned to me and said, 'We don't pay taxes; only the little people pay taxes.'"

In the end, the not-so-diminutive Helmsley was convicted of thirty-three counts of tax evasion. Her indiscretion: not paying the federal government more than $1.2 million by billing personal expenses for the couple's Greenwich mansion—including a $130,000 indoor-outdoor sound system and a $1.1 million swimming pool enclosure—to their company. U.S. District Judge John M. Walker Jr. sentenced Helmsley to four years in prison and fined her $7.1 million. "Your conduct was a product of naked greed," he told Helmsley, who broke down in tears before a packed courtroom. "You believed you were above the law and displayed no remorse or contrition. . . . No person—no matter how wealthy and prominent—stands above the law."

That indelible moment in December 1989 was a triumph for the concept of equal justice under the law, as Leona Helmsley got her very public comeuppance. But naked greed, of course, is still in quite abundant supply, even as those decadent eighties recede from memory. Indeed, there is a sizable cadre of Leona Helmsleys among us today who do not pay their taxes, although their ranks are populated with those who, unlike the felonious hotel queen, are not criminally or civilly prosecuted and who never become public figures. In our continuing national obsession with money and materialism, epitomized by bestselling books and hysterically popular TV game shows offering the allure of instant wealth, we overlook a salient, less glamorous reality: the millionaire next door might be a tax cheat.

A few years after the Helmsley trial, America got another garish glimpse of naked greed. But this time it was all entirely legal, as a rash of very wealthy Americans, motivated by a desire to sidestep the tax collector, simply abandoned their homeland in favor of foreign citizenship. Dubbed "Benedict Arnold billionaires" by the news media, the group of wealthy expatriates, whose fraternity includes heirs to such American corporate icons as Campbell Soup Company and Star-Kist Foods, Inc., skipped out with their wealth intact and their interests protected in absentia: their payroll has included a former member of Congress, who lobbied on their behalf in Washington. These well-heeled expatriates may relish their adopted tax-free surroundings, but they nonetheless tried to ensure that no one tinkered with their ability to revisit their birthplace—and to continue to profit from its unparalleled economy.

Increasingly, American companies have been playing the same game. But in their version of outwit-the-tax-collector, the strategies include relocating to Liberia, Bermuda, or any other offshore haven that won't subject them to those dreaded corporate income taxes. And for those companies wanting to maintain their desirable U.S. address, tax shelters and shams—some legal, some not—have provided the means of holding on to billions of dollars that otherwise would have been paid out in taxes.

For more than a decade, the Center for Public Integrity has conducted investigations into public service and ethics-related issues, most notably matters related to abuses of campaign finance laws. What we examine in *The Cheating of America*—the phenomenon of tax avoidance (that's legal), tax evasion (that's illegal), and tax "avoision" (catch us if you can)—also constitutes a significant distortion of our democracy. After all, if the most powerful economic interests can substantially dictate national public policy decisions such as tax rates, and also occasionally choose not to pay their fair share of taxes, then we may no longer have a government of the people, by the people, and for the people. We may have crossed the line between a democracy and a plutocracy.

And all this hasn't been lost on the American people, who are understandably suspicious and disgruntled about the fairness of their taxes. To their credit, however, most citizens are nonetheless reconciled to the words of Oliver Wendell Holmes Jr., the former justice of the Supreme Court of the United States, engraved in stone atop the entrance to the Internal Revenue Service headquarters in Washington: "Taxes are what we pay for civilized society."

Of course, in light of the Leona Helmsley spectacle, expatriate billionaires, proliferating corporate tax shelters, and an escalating mélange of abuses that threaten the very foundation of our voluntary tax system, it appears that the bill for civilization as we know it may one day be more than the "little people" can afford—or care—to pay.

Introduction

Moved by nostalgia for television of the 1980s, several hundred thousand people flock to the Southfork Ranch each year. About twenty miles northeast of downtown Dallas, Texas, the 220-acre ranch is the home of the famed series *Dallas,* which ran for twelve years and was once the world's most popular prime-time serial. With reruns of the series shown in ninety-six countries and translated into forty-three languages and dialects, the ranch truly has a worldwide pull.

Although indoor scenes were shot on California sound stages, the four-columned, two-story mansion is the highlight of the tour. Its twelve rooms have been decorated to reflect the show's characters, from Lucy's Yellow Rose of Texas–themed bedroom to the luxurious Jock Ewing living room to the elegant dining room reminiscent of the scenes of many a dysfunctional family dinner. With special permission—and about $3,500—a family or small group can spend the night in the mansion. The Dallas Cowboys cheerleaders enjoy this privilege—and the accompanying Texas-sized dinner and breakfast—at their yearly slumber party.

At Southfork's visitors center, guests dine on barbecued beef sandwiches and tortilla soup at Miss Ellie's Deli. They trace the Ewing family tree in the Dallas Legends: Fact to Fantasy exhibit, which houses five galleries of *Dallas* paraphernalia, including Lucy's Victorian-style wedding dress, J.R.'s white Stetson, and the pearl-handled Colt revolver used to shoot the villainous oil baron in the season-ending cliffhanger of 1980. In the middle of the Western gift shop, which peddles cowboy hats, fine jewelry, and expensive clothing, is Jock Ewing's 1978 Lincoln Continental.

The ranch also has a 63,000-square-foot event and conference center that holds various-sized ballrooms and an atrium with Victorian lampposts and Texas-shaped floor tiles. Southfork hosts 1,300 events annually and can accommodate such varied functions as political rallies, private rodeos, and wedding receptions. And recently, the ranch's owners discussed adding a 150- to 200-room resort hotel.

Southfork is one of twenty-three domestic properties owned by Forever Resorts. The Phoenix, Arizona–based company's list of holdings includes, among others, Signal Mountain Lodge at Grand Teton National Park and luxury houseboat rental operations on Lake Meade and Lake of the Ozarks.

Forever Resorts is owned by Rex Maughan, a onetime real estate entrepreneur. Having held several conferences at Southfork and having witnessed the continued enchantment with *Dallas* around the world, Maughan jumped at the opportunity to add the fabled ranch to his Forever Resorts holdings, shelling out $2.6 million for it at a 1992 auction. In addition to his other resort properties, Maughan owns a series of cattle ranches in Arizona and a ten-acre estate, complete with a 16,700-square-foot home, in Paradise Valley.

But Rex Maughan didn't make his fortune in real estate or resorts. Instead, this son of an Idaho cattle rancher hit it big by selling, of all things, aloe vera. His company, Forever Living Products International, is a multilevel marketing operation whose bestselling product is a drinkable aloe gel that looks like pineapple juice and, to hear some tell it, tastes like turpentine. Because of its specially patented stabilization process, the company claims, the gel retains its nutrients and active ingredients. High in vitamins, minerals, and amino acids, it has been touted as a treatment for everything from arthritis to ulcers. However, after being reprimanded by the Texas attorney general's office in 1992 for advertised claims that aloe gel could control diabetes, the company has taken its miracle-treatment spiels down a notch.

Forever Living Products' line of aloe goods also includes soap, tooth gel, shampoo, laundry detergent, and cosmetics. Although less popular than its aloe merchandise, the company also pushes about fifty bee products, from honey to bee pollen tablets. While the tablets are said to provide stamina and energy, doctors say that they're dangerous, even deadly, to those allergic to them.

Despite concerns and doubts about his products' actual health benefits, Maughan's business has made him a very wealthy man. In 1998, Forever Living Products had sales of over $1 billion, thanks to more than 5.5 million distributors in sixty-five countries. Maughan not only owns the distribution company, Forever Living Products, but also the production company, Aloe Vera of America, and even the aloe vera plantations from which the gel is harvested in Texas, Mexico, and the Dominican Republic. In 1997 and 1998, he was included as a member of the *Forbes* 400, a yearly listing of the wealthiest Americans. His estimated net worth in 1998: $525 million.

Maughan claims that his success is due to the fact that he offers his distributors a larger cut of the profits than other multilevel marketing companies and that he rewards them with bonuses for high sales or recruiting salespeople. In a 1995 interview with *Success* magazine, he said, "My father always told me that if I wanted to dance, I had to pay the fiddler."

And dance he has. But apparently, paying the fiddler does not include fulfilling his obligations to the Internal Revenue Service.

When Maughan expands his business to a new country, he establishes a local company there. That company, in turn, kicks back royalties to his U.S. company, and then to him, at which time federal taxes should be paid on the income. However, Maughan, who had a fair knowledge of the tax system from his business school years at Arizona

State and subsequent work in accounting, sought to lighten his tax burden on these royalties.

In 1994, the IRS issued a Notice of Deficiency to Maughan and his wife, Ruth, charging that they had understated their income for the years 1987 to 1990 and that they owed in excess of $4.7 million in taxes and penalties. Maughan's company, Selective Art, Inc.—aka Forever Living Products—received a similar notice for tax years 1987 to 1990, claiming the company owed over $4 million in taxes and penalties.

The story begins nearly a decade earlier, in 1985, when Forever Living Products sold global distributorship rights (excluding Canada, the United States, and Europe) to a nonresident United Kingdom company for $50,000—a price much lower than the actual value. Five days later, the distributorship rights were transferred to a different nonresident UK company. This company, in turn, licensed the rights to a Netherlands corporation called Batrax Rotterdam B.V. These transactions affected three of Forever Living Products' entities: Forever Living Products Japan, Forever Living Products Asia (Hong Kong), and Forever Living Products Australia PTY Limited.

Since Batrax held the distributorship rights, it received royalty payments from the Japan, Hong Kong, and Australia companies when their sales rose. However, instead of keeping the royalties, Batrax transferred them to International Marketing Company Limited, London (IMC London), the second nonresident UK corporation to receive Forever Living Products' distributorship rights. From there, the money was in turn sent to Swiss bank accounts under the IMC London name. Eventually, the royalty payments ended up in a pair of discretionary trusts, the Stratton Trust and the Peacon Trust, in the Channel Islands. The beneficiaries of the trusts were listed as charitable or educational entities in the Island of Jersey.

But the trusts made distributions to only one person: Rex Maughan. By directing royalty payments from the three Forever Living Products entities through foreign corporations and into the offshore trusts, Maughan and his company were able to avoid paying U.S. taxes on millions of dollars of income.

In reality, Batrax, International Marketing Company, and the other companies that were purported to hold distributorship rights and royalty payments are nothing more than sham corporations. None has any full-time employees, officers, production facilities, manufacturing expertise, experience in direct or multilevel marketing, or experience with the distribution of aloe vera products. And all but Batrax are owned, directly or indirectly, by a Swiss attorney named Dr. Richard Wengle and controlled by Maughan. Wengle, who was hired by Maughan in 1985 to set up the Batrax transaction, maintains active and inactive corporations, trusts, and other entities to use in his clients' business transactions. All told, Wengle used fourteen such companies—"shelf" corporations, as they're known—to set up the funneling of Forever Living Products' royalty payments.

As for the Channel Island trusts, they were also set up by Wengle, and the Swiss attorney was listed as the "protector" of the Peacon Trust. Although he did not hold that position for the Stratton Trust, Wengle nonetheless ensured that Maughan would reap its benefits. The deeds of the trusts were written with the understanding that their protector's requests would be granted, and the designated protector of the Stratton Trust was a man named Rjay Lloyd. Lloyd holds various positions at Forever Living Products, including director, assistant secretary, general counsel, and distributor. And in addition to being an accountant and an attorney specializing in taxation, Lloyd is also Rex Maughan's close childhood friend.

An IRS audit uncovered the tax avoidance scheme that allowed the Maughans and Forever Living Products to continue to reap sizable royalties from their foreign entities tax free. However, as often happens in large tax cases, the parties settled out of court. The Maughans got off paying $840,000 of the $4,736,538 they were assessed in the 1994 Notice of Deficiency—a mere 18 cents on the dollar. Maughan's company, Forever Living Products, fared even better: It paid only $500,000 of the $4,045,002 assessed by the IRS, or 12 cents on the dollar. But these weren't isolated cases. When Selective Art, Inc., received another Notice of Deficiency arising from the same tax avoidance scheme, the company paid $146,550 on a $1,921,891 tax deficiency—or just 8 cents on the dollar.

In fact, many millionaires, like Maughan, are able to avoid paying their fair share of income taxes by funneling their assets through shelf corporations, bogus trusts, and other financial devices which tax attorneys and crafty accountants create and exploit. They are able to engineer their finances so that they owe very little in taxes—sometimes none at all—while nonetheless reaping huge profits.

In 1998, Charles O. Rossotti, the commissioner of the Internal Revenue Service, testified before the Senate Finance Committee that noncompliance with the Internal Revenue Code—tax avoidance and tax evasion—costs each taxpayer more than $1,600 a year. Put simply, because some don't pay what they should, others must make up the difference. Some wealthy individuals and corporations are making the rest of us pay their share of the bill for our civilized society, to paraphrase the Oliver Wendell Holmes Jr. line that the IRS has engraved in stone.

From the beginning, the argument over taxation in the United States has been one over fairness—whether between classes, regions, or industries. From its earliest days as a nation, the United States has struggled with tax avoidance and evasion. Strapped with debts from the Revolutionary War—started in part by the colonists' revolt against unfair British taxes—the first Congress passed excise taxes on luxury items. Tobacco and snuff, refined sugar, carriages, property sold at auctions, various legal documents, and distilled spirits were covered by the tax, passed in 1794. Thus began the Whiskey Rebellion, when poor farmers in western Pennsylvania, who were dependent on selling distilled spirits for their meager incomes, revolted. Not only did they refuse to pay the tax, they also tarred and feathered the sheriffs who tried to collect it. President Washington deployed federal troops to quell the rebellion and enforce the tax.

America's first experience with an income tax came in 1861, when the Union needed extra revenue to fight the Civil War. At the beginning of the conflict, Congress increased tariffs and excise taxes and borrowed money to fund the war effort. But tariffs and excise taxes were consumption-oriented and regressive, and placed an increasingly heavy burden on the wallets of the country's lower-income citizens. The search for a fairer system of raising revenue led Congress to implement the income tax in 1861. Like those in later years, the Civil War income tax was based on the individual's ability to pay, imposing a 3 percent tax on any annual income over $800.

The Internal Revenue Act of 1862 was a more progressive measure that exempted the first $600 in income and imposed a 3 percent rate of taxation on income between $600 and $10,000 and a 5 percent rate on income over $10,000. The tax form of 1863 explained that the $600 exemption was "the amount fixed by law as an estimated computation for the expenses of maintaining a family."

Taxes were withheld from corporations' dividends and government employees' salaries. As the cost of the war grew, the income tax rates were increased, and the number of tax brackets expanded. In praise of the progressiveness of the income tax, Thaddeus Stevens, a Republican representative from Pennsylvania, said, "The food of the poor is untaxed; and no one will be affected by the provisions of this bill whose living depends solely on his manual labor."

After the war, the government's revenue needs decreased dramatically, and most taxes were repealed, including the income tax in 1872. Taxes on liquor and tobacco were the main source of government revenue by 1868 and made up nearly 90 percent of government income from then until 1913, when the income tax became a permanent feature of American life.

On February 25, 1913, four years after it was proposed by Congress, the Sixteenth Amendment to the Constitution was adopted. It states, "The Congress shall have the power to lay and collect taxes on incomes, from whatever source derived, without apportionment among the several States, and without regard to any census or enumeration." Sereno Payne, a Republican representative from New York, introduced the amendment in the House. He was under no illusions about the potential for well-heeled taxpayers to avoid paying the tax. "I believe it is the most easily concealed of any tax that can be laid, the most difficult of enforcement, and the hardest to collect," he said on the House floor in 1909. "[I]t is, in a word, a tax upon the income of honest men and an exemption, to a greater or lesser extent, of the income of rascals."

Congress began exempting the incomes of rascals with the passage of the Tariff Act of October 3, 1913. As predicted by Sereno Payne, over the years, collecting it would prove difficult.

With the entry of the United States into World War I, the tax laws were revised and expanded to generate revenue to fund the military effort. By 1918, there were fifty-five income brackets, a maximum individual tax rate of 77 percent, and a corporate rate of 12 percent. Still, 95 percent of the population paid no income tax.

With the beginning of the Great Depression, individual and corporate incomes—and subsequently income tax revenues—declined sharply. Congress again raised the tax rates and lowered exemptions in order to raise government revenues. By 1932, corporate rates had increased to 13.75 percent. Individual rates doubled. Nevertheless, the richest Americans still found ways to avoid their income taxes.

In 1933, average Americans were shocked to learn that all twenty partners of J. P. Morgan & Company, the giant Wall Street banking firm, had paid no income taxes the previous two years. Newspapers of the day trumpeted the disclosure as tax evasion by the firm's partners, although they had broken no law. They had merely taken advantage of loopholes in the laws to avoid their taxes. J. Pierpont Morgan Jr., the son of the firm's founder and his successor at its helm, later remarked, "Congress should know how to levy taxes, and if it doesn't know how to collect them, then a man is a fool to pay the taxes. If stupid mistakes are made, it is up to Congress to rectify them and not for us taxpayers to do so."

The distinction between avoidance and evasion may have been lost on the public, but Congress understood the difference, and began tinkering with the tax laws to prevent the wealthy from paying nothing to the federal treasury. By 1936, the maximum individual tax rate had jumped to 79 percent. A number of other taxes were implemented as well, including taxes on capital stock and dividend receipts. The Social Security Act of 1935 imposed a wage tax—half paid by employers, half by employees—for a system of federally funded retirement benefits.

The wealthy, meanwhile, were finding new ways to opt out of the New Deal. Alfred P. Sloan Jr., the chief executive officer of General Motors and one of the highest-paid executives in the country, set up a personal holding company called the Rene Corporation. The company owned his 235-foot yacht, the *Rene*. Sloan, whose annual income totaled $2.9 million in 1936, wrote off the costs of maintaining his yacht—about $150,000 a year—to lower his taxes.

Other well-heeled individuals established personal holding companies in offshore locales like the Bahamas and Panama—countries that, unlike the United States, had no personal or corporate income taxes. The offshore companies accumulated tax-free wealth for America's millionaires. After holding hearings on the issue, Congress added foreign personal holding company provisions to the tax laws in 1937. U.S. shareholders had to pay taxes on their share of income that accumulated in Caribbean and Central American corporations. Although these provisions have been revised many times over the years, offshore tax havens continue to do a thriving business sheltering the income of affluent Americans.

All the changes made the tax system ever more complicated. In 1938, President Franklin Delano Roosevelt sent a letter to the commissioner of internal revenue along with his 1937 tax return explaining his problems in determining the amount of tax he owed: "As this is a problem in higher mathematics," he wrote, "may I ask that the Bureau let me know the amount of the balance due?"

Higher math wasn't the only problem. The tax laws had never been gathered together. In 1939, Congress ordered that the tax rules contained in the Statutes at Large be codified, and the first permanent tax code—later renamed the Internal Revenue Code of 1939—was born.

When Pearl Harbor was bombed on December 7, 1941, the country was shaken out of the doldrums of the Depression. The twin threats of Nazi Germany and imperial Japan demanded an all-out effort from the American people. Congress cut exemptions for individual and married filers nearly in half, dramatically expanding the reach of the income tax; the number of taxpayers grew from 4 million to 43 million from 1939 to 1945. In the span of five years, from 1940 to 1944, rates were raised from 4 percent to 19 percent at the bottom tax bracket, while the top bracket increased to 88 percent. Because of the increased tax rates, it was difficult for taxpayers to come up with a lump sum once a year to pay their taxes. Withholding tax from paychecks, first instituted during the Civil War, was reintroduced.

In 1953, the Bureau of Internal Revenue changed its name to the Internal Revenue Service, following an internal reorganization. The tax code was reorganized once again and clarified in the Internal Revenue Code of 1954. And in 1959, the IRS earned the distinction of becoming the world's largest accounting, collection, and forms-processing organization.

With numerous revisions and expansions over time, the tax code has become riddled with special provisions, called tax shelters, that allow the well-heeled to forgo—or at least drastically reduce—their tax obligations. By abusing these tax shelters, tax attorneys have been able to create complex investment schemes that have saved the wealthy thousands, or even millions, of dollars in taxes.

Cutting rates for the wealthy in the Tax Reform Act of 1986, for example, did not reduce their evasion any more than it did in the 1920s. In 1998, IRS Commissioner Rossotti testified to the Senate Finance Committee that taxpayer noncompliance costs the federal government $195 billion a year. The actual figure is probably much higher, since the commissioner's estimate is based on forward projections of survey data gathered in 1988.

Those numbers do not even include the usual games corporations play, such as incorporating offshore. For example, for years the largest, essentially American cruise lines have avoided American taxes simply by incorporating outside the United States. Royal Caribbean, for instance, is incorporated in Liberia; Carnival Cruise Lines is incorporated in Panama. Both companies thus have eluded paying hundreds of millions of dollars in U.S. taxes.

In March 2000, the *New York Times* reported that half a dozen U.S. insurance companies no longer pay income taxes because they moved their corporate headquarters to Bermuda (which has no corporate income tax) or they were acquired by a Bermuda insurer. Treasury officials estimated that if all U.S. property and casualty insurers did this, they could avoid $7 billion in U.S. taxes annually. By moving their headquarters to Bermuda, these insurance companies can place their considerable investment income on the Bermuda books—beyond the reach of the Internal Revenue Service—and keep the unprofitable part of the company on the United States ledgers. According to a 1993 study of 200 U.S. corporations by four economists, "the average multinational firm with subsidiaries in more than five regions uses income shifting to reduce its taxes to 51.6 percent of what they would otherwise be."

Along these lines, federal authorities have noticed a striking divergence between the actual taxable income companies have reported to their shareholders and to the IRS. In 2000, for example, it was estimated that less than 70 percent of profit reported by corporations to shareholders was reported to the IRS as taxable; in 1990, the number was 91 percent. In fact, for 1995, the most recent year for which federal data are available, for the nation's largest corporations with assets of $250 million or more, 1,279 out of 7,537, or 17 percent, reported no net income to the IRS and therefore paid no taxes.

Tax avoidance by corporations has been increasing in other ways: corporate tax shelters. In recent years, well-known companies, including Colgate-Palmolive, Compaq Computer, and United Parcel Service have been involved in schemes that allowed them, collectively, to avoid billions of dollars in taxes via tax shams. According to a Treasury Department analysis, "Corporate tax shelters breed disrespect for the tax system—both by the people who participate in the tax shelter and by others who perceive unfairness. . . . These tax-engineered transactions may cause a 'race to the bottom.' If unabated, this could have long-term consequences to our voluntary tax system far more important than the short-term revenue loss we are experiencing."

Forbes magazine and others have estimated conservatively that corporate tax shelters cost the U.S. Treasury at least $10 billion each year, and that number is increasing significantly. In terms of tax law enforcement, Treasury Secretary Lawrence H. Summers declared in 2000 that, "Corporate tax shelters are our No. 1 problem."

For a number of reasons and in a variety of ways, then, U.S. companies generally are paying *fewer* corporate income taxes today. For example, taxes paid by corporations on profits reported to the IRS dropped from 26 percent to 20 percent between 1990 and 1997. By comparison, in 1997, 15 percent of Americans' income went to the IRS, an increase from 13 percent in 1990.

In other words, the federal tax burden resides more and more with individual citizens. In 1997, corporations spent $60 billion less in income taxes than they would have paid in 1990, at the same rate. Meanwhile, individual taxpayers paid $80 billion more in annual income taxes between 1990 and 1997.

Unlike the nation's corporations and wealthy elite, the "little people" cannot afford to move to the Bahamas or hire expensive accountants and lawyers to hide their money in clever tax shelters and other tax avoidance schemes. This disparity is what two-time Pulitzer Prize–winning investigative reporters Donald Barlett and James Steele have referred to as "the two-tax, two-class society." At the high end, there were 998 families and individuals with incomes of $200,000 or more who paid no income tax in 1995, for an effective tax rate of zero. And 9,188 families and individuals in that income stratosphere who *did* pay their taxes, paid them at an effective tax rate of under 7 percent. Another 17,959 wealthy filers in that income bracket paid less than 12 percent of their income in taxes. Most individuals and families with incomes over $200,000, it is reassuring to note, actually paid their taxes without avoidance jujitsu: there were 1,271,510 taxable returns, reporting $639.4 billion in combined adjusted gross income, paying nearly $182.5 billion in total income tax, for an effective rate of 28.5 percent.

The issue is not whether America's wealthiest citizens generally pay their taxes today. They do. What most intrigues us is the extraordinary extent today of naked greed and betrayal. In *The Cheating of America*, we investigate the people and companies who have benefited most from our society and our way of life and then chosen to thumb their noses at the rest of us, by paying little or no taxes. As mentioned earlier, nothing rubs the American psyche raw more than the specter of the rich ducking taxes at the expense of the poor and middle class.

For example, of those families and individuals with incomes between $30,000 and $40,000, some 2,700,965 filed returns whose effective tax rate was between 12 percent and 15 percent. More than 4.5 million tax returns were filed by the upper income bracket of the working poor—those earning between $15,000 and $20,000—who paid between 7 percent and 10 percent of their incomes in taxes. But some 45,000 returns were filed by individuals making $100,000 or more a year, who paid less than 7 percent of their earnings into the federal treasury.

To add insult to injury, wealthy families and individuals are audited less frequently today than in the past. According to a 1996 General Accounting Office (GAO) report, IRS annual audit rates—although generally higher for higher-income individuals—have "decreased since fiscal year 1988 for the highest-income individuals, while increasing in the past two years for the lowest-income individuals." In fiscal years 1994 and 1995, Americans earning less than $25,000 saw their audit rates double. In the meantime, audit rates dropped to one-fourth of what they had been in fiscal year 1988 for those making more than $100,000.

Those GAO findings were bolstered in 1999, when it was widely reported that the IRS audited 1.36 percent of all income tax returns filed by people earning less than $25,000 a year in 1998, but audited only 1.15 percent of returns filed by taxpayers who made $100,000 or more. Since 1988, audit rates have increased by almost a third for the poor, from 1.03 percent to 1.36 percent, and dropped 90 percent for the most affluent, from 11.4 percent to 1.15 percent of tax returns. According to an exhaustive analysis of IRS audit and enforcement actions by a Syracuse University research organization, the Transactional Records Access Clearinghouse, the audit rate for the largest U.S. corporations also dramatically decreased in 1999. For corporations with more than $250 million in assets, 34.5 percent were audited, down from 54.6 percent in 1992.

Why would the IRS focus so much of its audit and tax enforcement energy on the poorest of this country when many corporations and wealthy individuals are hiding *billions* of dollars from the United States each year? IRS officials—who supplied the massive government data to the Syracuse researchers—attributed the rise in audit rates for the working poor to congressional and White House pressure put on the IRS to closely monitor misuse of the Earned Income Tax Credit program. Begun in the 1970s and designed to help low income families, the program was criticized in 1995 by former Speaker of the House Newt Gingrich and the Republican Congress, who wanted to downsize it. The Clinton administration, meanwhile, responded with calls to increase IRS scrutiny of program fraud and abuse. All of that heat resulted in greater audit scrutiny of those tax returns claiming earned income tax credits—i.e., the poor—which has distorted the overall IRS audit rate picture.

Meanwhile, no one in government seems terribly concerned about the sharp drop in large corporate audits. In fact, the broader, more fascinating question is: What has happened to the IRS? The overall percentage of individual taxpayer and corporation audits has been decreasing for years. Perhaps that is because while the number of IRS staff has stayed the same since 1983, the total number of tax returns has increased by a third. The number of annual IRS property seizures to pay back taxes has fallen to 161 from 10,000 a decade ago. In 1999, there were only 722 tax-related criminal prosecutions in the United States, half the number in 1981.

Given all the evidence of IRS audit and enforcement reticence when it comes to the rich, it is hardly surprising that the American people today are suspicious and disgruntled about the fairness of their taxes. According to the Gallup polling organization, fully two-thirds of the public believes that "upper-income" Americans pay too little in taxes.

It is interesting today that not only do most Americans think the current tax system unfairly favors the rich, they *also* have historically significant distrust of politicians at all levels. In the 1996 and 1998 elections, the United States had the lowest voter turnout in half a century; 100 million Americans do not participate in our democracy.

There is an intriguing overlap between popular resentment over tax unfairness and disgust toward our elected officials who promulgate those tax laws and enable their enforcement. That visceral skepticism is well founded. Many of the wealthiest and most powerful people and corporations in America today not only have high-priced legal and accounting talent at their beck and call, they also are, of course, very well acquainted with Washington. They contribute billions of dollars to the two political parties and the political campaigns of the most important elected officials in our nation's capital. And they retain the best lobbyists money can buy. At the same time, 96 percent of the American people—Leona Helmsley's "little people"—do not contribute to *any* politician or party at the federal level. The maximum allowable contribution to an individual candidate, $1,000, comes from less than 0.1 percent of the American people.

So perhaps it is not surprising that Congress and a succession of presidents over the past few decades have accommodated the wishes of their most ardent financial sponsors. Since the 1970s, Republicans and Democrats have substantially reduced both the top income tax rate and the tax on capital gains. Over the years, Congress has repeatedly cut taxes for corporations and wealthy individuals, and it shows. In 1956, corporate income taxes accounted for 28 percent of all federal tax revenue. Today that number is down to 10 percent. And in the 2000 presidential campaign, the major party candidates—both millionaires themselves, incidentally—did not advocate tougher new laws to make the rich pay their fair share of taxes. George W. Bush and Albert Gore Jr. cumulatively raised nearly $100 million in campaign contributions from America's wealthiest interests in 1999.

At the Center for Public Integrity over the past five years, we have written extensively about how powerful, moneyed interests have been distorting our democracy, in such books as *The Buying of the President, The Buying of the Congress,* and *The Buying of the President 2000.* Now, with *The Cheating of America,* we investigate a different kind of distortion, which also causes enormous distrust and cynicism about the laws, the policies, and the people who govern us. What you are about to read is the result of an exhaustive, unprecedented investigation of U.S. tax records by a dozen researchers, writers, and editors. This book is not a systematic analysis of all the exemptions wealthy individuals and corporations take. Rather, it is a series of case studies, painstakingly assembled over the course of more than two years, that show how some affluent individuals have avoided paying their fair share of federal income tax. A few have done so through illegal means, but the vast majority of them have taken advantage of perfectly legal loopholes in the Internal Revenue Code to shield millions of dollars in income from the taxes that ordinary Americans have to pay.

In the course of preparing this book, we reviewed years of statistical data published by the Internal Revenue Service to determine which deductions and credits are most favored by wealthy individuals and corporations to reduce their tax burdens. We scoured records at the U.S. Tax Court, delving into the minutiae of tax disputes, while never losing sight of the larger story those documents revealed. We interviewed dozens of experts, tax attorneys, law enforcement officials, former IRS insiders, and ordinary Americans. We traveled across the country and to tax havens like the Bahamas and Belize to interview some of the wealthy individuals we've profiled.

Most of these people have broken no criminal law. Many of them are prominent citizens in their local communities, well regarded by their peers. Some have given sizable amounts to charitable endeavors. A few have endowed educational institutions.

What they have not done is pay the price for our civilized society.

All told, we chronicle the activities of dozens of memorable people and companies whose essential characteristics seem to be almost breathtaking chutzpah and attitude. Most of them have confounded the IRS over the years; the dirty little secret of this book actually is the stunning ease by which these tax finaglers can nimbly avoid or wear down federal authorities. To these wealthy individuals and companies, the annual tax bill seems to be more of a recommendation than an actual requirement—something to be worked out over time with the IRS, for pennies on each dollar owed.

The Cheating of America is not intended to be a book about the IRS. Nor is it intended to be a "how-to" manual for would-be tax scam artists. Nor is it intended to be a simplistic screed against wealth and people with money. Most Americans, even most millionaires, pay their taxes.

What interests us are the people and companies who have bene-fited and profited handsomely from the American economy and quality of life, but who have chosen to opt out of the system. At some point, they have decided to abandon their country, or at least minimize their contribution to it. And meanwhile, an entire tax avoidance industry has evolved to encourage it, proselytizing directly to the wealthy that the United States is headed unavoidably for the abyss. One proponent of the "coming apocalypse" is Jerome Schneider, who wrote in *The Complete Guide to Offshore Money Havens*, "You need to accept that the domestic scene is hopeless, and you need to create a financial escape route for yourself and those who depend on you. Stop beating your head against a brick wall. America is crumbling, and you need to get out." He could as well have said, "Leave the remains to the little people."

Finally, beyond the recurring motif of "naked greed" throughout *The Cheating of America*, in the conclusion we suggest some obvious, potential remedies. And we explore some rarely discussed, disturbing issues about the unprecedented mobility of money today, and the logistical havoc that it is wreaking on governments, which must raise revenue from their residents. According to the IRS, today an estimated $3 trillion in assets are held as bank deposits offshore. But beyond the scores of jurisdictions offering competing "offshore services" to wealthy individuals and corporations, the new technologies mean that money today has no real home. We now have virtual banks and virtual brokers, virtual money and virtual securities, all confounding to law enforcement authorities around the world whose work is still structured the old-fashioned way: by crime, by country, and by territorially based laws and regulations. Cyberspace, encryption, and other forces of technology and globalization are ensuring virtual secrecy and rendering the essential, nation-state task of taxation increasingly difficult.

As one futurist treatise ominously predicting nothing less than the end of the modern phase of Western civilization observed, "The state has grown used to treating its taxpayers as a farmer treats his cows, keeping them in a field to be milked. Soon, the cows will have wings."

Some of them, we learned, already do.

1

No More Than a Living

Jane Morgan is the kind of person upon whom the voluntary tax system depends. Conscientious, organized, and honest to a fault, Morgan faithfully filled out her income tax returns year after year, declaring her earnings, her deductions, and how much she owed in taxes. Like many other middle income taxpayers the Center contacted who had run-ins with the Internal Revenue Service, she was reluctant to speak on the record; her name has been changed to protect her privacy.

A self-employed consultant, Morgan has had contracts with universities and the federal government. To supplement her consulting income, she's worked as a substitute teacher in her local public school system. Like many who are determined to be their own bosses, she's never gotten rich from her efforts, but she has made a living selling her expertise to a wide variety of clients. Unlike an employee of a company who expects a weekly or biweekly paycheck, Morgan's compensation comes at irregular intervals. When she's paid for a long-term project, times are good. During other months, however, she's sometimes forced to dip into assets to pay her bills.

In 1996, while preparing her 1995 return, she was confused by the instructions explaining the penalties for early withdrawals from an Individual Retirement Account. On page 16 of the instruction book the Internal Revenue Service mailed to taxpayers, she read the following passage: "Caution: You may have to pay an additional tax if (1) you received an early distribution from your IRA and the total distribution was not rolled over or (2) you received a distribution in excess of $150,000 or (3) you were born before July 1st, 1924, and received less than the minimum required distribution. See instructions for line 51 for details."

Morgan, who was in her early fifties at the time, had in fact taken a distribution from her IRA in 1995. "I knew I was supposed to declare it on my income tax that year and I did not know how I was supposed to file it," she said. "And so I called the IRS. I do my own taxes."

Morgan wasn't alone. Every year in the months leading up to April 15, IRS employees answer phones to help taxpayers decipher the complicated jargon in the Service's instruction booklets and the myriad forms that accompany them.

In 1999, Form 1040, the basic tax return, had twenty separate lines for reporting income, eleven lines for reporting deductions, one line for reporting personal exemptions, nine lines for reporting tax credits, seven lines for reporting taxes owed, and five lines for reporting payments. There were another ten schedules, used to report business income, self-employment taxes, itemized deductions, capital gains, rental income, and farm income. The seventy-two-page instruction booklet that accompanied each tax return estimated that the total time needed to do just Form 1040 was nearly thirteen hours. The unlucky taxpayer who had to fill out every schedule (assuming such a taxpayer existed) would have required, on average, fifty-six hours and six minutes to complete all the paperwork. In addition to the schedules, there were sixteen more forms specifically referred to by the 1040, used to report moving expenses, to claim the child tax credit and the adoption tax credit, to declare foreign taxes paid, and to report "other gains or losses" not covered by the other forms.

Every taxpayer, no matter what his net worth or employment status, is required to accurately report all of his income on those forms. When the IRS or the Treasury Department describes the system as voluntary, this is what they mean: taxpayers voluntarily report all their income to the government. Of course, matters don't end there. The typical W-2 Form, which reports an employee's wage or salary income to the IRS, contains some variation of the following phrase: "This information is being furnished to the Internal Revenue Service." Form 1099, used to report interest on a savings account, dividend income, or payments made to an independent contractor, carries a similar warning. Each year, the IRS receives copies of roughly 1 billion documents, which it matches electronically, using the Social Security number on each form, to the more than 100 million tax returns submitted by individual and joint filers. The Service checks up on virtually everyone through what it calls the information returns program. If a filer of a Form 1040EZ tries to understate his income as detailed on his W-2, for example, the IRS will catch the understatement. If a filer of a 1040A omits his dividend income, the IRS receives word of it from his broker. If a filer of a regular 1040 doesn't report her interest income, the IRS is tipped off to that omission by her bank.

Even if one merely makes an honest mistake—anything from a math error that inadvertently understates income to forgetting to report the interest on a checking account—the IRS, if it catches the error, will charge the extra taxes plus interest. There may even be a penalty assessed, depending on the nature of the mistake and whether the Service believes there was an intent to pay less than what was owed.

Morgan ran into trouble with lines 15(a) and 15(b) on her 1040, on which taxpayers are supposed to declare any IRA distributions—that is, money they've received from their retirement accounts, along with any penalties (additional taxes for either withdrawing money before reaching age fifty-nine or for not withdrawing enough after turning seventy). "When it came to that portion I did not know how to do it," she said. "And I called the IRS and that's where the problem started."

About two years later, on January 17, 1998, Morgan received a letter from the IRS: $1,234 was owed to the government, it said, for taxes due in 1995. A perplexed Morgan had no idea what the bill was for, but two days later she found out the source of her troubles: the IRS had given her incorrect instructions when she called the agency in 1996 for help.

That year, instead of getting a refund of $329, she should have actually paid an additional $721—an error that Morgan attributed to the bum advice doled out by an IRS employee. Over the next fourteen months, she struggled to resolve the matter with a host of IRS officials. "Please know that I am not trying not to pay the amount I owe, however, I did make the effort to find out what I was supposed to do," she wrote to an IRS manager on January 21, 1998. "If the IRS had provided all the information for filing my return in 1995 as I requested, I would have owed $721, which is the fair amount I would have paid in 1995. Instead, two years later, I am informed that I must pay $1,234 and if I don't meet the allotted time requirements, I will be charged additional interest."

She made every effort to resolve her tax problem, and kept detailed logs of her futile attempts. A sampling shows the maddening lack of progress she made in her case:

January 26: Took day off, no work, waited all day for a call from [an IRS agent], she never called.

January 31: Saturday, IRS Problem Solving Day (found out about this day when I called [her congressman's] office and immediately made arrangements to attend. The IRS did not tell me about it). The session with the IRS representative was non-productive. He did not have any knowledge or experience with my type of audit. He left me twice during our discussion and both times said he was going to ask his bosses for clarification and direction. . . . Both times he returned and said his bosses/managers did not know anything either. . . . [He] admitted . . . that I had been given "bum" information by the IRS in 1995. He also said that I had been given a run around by the IRS representatives I have previously contacted.

February 5: Todd [an IRS problem resolution officer] . . . called. The discussion was unproductive. He listened and his response to my concerns were: I should fill out Form 843 because the Letter of Compromise [an offer a taxpayer can make to settle for less than the IRS wants] is intended for large sums of tax owed to the government. . . . Todd has already made up his mind even before he has read anything about my situation. He said the IRS would take whatever assets I have. Todd also asked if I filled out my 1997 return and if I was getting a refund, because if I was the IRS would take that.

February 13: I waited all week for Todd's letter. To date, I have not received it.

Morgan didn't hear back from the IRS until July. In the meantime, she wrote letters to her representative in Congress; her two senators; President Bill Clinton and Vice President Al Gore; and Charles Rossotti, the commissioner of the Internal Revenue Service. Her representatives in Congress referred her to various IRS officials in her state. Gore's office responded with the advice that Morgan, for whom the $1,234 tax bill coming out of the blue was a hardship, should hire a tax attorney and settle the affair through legal means. "Without funds," she wrote in her log of contacts with the government, "how do I obtain 'legal means'? What a joke."

On July 6, 1998, one of the IRS agents instructed Morgan in a phone conversation to send a petition to the U.S. Tax Court. "Not exactly sure what Tax Court is," she wrote in her log. "Guess it's my only option. Why didn't he tell me about it before?"

Congress created the U.S. Tax Court in 1924 to give individuals a judicial forum for disputes with the IRS. The president appoints the court's nineteen judges, who hear cases in Washington, D.C., or in federal buildings in locations more convenient to taxpayers. The vast majority of cases filed with the court never go to trial, but are settled through a negotiation process between the taxpayer (the petitioner) and the IRS (the respondent). The burden of proof rests on the tax-payer. Even when a case does go to trial, an effort is made to resolve most of the issues prior to the testimony. The judge will then decide any remaining issues and issue findings of fact, an opinion, and a decision stating either the amount owed by the taxpayer, if any, or his over-payment.

On July 14, Morgan sent a petition to Tax Court. She wrote that she wanted to resolve her tax situation, but added, "I do feel the IRS is also responsible for the current situation. In January of 1995 I called the IRS information line and requested a line-by-line explanation of the 1995 1040 forms and instruction publication, page 16, lines 15(a) and 15(b), IRA distribution. I followed the direction given to me by the IRS. I entered the amount of the IRA withdrawals on lines 15(a) and 15(b). When I asked about the caution note, I was told 'it did not apply to me.' I have been told that since I do not have anything in writing and thus can not prove what an IRS representative told me in 1995 about my IRA distribution amount, that the IRS is not responsible."

On September 23, Morgan received an answer to her petition. It was written by an attorney in the Office of the District Counsel, one of the legal arms of the IRS. "Didn't understand it," Morgan wrote. "Called and received an explanation. Was told my case went to IRS Appeals Department before it goes to Tax Court. Must call appeals office. Now what?"

Once again, Morgan tried to resolve her tax troubles amicably. She met with yet another IRS official, the appeals officer assigned to her case—a meeting Morgan described as "useless." "Meeting was to set-tle and resolve my situation without going to trial," Morgan wrote in her log. "She was not prepared, had no paper work or information about me."

After the appeals process went nowhere, Morgan prepared to go to trial. She called the IRS attorney who had written the Service's answer to her petition, to discuss the case. Morgan's log from December 23 notes that the attorney suggested a Letter of Compromise. "When I told her I had tried that and was refused, she didn't understand. I told her about all the people I had contact with. She said she had not heard of any of them, that she knew them all and did not recognize any of the names. . . . She's an attorney and doesn't know all that is involved. But I am supposed to." The IRS attorney also said she would draw up a stipulation of facts—an agreement between the two parties in a Tax Court case on what is not in dispute. The stipulations allow Tax Court judges to focus on narrow issues of the tax law, alleviating the necessity of having to establish all the facts of a case during trial.

On February 3, 1999, Morgan received a pretrial memorandum, laying out the issues and arguments that the Service's attorney would make against her in Tax Court. "Didn't even bother to read it, especially when I saw it was full of different cited cases," Morgan wrote. "I don't have money to hire an attorney who can find cases or make legal points for me. Where are my rights?"

On February 17, 1999, more than three years after she called the IRS for help preparing her tax return, Morgan finally wound up before a special trial judge of the U.S. Tax Court. The IRS sent an attorney, the same one who had written the Service's answer to Morgan's petition, to represent its interests. Morgan represented herself.

"The reason I'm here today," the consultant said in her opening statement, "is I'm not sure how I got here. I got here because I kept saying I disagree with . . . whoever I talked to and they said, 'Well, these are your options,' and I kept taking options and the next thing I know I'm here in court because I marked a little box on a piece of paper which gave me the right to be here."

Her adversary's opening statement was markedly different: "At issue in this case is whether the ten percent premature pension distribution penalty under IRC 72(t) [Internal Revenue Code section 72(t)] applies to the distribution paid to petitioner in 1995 from her individual retirement account."

Jane Morgan was the only witness called, and during testimony she explained how she had tried to settle the matter with the IRS. "It's very frustrating when you talk to people and you get different things being told to you and they don't agree," she said. "If you ask questions, they don't know what to tell you. If you ask for advice, they don't know what to tell you. And that's why I said I don't know how I ended up here in Tax Court. I have been trying to get this resolved.

"I feel that they gave me the wrong information. I at no time was trying to withhold money from the government or not pay my taxes. I did what the guy said to do. Two years later I find out it's not what I was supposed to do. . . .

"They don't know what they're doing. . . . God forbid you talk to somebody from a different department. 'No, that's collections, I don't have anything to do with collections. You've got to talk to collections.' I talk to collections. 'I'm not on that case anymore.' Oh, who is? 'Well, we don't know.' "

Morgan's frustrations were only compounded as the case dragged on: during the entire time she was trying to resolve the situation with the IRS, the size of her debt to the government kept growing. "What's scary is they tell me that the interest is just going to accumulate and it's like, well, I'm going to go to my grave owing the IRS money."

The judge questioned Morgan, then dashed her hopes of getting satisfaction. "To tell you the truth," he said, "you have a very slim chance of prevailing in the Tax Court. I'm going to go back to Washington. I'm going to look this case over. . . . If the Government wins, you will owe the tax."

On March 8, 1999, Morgan wrote a letter to the judge, in which, among other things, she apologized for "taking up the court's time." But, she added, "I do feel that what I have been put through this year has added needless stress to my life. It could have been handled efficiently and effectively, but it was not. I am being penalized because a government IRS representative gave me inaccurate information."

She added a final sentiment: "Though I know this would not hold up in court, the American writer Henry David Thoreau argued, 'people have a duty to disobey laws they consider unjust,' but it is how I feel."

In the end, the IRS prevailed. "[P]etitioner contends that the application of section 72(t) in this case is inequitable because she made a good faith effort to correctly file her 1995 Federal income tax and relied on IRS advice. This Court has previously held that the authoritative sources of Federal tax law are statutes, regulations, and judicial case law and not informal IRS sources," the judge's opinion read. "Though it is unfortunate that petitioner may have received unhelpful or incorrect tax advice from IRS employees, that advice does not have the force of law."

Morgan was ordered to pay the entire amount owed, including interest. She came away from her Tax Court experience poorer, but wiser. "The IRS needs to improve in how it does its job," she told the Center. "But the IRS is not responsible for the tax laws and other policies that are decided and voted in by the Congress. It is the judicial, legislative, and executive branches who decide how Americans will live their lives."

And one of the most important ways they decide how Americans live their lives is through the promulgation and enforcement of the Internal Revenue Code, a behemoth of rules, regulations, and fine print that even the IRS has conceded is far too complex for most taxpayers to understand.

The Sixteenth Amendment to the Constitution, which authorizes Congress to levy and collect a tax on incomes from whatever source derived, contains just thirty words. The original income tax law was eighteen pages long. Today, the Internal Revenue Code, the law of the land, stretches to well over 17,000 pages in some editions. The IRS refuses to say how long the tax code is. "It's a meaningless question," Steve Pyrek, a public affairs officer for the Service, told the Center in an interview. "There's no definitive version."

After passing the first tax law in 1913, Congress changed it seventy-five times in eighty years, or once every thirteen months. After the House and Senate pass new tax legislation, and the president signs it into law, the Treasury Department and the IRS write regulations implementing the changes. There are permanent and temporary Treasury regulations; there are private letter rulings that the IRS sends to tax-payers requesting guidance on particular tax problems; there are court decisions and revenue rulings. There is a vast library of complicated rules to decipher, and it has come to pervade just about every aspect of the economic life of the United States.

In the 1930s, for example, in addition to raising revenue, New Deal economists recognized that the tax code could be used to control inflation and limit consumption by draining purchasing power out of the economy. People who paid more in taxes had less money to spend on goods and services. In the 1940s, during World War II, Congress worried that the demands of labor unions for higher wages would lead to inflation. They made fringe benefits like health insurance tax deductible for employers, which gave employers an incentive to offer benefits in lieu of wages to their unions. Some fifty-six years after the need to control inflation in a wartime economy has gone away, health insurance is still a tax-deductible benefit that employers provide to employees (at least, when they wish to).

In the 1950s, when the majority of married women didn't work, the tax code benefited them and taxed single individuals at a higher rate; in the 1960s, Congress revised the code to make it fairer to unmarried individuals, which has led to today's marriage penalties paid by couples in which both spouses work. At various times, Congress has given preferential treatment to oil and gas producers, to real estate investors, to middle-class workers saving for their retirement, and to retirees. At other times, it has taken away those preferences.

In 1981, Congress passed the Economic Recovery Tax Act, an overhaul of the nation's tax laws. Among the bill's provisions was one that broadened the eligibility of workers to establish IRAs. William Frenzel, a Republican representative from Minnesota, explained the changes in 1981. "Under current law, many employees are barred from making contributions to an individual retirement account because they are active participants in an employer-sponsored pension plan, even though the benefits that they eventually will receive from the plan are very small, or they are not vested in the plan at all. Therefore, these individuals are denied the opportunity to prepare adequately for their retirement by receiving a tax deduction for their contributions to a retirement savings plan."

Five years after the IRA deduction became part of the tax law, a new massive overhaul of the nation's tax laws, the Tax Reform Act of 1986, was passed. Senator Bill Bradley, a Democrat from New Jersey, explained the principle behind that bill. "The choice of tax reform is that you get lower rates in exchange for giving up certain credit exclusions or deductions," he said. "You give up those loopholes which only some people use, so that the tax rates on everyone can be lowered dramatically." Among the loopholes Bradley proposed giving up was the IRA deduction, passed in 1981 to allow workers to prepare adequately for their retirement.

Congress isn't the only legislative body with the authority to levy taxes. State and local governments also have their own revenue codes, and they enthusiastically tax income, assets, and sales of merchandise. More than 268 million Americans pay taxes on everything from candy bars to capital gains, from airline tickets to income, all of which adds up to a staggering amount of money.

In 1997, for example, the total tax burden amounted to some $2.6 trillion. To put that in perspective, the gross domestic product that year—the total economic output of the United States—was $8.1 trillion. Of every dollar earned, governments seized 32 cents in taxes. The federal government took in the lion's share, some $1.6 trillion. More than half of that—some $825 billion—came from individual income taxes. Employment taxes, which pay for programs like Social Security and Medicare, accounted for about a third. The corporate share was $204 billion—a little more than one-eighth of federal revenues.

That year, according to the Internal Revenue Service, the federal per capita tax burden was $6,045. That figure doesn't include the $869 billion that state and local governments raised from taxes and fees (like those for a driver's license or building permit); tack those on, and the per capita tax burden climbed another $3,244, to nearly $9,300. That's $9,300 in taxes for every man, woman, and child in the United States, a far cry from what Americans once paid. Just twenty years earlier, the combined federal, state, and local per capita tax burden was $2,635, or $6,979 adjusting for inflation.

The per capita figures, of course, can be misleading. How much tax an individual owes depends in large measure on his income, where he lives, whether he's married and has dependent children, even what his habits and preferences are. Internal Revenue Service publications caution that there is no such thing as an "average taxpayer," and given the wide range of individual circumstances, that's not an unreasonable assertion to make. Residents of Alaska, Florida, Nevada, South Dakota, Texas, Washington, and Wyoming pay no state income tax; workers in Philadelphia pay both a city and a state tax on their wages. Someone who lives in the City of Brotherly Love and relies on the local mass transit system will never pay the state and federal gasoline tax; indeed, because the Southeastern Pennsylvania Transportation Authority—or SEPTA, as it is known—receives part of its budget from local, state, and federal subsidies, her subway trips are partially paid for by other taxpayers. Someone who's too terrified to board a plane won't have to pay the 10 percent federal surcharge on airline tickets, but he might have to pay the $3 tax to cruise on a passenger ship. An individual whose sole source of income is dividends from stocks will pay no taxes to the Social Security and Medicare trust funds, whereas someone who receives all his money from a paycheck surrenders up to 7.65 percent of his income for those social insurance taxes. And a self-employed individual like Jane Morgan had to pay 15.3 percent of her income—both her share and the employer's share of the tax.

Each taxpayer's circumstances are unique, and the Internal Revenue Code is an attempt to fairly levy taxes on each of those taxpayers. And fairness depends, in large part, on the eye of the beholder.

The first income tax law, the Tariff Act of 1913, exempted from taxation all income under $4,000 for married couples. Those who earned more than that were taxed at a rate of 1 percent, so a couple with an income of $4,001, for example, would have paid one penny to the federal government. By contrast, income over $20,000 was taxed at graduated rates between 2 and 6 percent; the top bracket kicked in for incomes over $500,000. "There are those who say that we should begin at $1,000 in lieu of $4,000," Representative William Henry David Murray, a Democrat from Oklahoma, explained on the House floor during the debate over the Tariff Act. "They forget the principle on which this tax is founded, and that is that every man who is making no more than a living should not be taxed upon living earnings, but should be taxed on the surplus that he makes over and above that amount necessary for good living." In other words, income taxes would be assessed on one's ability to pay; those who earned the most would pay the most, whereas those who were "making no more than a living" would not be taxed at all.

Adjusted for inflation, Murray's "living earnings"—that first $4,000 of tax-free income—would be worth nearly $65,000 in 1997 dollars. If the first income tax law remained in effect, adjusted for inflation, anyone earning that amount or less would pay no income taxes. Over the years, however, Congress sacrificed the principle Murray expounded (the ability to pay), in order to raise revenue. The process started just four years after passage of the Tariff Act, when the United States needed money to pay for its entry into World War I. In the ensuing years, the Great Depression, World War II, the Korean War, Vietnam, and the four-decade-long Cold War all required a greater tax bite. So did the creation of the Social Security system, Medicare and Medicaid, Aid to Families with Dependent Children, and all the other social safety net programs the government has created since the first income tax law took effect. So did the space program, the air traffic control network, and the interstate highway system. Through it all, year after year, those "making no more than a living" paid a greater and greater share of their income to the federal treasury. And to state treasuries. And to local treasuries. Over the last half century, in fact, the growing tax bite on the incomes of the middle class has been staggering.

To see how staggering, consider the taxes paid by two families living in Wichita, Kansas, one in the 1950s and the other in the 1990s. In 1956, a family of four—let's call them the Smiths—earning the annual median family income (half of all families earned more, half earned less) would have had $4,780 in income. The personal exemption that year was $600, so the Smiths would have started with $2,400 in tax-exempt income. The standard deduction was 10 percent of adjusted gross income; for the Smiths, that would have knocked another $478 off their taxable income. All told, they would have owed $380 in federal income taxes. The Smiths would have owed an additional $84 in social insurance taxes—used to fund Social Security, the government-run retirement system—and another $30 in state income taxes, for a total tax burden of $494. Altogether, the Smiths would have paid a little more than 10 percent of their income in taxes.

Forty years later, their counterparts—call them the Joneses—would have had income of $42,300, the median family income that year. Their personal exemption would have been worth $10,200—a mere quarter of their income. They would have paid $3,814 in federal income taxes, another $3,236 in social insurance taxes, and $1,026 in state income taxes. The total tax burden for the Joneses would have amounted to $8,076, or 19 percent of their income.

By far the largest source of disparity between the two families are the social insurance taxes. The Smiths paid $84, or 2 percent of their income, to the Social Security trust funds, while the Joneses paid 7.65 percent. Operating right alongside the progressive income tax system is a regressive tax, called the Federal Insurance Contributions Act, or FICA.

FICA taxes are levied solely against wage and salary income—the income reported on a W-2 Form that workers receive from their employers or the 1099-MISC Form that independent contractors and the self-employed receive. Capital gains, along with dividend and interest income, are exempt from the tax. Unlike the income tax, there are no personal exemptions—FICA taxes are levied on the first dollar of income. Further, higher levels of income are taxed at a lower rate: in 1999, for instance, income up to $72,600 was taxed at a rate of 7.65

percent; any dollar earned above that amount was taxed at a mere 1.45 percent. So, a family of four with wage or salary income of $72,600 would pay $5,554 in FICA taxes—7.65 percent of their income—plus whatever they owed in federal income taxes. An athlete with a multi-million-dollar contract paying him one hundred times as much would pay just 1.5 percent of his income to the trust funds.

FICA taxes give the most affluent Americans a free ride. And the affluent with enough savvy to manipulate the tax code to their benefit can reduce their income tax rate to a similarly low level.

Consider, for example, Roy M. Speer, the millionaire founder of the Home Shopping Network, who paid just 1.2 percent of his income to the Social Security and Medicare trust funds in 1989. Speer, a brash, self-made millionaire, possesses a towering ego, an imposing six-foot, 200-pound body, a face more suited to a pugilist than an entrepreneur, and a nature not given to compromise. The native Floridian worked his way through college, served in the Navy, went on to law school and graduated in 1959. He worked as an assistant Florida attorney general, a trial attorney for the National Labor Relations Board, and special counsel for the city of St. Petersburg, Florida, where he specialized in water law and legislative work. Not a bad résumé for an attorney, but Speer wasn't satisfied. "One day I woke up and decided that if something happened to me and I couldn't go into [the] law office, I couldn't make any money, and I had nothing to protect my family with, so I decided to be an entrepreneur," Speer once said.

In midlife, Speer changed careers. He went into land development, building, construction, the concrete business, marine construction, and dredging. He tried his hand at oil around the time that prices peaked in 1982, but he lost money when the bottom fell out of the market. "That was something I have been trying to forget," he said of his experience in the energy business. Through it all, however, he was indefatigable. "I am what has been termed as a workaholic. I don't golf; I don't belong to country clubs. I make it a point to spend Sunday with my family. And my day starts about seven and stops at about ten or eleven at night. . . . Six days a week; I work on Saturday. I try not to work on Sunday."

In 1981, Speer set up Home Shopping Channels, Incorporated, a company that sold retail merchandise over the airwaves in the Tampa Bay area of Florida. Initially, shoppers who ordered from the show drove to one of Home Shopping's warehouses to pick up their purchases; when the channel went national in 1985, renamed Home Shopping Network, Incorporated, it began shipping its sales directly to customers' homes. "Most people look at home shopping on the television and they think it is simple," Speer said of the business. "It is probably the most complex array of merchandising and computers that you will ever find."

Home Shopping Network went live on July 1, 1985, broadcasting nationally for five hours each day via satellite. Speer owned 60 percent of the company, and he held the reins tightly. "I have a principle in my business: If I don't control it, I don't own it," he once testified in a Tax Court case. "The reason for that is that if it gets in trouble, I am the one that is going to have to bail it out, and I want to be in the position of a controller. . . . I have done it several times the other way in my life, and every one of them have been disasters."

Speer's hard work, along with the cable and credit card booms of the 1980s that fueled impulse buying, made the Home Shopping Network a huge financial winner. When Speer cashed out in December 1992, he was paid $160 million for his controlling stake by Liberty Media Corporation, a cable television programmer. He sold the rest of his shares in 1993, for another $100 million, and relinquished his position as chairman.

It wasn't the profits Speer reaped from the sale of his stake in Home Shopping Network that caught the attention of the IRS, but rather the way he ran the firm. Pioneer Data Processing, a company that Speer once owned, developed the software program that Home Shopping Channel—the Tampa Bay–area predecessor to the national Home Shopping Network—used to take its orders from the throngs of cable TV viewers.

When Speer launched the Home Shopping Network in 1985, he hired Burroughs Corporation to rewrite the program in a different computer language, and he paid the computer company $55,250 for its efforts. He agreed to pay Pioneer, whose program he was no longer using, a far more generous sum. Speer signed a licensing agreement with the firm guaranteeing it 1 percent of the annual gross profits of Home Shopping Network. The agreement was open-ended.

Speer signed the document for Pioneer even though he didn't own the software firm. He was just exercising his parental prerogatives: his son, Richard Speer, owned Pioneer.

After auditing the returns of Pioneer software and Roy and Richard Speer, the IRS concluded that the licensing agreement was a sham—that it was merely an attempt to divert income from Home Shopping to Pioneer and Speer's son, Richard. Pioneer, in turn, paid hundreds of thousands of dollars in consulting fees to companies owned by Roy Speer, which the IRS discovered in a 1991 audit of the closely held software developer.

On December 2, 1988, Pioneer wrote a $300,000 check to Tahitian Investments, Incorporated, for consulting fees, and later deducted it from its tax returns as an ordinary and necessary business expense. Roy Speer, it turned out, owned Tahitian Investments, and the $300,000 in consulting fees was for his time. "Roy Speer stated that as a matter of family tradition," an IRS agent who audited the Pioneer tax returns wrote in his report, "he and his family would discuss business on the weekends, which is when he discussed many of Pioneer Data Processing's business affairs with his son, Richard." Unlike most fathers, however, Roy Speer charged his son for his weekend advice. "He thought about the time that he spent on Pioneer Data's business affairs, and based on his business experience, he pulled a number from the air which he thought represented a fair fee. He stated that he believes in making his children pay for the things that they get, and that they should work for their money. Thus, he makes his children pay for his services." The IRS auditor decided to disallow the deduction from Pioneer's tax returns.

The audit of Pioneer led the IRS to audit the Speers as well. When the Service concludes from an audit that additional taxes are owed, it sends a Notice of Deficiency, stating the amount of tax owed and any interest or penalties assessed. If there's a dispute, the taxpayer may contact the revenue agent to discuss the case. If the matter can't be resolved, the taxpayer has the option of filing a petition with the U.S. Tax Court. In 1994, Roy Speer did just that after he and his wife, Lynnda, received Notices of Deficiency for more than $9.9 million.

The IRS challenged the licensing agreement between Home Shopping Network and Pioneer, arguing that Speer was funneling money from Home Shopping through Pioneer and back to himself. This challenge of the licensing agreement accounted for the bulk of the amount of unpaid taxes assessed against Speer; other deficiencies included losses the workaholic claimed from the operation of various businesses he owned while he ran Home Shopping.

Like Jane Morgan, the combative Speer was unable to resolve the dispute with the IRS through negotiations, and in January 1995, the case went to trial in Tampa. Unlike Morgan, Speer had a team of high-priced lawyers, including James A. Bruton III, who had worked in the IRS chief counsel's office. The Tax Court testimony lasted five days. Among the witnesses called by Speer's half dozen attorneys and the IRS were experts on computer programming; among the exhibits entered into the record was the 1981 program itself. Speer also took the stand. Senior attorney Francis C. Mucciolo, who tried the case for the IRS, asked Speer about the $300,000 his son paid him for his advice. "Probably should have charged him half a million instead," he replied. "He got a break." Mucciolo asked Speer about his home in the Bahamas, which one of his companies bought for him in 1991. "I have probably quadrupled it since then. I have built onto it." Mucciolo asked Speer whether he'd used a 68-foot yacht that his son's company bought. "I think it's a 63-footer, but we might have stretched it a little bit. . . . I am sure I have used it on occasion."

Among the documents entered into the record were joint tax returns filed by Roy and Lynnda Speer. Speer reaped rewards from his cable business that put him, in terms of income, among the top 1 percent of all Americans. In 1989, for example, his salary from Home Shopping Network was more than $400,000. Tahitian Development—the company to which Pioneer Data Processing paid $300,000 in 1988—paid Speer a salary of $48,000. Altogether, Speer and his wife earned more than $550,000 in salary. They also received just over $1 million in taxable interest income, another $157,000 in capital gains, and $490,000 in tax-exempt interest income from investments in municipal bonds and the like. Altogether, the Speers' total income amounted to $1.2 million.

Not everything Speer touched turned to gold, as his tax returns show. In 1989, for example, he claimed losses of $1.1 million from Maximo Marina, Incorporated, a full-service marina operating in St. Petersburg, Florida. Speer, as was his habit, owned a controlling interest in Maximo, and could claim those losses on his Form 1040. He claimed losses of $78,000 from another of his companies, Gateway Marine, Incorporated, a tug and barge business. Altogether, he claimed losses from his other business ventures of nearly $1.2 million.

That left the Speers with an adjusted gross income of $578,000—still not a bad year. The personal exemption that year was $2,000; Speer claimed one for himself and his wife. The standard deduction for a married couple filing a joint return in 1989 was $5,200; the Speers instead claimed itemized deductions of more than $400,000. They deducted $61,000 paid in local and state taxes, another $142,000 for interest paid on loans they took out to invest in various businesses, and nearly $200,000 for donations made to various charities.

Altogether, the Speers were left with a little less than $174,000 in taxable income, or about 15 percent of their $1.2 million in gross income. They claimed they owed $89,600 in federal income taxes. In a year in which the Speers, by their own admission, received more than a million dollars in income, they paid taxes at an effective rate of 7.4 percent. Remember the Joneses, the hypothetical family from Wichita earning the median income? Their total federal income tax burden amounted to 9 percent of their gross income. Tack on the Joneses' social insurance and state income taxes, and they paid 19 percent of their income in taxes. The Speers, among the wealthiest Americans, paid $7,200 in payroll taxes and another $61,000 in state and local taxes. Altogether, the Speers' tax burden amounted to a little more than 13 percent of their total income.

In the 1994 Notices of Deficiency, the IRS reduced the losses from both Maximo Marina and Gateway Marine that the Speers claimed in 1989. The Service argued that the losses were passive, not active; a taxpayer can claim only a portion of a passive loss rather than the full amount from a business in which the taxpayer "materially participates." The Internal Revenue Code requires an individual to spend just 100 hours a year on a business to claim active participation.

Speer testified that he was involved with all the business decisions made by Maximo and Gateway. "My money has been hard to come by," he testified in the Tax Court case, "and I am usually very close to it whenever it is spent." He estimated that he spent about 400 hours a year on the two businesses, but could provide no documentation to back up the assertion.

In the end, Judge Robert P. Ruwe ruled that the program owned by Pioneer Data had value, it was the basis of the program Burroughs later wrote, and that the licensing agreement was legitimate. As a result, Speer did not have to pay the bulk of the deficiencies assessed against him.

But the judge dismissed the "ballpark guesstimate" offered by Speer's attorneys of his activities involving Maximo Marina and Gateway Marine. His losses were reclassified as passive, and Speer had to pay taxes on an additional $1.7 million in income—pennies on the dollar, it turned out, of the nearly $10 million that the IRS sought in its original Notices of Deficiency. That result was par for the course for the IRS. In cases in which $10 million or more is at stake, the Service recoups on average just 17 cents on the dollar. In smaller cases, with less than $10 million at stake (the vast majority of them), the IRS recovers 42 cents for every dollar it claims is owed.

———

Had Speer been able to document the time he spent on his other business—had he met the 100-hour threshold for active participation in the affairs of Gateway and Maximo—his losses would have been tax deductible. By contrast, Jane Morgan's IRA distributions, which she reluctantly took to cover basic living expenses like rent, health insurance premiums, and car payments, were subject to a penalty. The tax code treats different kinds of money differently. Money spent to make more money is tax deductible. Money spent to meet one's basic needs is not.

Consider the IRS's audit of Pioneer Data Processing. After discovering questionable items on its returns from the 1980s, agents interviewed the Speers—part of the audit process, in which a taxpayer can give his side of the story.

In 1987, Pioneer paid $525 in country club dues for Roy Speer and deducted the cost from its taxes as a necessary business expense. "It has been determined that Roy Speer provided a valued service to the taxpayer and the 'dues' in question represent an ordinary business expense to the taxpayer," said the summary of the audit, called a revenue agent's report. Pioneer paid $20,304 for a security fence for Richard Speer's home and deducted that; the IRS chose not to challenge that expense either. "In light of the fact that Richard Speer made loans to [Pioneer], subsequent to the building of the fence at issue, the Service is conceding this issue in full." Pioneer also paid an architect $5,798 to design a home for Roy Speer and his wife on land owned by the company; the IRS allowed Pioneer to deduct the architect's fees.

The Speers didn't persuade the IRS agents that all of the company's deductions were legitimate, however. In 1988, Pioneer claimed a $41,045 depreciation deduction for a Rolls-Royce limousine purchased the previous September. "The Rolls Royce was never rented or advertised for rent," the revenue agent's report stated. "The Rolls Royce was never permitted or licensed by the taxpayer to be operated as a commercial limousine." An agent interviewed Richard Speer about the car, and in his report wrote: "Richard Speer stated that he intended to lease the limousine when he originally purchased it, but, after he saw the car, he was afraid to let anybody drive it. . . . He said the limo was kept under cover in a carport at his house."

After determining that the limo had no business purpose, the agent addressed the question of whether it had in fact depreciated in value. This time he interviewed Richard's father. "According to Roy Speer, only a limited number of these limousines were made by Rolls Royce; thus, they are a collector's item. This particular limo was originally purchased by a lady in Las Vegas, but she died before, or shortly after, it was to be delivered to her."

On the basis of his interviews with the Speers, the agent didn't allow the company to write off the costs of its limo. "The taxpayer is not entitled to claim depreciation on the Rolls Royce limousine in taxable year 1988. The limousine was never placed into service and is tantamount to investment property that is more likely to appreciate rather than depreciate in value."

A corporation can deduct half the cost of providing entertainment to its clients or customers. If it pays for tickets to baseball games or Broadway musicals for its employees, it can deduct 100 percent of that cost as a fringe benefit. In 1997, the IRS even allowed a corporation to deduct 80 percent of a contribution it made to a university in return for a ten-year lease on a sky box in the university's football stadium. Think of it this way: a father who takes his son to a ballgame can't write off the cost. A corporation that sends its employees and customers to a game can. Similarly, a corporation that pays for health insurance for its workers can deduct the cost. An employee of a company that doesn't provide health insurance can buy coverage for himself and his family, but he can't deduct the premiums. A corporation that buys a fleet of automobiles can deduct the expense; as the cars lose value, the corporation can write off the depreciation. An individual who buys a car cannot write off the expense; as the car's value shrinks over time, he bears the loss himself. A corporation that's sued because its product injured someone can write off the costs of its defense, plus any monetary judgment against it; an individual who's sued for causing an injury, say in a car accident, can write off neither the costs of his defense nor the costs of a settlement. A corporation that goes deeply into debt can deduct its interest payments. An individual who runs up a fortune in credit card bills can't do the same.

The disparities are simple enough to explain. The Internal Revenue Code treats certain kinds of spending differently. In essence, money spent to make more money is tax deductible; money spent on oneself, whether it's for rent, groceries, or a family car, is not. The income tax is essentially a tax on money used for consumption—on "living earnings," as Representative Murray opined in the 1913 debate over the income tax. Those who earn a surplus "over and above that amount necessary for good living" can play by many of the same rules corporations use— provided they're willing to use their money to make more money.

Consider interest expenses. A young couple who buys a cradle, bassinet, changing table, and so forth on an installment plan may not deduct the interest payments on the furniture as they await their bundle of joy. By contrast, a millionaire like Roy Speer, who borrows to invest in a slew of ventures, may write off on his taxes the interest he pays on those loans. In 1995, more than 39,700 millionaires deducted more than $4 billion from their tax returns for interest paid to invest in everything from the latest high-tech company to the most old-fashioned speculative property, real estate. Those millionaires, incidentally, represented a mere 3 out of every 10,000 taxpayers; collectively, they claimed 38 cents of every dollar in deductions for investment interest expenses.

The IRS, of course, is the federal agency charged with determining whether all those deductions, made by corporations and individuals, are proper. In 1997, the IRS spent more than $1.6 billion examining returns, employing a staff of more than 17,000 revenue agents and auditors. Of the 118 million individual income tax returns filed that year, the Service conducted formal audits of just 1.5 million of them, or 1.28 percent. Two-thirds of those returns were from taxpayers declaring incomes of under $50,000. The IRS recommended additional taxes and penalties of $3.6 billion against them—an average of $3,520 per audit. For the 119,000 audited with incomes over $100,000, the Service recommended $1.78 billion in additional taxes and penalties—an average of $14,900 per audit.

Few agencies have a greater talent for arousing outright hostility than the IRS. Either they're bureaucratic incompetents, as Jane Morgan found, or jackbooted thugs, as several taxpayers testified before the Senate Finance Committee in 1996, when Senator William Roth, a Republican from Delaware, held a highly publicized series of hearings aimed at curbing the Service's power. Roth later coauthored *The Power to Destroy*, which described the horrors that taxpayers endured at the hands of the Service. Roth's hearings led to the passage of the IRS Reform and Restructuring Act of 1998, which implemented the Taxpayer Bill of Rights—a manifesto that Morgan concluded was ignored in her case.

On January 18, 1999, the IRS began sending out a redrafted letter to all the subjects of audits warning that agents may need to contact third parties. "Third party contacts may include, but are not limited to, neighbors, employers, employees and banks," the letter explained. "We may use these contacts to help us determine your correct tax liability, identify your assets, or locate your current address." The new wording, part of the Service's attempt to comply with the Reform and Restructuring Act and become more "taxpayer friendly," fell well short of the mark.

While the IRS withdrew the letter, it has continued to target its audits toward middle- and lower-income taxpayers. This astonishes Jane Morgan. "Why was I put through this ordeal for over a year," she asked. "What has the government to gain? How much has it cost the government? More than the amount I owe!"

The Jane Morgans of the world, of course, pay their taxes. There's a wide assortment of experts who help the wealthy avoid theirs.

2

Haven's Gate

Jerome Schneider believes in American entrepreneurship. The Vancouver, Canada–based financial consultant is often amazed by the hard work and ingenuity his clients employ to achieve the American dream, traits that he calls "the things that have made the United States the success story it is today." He believes in wealth, and he celebrates those for whom increasing net worth is a constant preoccupation. He believes that each generation of Americans should have a better life than their parents, that hard work and successful risk-taking should be rewarded, and that there's nothing wrong with wanting to be rich. In this respect, he's not much different from most Americans. But Schneider, who's a self-described expert on offshore tax havens, doesn't believe that those who achieve the American dream should feel any obligation to pay their share of U.S. taxes.

"I'm convinced the United States is currently on the road to ruin," he wrote in the third edition of *The Complete Guide to Offshore Money Havens: How to Make Millions, Protect your Privacy, and Legally Avoid Taxes.* The book, one of six he has authored, is part how-to, part why-to, with a healthy dose of self-promotion thrown in for good measure. Schneider cites a litany of reasons the United States—"the success story" where all his clients have made their fortunes—is falling apart, everything from the massacre in Littleton, Colorado, to Monica Lewinsky. According to Schneider, political power is in the hands of the poor, the courts are out of control, the culture is saturated with violent video games and films, and the government does nothing but raise taxes and fritter the money away on wasteful spending.

But there is an alternative. "Just like a blinking lighthouse can guide a ship into the safety of an island harbor, I can show you how to physically and financially escape America's roadblocks," he declares in his book, which is full of advice for the potential tax avoider. "If your accountant isn't working with you to plan intelligent tax avoidance strategies," he writes at one point, "I'd suggest you look for a new accountant." Elsewhere, he suggests that the IRS is nothing to be frightened of. "The IRS is so understaffed that it will not have the manpower to challenge everything on your return," he says, adding one page later, "It helps to realize that the audit process is not so much an investigation as a negotiation. Your tax return was like your first offer to the IRS."

But the brightest blinking beacon he holds out avoids all that potential unpleasantness. Schneider counsels his readers to move their wealth out of the United States into one of several recommended offshore tax havens—jurisdictions with low levels of taxation and a high degree of confidentiality maintained by their financial institutions. His pitch on behalf of those countries is part travel agent, part tax avoider: "There's no question that it's more fun to do business while relaxing on the beach of some Caribbean paradise than while cooped up in your office back home. But there's more to the offshore world than the sunny climate. There's freedom and privacy beyond your wildest imagination. Off come the shackles of government regulation and the handcuffs of excessive taxation."

Thus Aruba, the book informs, is "located just twelve miles off the coast of Venezuela. The climate is incredible. I would highly recommend you consider it for any vacation." The country also offers something called "the Aruba Exempt Corporation. This is a fully tax-exempt company that is very easy to maintain." St. Vincent "is a picturesque group of seventeen islands in the Windward region of the Caribbean. Yachtsmen absolutely love it." It's also a place where "companies deemed 'nonresident' don't have to pay an annual fee and don't have to pay tax on income from foreign sources." Schneider profiles some forty tax havens, from Andorra (in the heart of the Pyrenees) to the Vatican, from the Bahamas to Vanuatu, a chain of more than 100 tiny islands in the Pacific Ocean, all of which offer pleasant environs and the opportunity to move one's wealth beyond the reach of the IRS.

In appendices, he helpfully explains how to open a foreign bank account, and lists local banks in each country, complete with addresses, phone and fax numbers, e-mail addresses, and telex and cable codes. They range from the exotic, like the Caribbean Commercial Bank in Anguilla or the Altajir Bank in the Cayman Islands, a subsidiary of a Liechtenstein bank, to familiar names like Citibank and Chase Manhattan. Above all, he advises that, before contemplating a jump offshore, his readers seek professional advice.

Schneider happens to offer it. He claims that he has helped hundreds of well-heeled Americans legally avoid millions in taxes by setting up offshore banks, trusts, or corporations, or some combination of all three. Schneider has also helped five governments of tax haven countries to rewrite their tax and banking laws to attract wealthy tax avoiders. His services, advertised in magazines and newspapers and on the Web, aren't cheap. He charges clients tens of thousands of dollars for setting up recommended offshore vehicles, plus $150 an hour for his time. When the Center contacted his office in Vancouver explaining the nature of this book and requesting an interview, Schneider's office responded that we too would have to pay for his time. We politely declined.

Schneider, who has been called the foremost promoter of offshore banking, is just one of hundreds of operators who offer wealthy Americans the advantages of moving portions of their net worth beyond the reach of the U.S. tax authorities. Some hawk offshore trusts or banks, others sell domestic vehicles. Some are canny former IRS insiders, others are tax protestors who advise that the entire Internal Revenue Code may be ignored because the Sixteenth Amendment, which authorized the income tax, was never properly ratified. Some work for the biggest accounting firms, others have little more than a Web site and a post office box. But they all have one thing in common: they try, with varying degrees of success, to help their clients minimize the taxes they owe. And there's very little the government can do to stop them.

From his base in Vancouver, Schneider trumpets one of the most popular schemes: moving offshore. The advantages are obvious. The Bank Secrecy Act of 1970 requires all U.S. banks to provide the IRS with information on the deposits and interest accumulated by U.S. citizens. For nonfilers and those who fail to report income, the IRS can access bank records that show how much money was deposited over time to reconstruct an individual's income. Banks in tax haven countries, by contrast, operate under laws designed to ensure both the anonymity of the depositor and the confidentiality of his account activity. It's not illegal for a U.S. citizen to have a bank account in a tax haven, provided he reports its existence, and any interest income he earned from it, on his tax return. The bank secrecy of the offshore havens ensure that, should an individual decide not to report his account, there's very little chance the IRS would discover it. The amount of American money stashed away in tax havens is unknown. One estimate, prepared by the International Monetary Fund, put the total figure of all foreign deposits in low-tax jurisdictions at $4.8 trillion.

John M. Mathewson, a San Antonio businessman who was chairman of the Guardian Bank & Trust Limited, a Cayman Islands bank, was arrested on June 27, 1996, by the Federal Bureau of Investigation for his part in a cable television piracy ring. Mathewson offered a plea bargain: he'd turn over the computerized records of his secret offshore bank. More than 1,500 Americans had established secret, unreported accounts at the bank in violation of U.S. law. Among them were doctors, businessmen, and other affluent individuals. American companies had also established secret accounts.

Mathewson not only got his depositors' money into secret offshore accounts, he helped disguise it on its return trip to the United States. The bank set up phony Dutch corporations that appeared to issue mortgages to depositors; in reality, they were secretly "borrowing" funds from their own bank deposits. If the IRS challenged the source of the money, they could point to the loan documents and show that they were repaying the loans. Mathewson explained to federal prosecutors that the loans also provided sham tax deductions for mortgage interest that his customers were paying to themselves.

Within three years, thanks to Mathewson's records and inside information, the IRS and the Department of Justice recovered $50 million in back taxes and penalties after dozens of audits and prosecutions. Mathewson's records, covering a fourteen-month period, might result in the recovery of some $300 million more in taxes. And that's just one bank. Schneider has sold hundreds of banking licenses. That's how he makes his money.

The banks Schneider's clients set up didn't have ATM machines, or windows staffed by tellers, or even buildings. They existed, for the most part, on paper. Sometimes referred to as suitcase banks, most of them possessed no physical assets whatsoever. The money they held was deposited, in their names, in other banks—run by more reputable firms. At most, each of the banks Schneider peddled had a local agent who handled its affairs and got its mail in the tax haven country, and perhaps sported a brass plate in the lobby of the agent's building.

In 1983, Schneider was called before the Senate Permanent Subcommittee on Investigations to testify on the growing market for offshore banks. At the time, he was running a Beverly Hills–based company called WFI Corporation. He testified that he'd set up 150 banks in tax havens around the world. He bought the licenses to charter 120 of the banks for as little as $350 and sold them to clients for up to $35,000. That's a potential profit of $4 million.

Schneider, who cautions his readers and clients alike to know the people they do business with, didn't talk much about his background that day. In his book, he explains that he worked for a Wall Street brokerage, and made a fortune for a client in 1974 by telling him to short the market—that is, bet that stock prices would decline—because he expected that Richard Nixon's pending impeachment would cause economic chaos. He omits from his book any mention of the forty days he served in jail in 1972 for stealing equipment from the Pacific Telephone Company. After his release, he tried unsuccessfully to launch a consulting business focused on ways to avoid corporate computer theft. Then, in 1975, he formed Jerry Schneider & Company, the predecessor to WFI, and began the profitable business of selling offshore banks.

In his 1983 testimony, Schneider suggested that there was nothing improper about his business, and hailed as a success story a bank he had set up for J. David Dominelli, an investment adviser from La Jolla, California, on the tiny Caribbean island of Montserrat. "J. David Banking," he told the senators, "is used as an intermediary for foreign exchange currency trading to channel investment dollars into the United States in a wholly legitimate manner. It is this type of activity that underscores the legitimate uses of offshore banks." Dominelli later pled guilty to bilking investors out of $80 million; he was sentenced in 1985 to twenty years in prison.

Schneider set up more than 200 banks on Montserrat, the majority of which were closed in 1992 by the Bank of England after an investigation into their practices by Scotland Yard alleged that most of them were used for tax evasion, money laundering, or other criminal activities. Montserrat banned Schneider from the island; he soon turned his attention to Grenada, where he continued to sell banks to investors. Grenada had no law authorizing offshore banks at the time. That country banned him too, but not before another of his clients used one of his banks to run a swindle.

Daisy Johnson Butler, a Texas con artist, told would-be loan applicants that her family "owned most of the Bahamas" and was worth $2 billion. She promised them loans through her Houston loan-brokerage company, and the European Overseas Bank Ltd., on Grenada, backed her up by certifying that she had funds on account there. Some sixty people who ponied up $1 million in up-front fees were taken in by her. European Overseas was set up by Schneider and his company, WFI, and sold to Butler; she received official bank documents, including certificates of deposit forms and sample letters of credit, for the fee she paid him. She used the documents to trick her depositors, who never got the loans they sought or their money back. She was sentenced to seven years in prison in Texas.

The Office of the Comptroller of the Currency, a branch of the Treasury Department concerned with, among other things, bank fraud and money laundering, wanted to shut down Schneider's operation as early as 1984. In response, Schneider wrote an eight-page proposal to John W. Shockey, a senior regulator in the comptroller's office who had been a particularly strident critic of the tax haven expert. "Let's work together to put an end to offshore bank fraud," he wrote on August 21, 1985. "We've been in business for 10 years and established over 200 offshore banks. Only a few have been under legal scrutiny." Schneider asked the comptroller's office to vet his potential clients for him, thus giving an official stamp of government approval to the offshore banks he was creating. Shockey declined to meet with him.

"I tried to get the U.S. attorney's office to indict him for aiding and abetting fraud," Shockey, who retired from the comptroller's office but still keeps an eye on Schneider, told the Center. "It looks like they just didn't want to indict him, that they thought the evidence wasn't strong enough. I've been looking at him for fifteen years now, and I'm surprised he's not behind bars."

Not only is he a free man, he's a prosperous one, and still sells foreign banks to clients. What's more, the government retains an interest in him. In 1999, for example, at his "Offshore Wealth Summit '99" in Vancouver, the featured speakers included U.S. Representative Billy Tauzin, Republican from Louisiana, who is quoted prominently on the cover of the third edition of Schneider's book on offshore banking. "A serious contender for the best book on offshore banking I've ever read," Tauzin wrote.

"The reason [the wealthy] are trying to shelter their income offshore is because we have a punitive tax code," Tauzin spokesman Ken Johnson said, noting that the congressman supports replacing the Internal Revenue Code with a national sales tax. "Representative Tauzin is saying, 'Quit trying to hide your money. We can make it so you won't have to.' "

According to Shockey, U.S. attorneys rely on Schneider as an expert when they unravel cases involving offshore bank fraud. "It's disgusting," he said of the government's working with Schneider. "He knowingly provides an instrument for fraud. He's misleading his own clients. He's not selling them a bank, he's selling them a piece of paper."

"We'll go after the promoters when we believe we have the evidence," IRS criminal investigations analyst Ed Hannon said. "But offshore banking records are obviously hard to come by."

Going offshore isn't always necessary. The Internal Revenue Code is loaded with plenty of havens for the well-off. The bulk of the deductions and credits that the code allows disproportionately benefits wealthy taxpayers. In 1995, the last year for which complete statistics were available, there were more than 1,272,500 returns filed by taxpayers earning $200,000 or more, representing 1 percent of all taxpayers. That 1 percent claimed 15 percent of the total itemized deductions. They enjoyed 40 percent of the tax-exempt interest income that municipal bonds and the like pay. They claimed nearly 50 percent of the write-offs for losses from partnerships and closely held corporations.

To take advantage of those provisions in the code, one doesn't need a Vancouver address, an Aruba Exempt Corporation, or a foreign bank account. All it takes is a certain technical skill and a lot of money. Schneider, the offshore-tax-haven promoter, wrote in his book, "With the help of an experienced financial consultant, you can turn the ambiguities and inconsistencies of our tax code to your own advantage. You can break away from the uninformed majority and revolutionize your economic life."

Aron B. Katz has done just that. And he didn't need to move a dime to offshore tax havens.

Katz, who lives in Boulder, Colorado, is a real estate investor. He is currently president, director, or chairman of more than twenty companies in four states—all privately held businesses with names like MM Investments, American Residential Properties, AmeraCQ Incorporated, Cash Management Company, and the Aron B. Katz Company. Like their founder, the companies maintain a low profile. Except for the vanity license plate on his car, which reads "XS," there's very little that's showy or ostentatious about Katz.

His wife, Phyllis A. Katz, is the more famous of the pair. A prominent social psychologist and author, she is the founder and executive director of the Institute for Research on Social Problems, a well-respected think tank with a steady stream of grants from the federal government. In the 1970s, the institute did groundbreaking research on gender distinctions; its Baby X experiments showed that adults treated the same baby very differently depending on whether they thought the child was a boy or a girl. More recently, she moderated President Bill Clinton's Initiative on Race meeting in Denver.

Phyllis and her daughter, Margaret Katz, cowrote the 1997 book *The Feminist Dollar: The Wise Woman's Buying Guide*, which scrutinizes the attitude of 400 companies toward their female employees. "As a mother who's tried part-time work, not working, running a home business and working full time, it's a big deal when companies make a conscious effort to make it easier on women," Margaret told a *Denver Post* reporter.

The collaboration on the book is somewhat typical of the close-knit family. Aron Katz is a director of Phyllis's Institute for Research on Social Problems. So in their son, Martin Katz. Phyllis is executive vice president of the Aron B. Katz Company. Their children are involved in any number of the Katzes' companies, either as shareholders or directors. And the family has stuck together through annual audits and sixteen separate Tax Court battles with the Internal Revenue Service.

The issues are complex, but the end result is the same: year after year, family members file tax returns claiming they had either no income or negative income. Year after year, the IRS audits them and claims that their income was actually in the hundreds of thousands or millions of dollars. Year after year, the Katzes battle the Service in Tax Court. And they win.

Josh Ungerman, who has represented the family in its dealing with the IRS, wrote in a September 1999 Tax Court filing, "The Katz family and related entities have been continuously audited on and off since the 1970s. Each audit has proceeded in the same manner. The auditors produce reports that are processed as the Notices of Deficiency. After petitioning the Tax Court, the groups of cases have been settled after lengthy negotiations with the IRS Appeals Division, resulting in little or no liability."

Until 1986, Katz was able to avoid taxes by structuring the family's businesses to take advantage of various tax shelter provisions built into the Internal Revenue Code. Real estate investments received generous deductions for debt that allowed an investor to offset on paper the income he earned from a property. Katz received income from hotels and apartment complexes, but could declare losses on the properties because the amount of money he had invested in them—most of which was borrowed—was far greater than the revenue returned. American Residential Properties, Katz's flagship company, had soaring revenues through the 1980s, but neither the company nor Katz paid very much tax on the revenue.

The Tax Reform Act of 1986, which eliminated most real estate shelters, changed all that. "The whole organization took some turns," Terrie Thompson, former head of marketing and investor communications at American Residential Properties, said. "Prior to 1986 everything was structured and very leveraged. And then after the '86 tax reform it didn't make those kinds of investments profitable because the write-offs were no longer available. As a result he had to go into a lot of Chapter 11 [bankruptcy proceedings] and try to restructure and finance."

At the time, Katz owned more than 144 properties around the country, ranging from multifamily housing projects for low-income tenants to a Hilton Hotel in Los Angeles. According to Thompson, he and his partners lost many of their real estate holdings in the aftermath of the Tax Reform Act of 1986. "It was not a pretty picture by any means," she said. "A lot of the properties went away."

But Katz was hardly wiped out. He held on to many of his companies, including those that had lost millions because of the new tax climate. They would prove to be his best weapon against the IRS. Because the Internal Revenue Code allows taxpayers to carry net operating losses from businesses forward for fifteen years, he was able to use those losses to wipe out any taxable income he and his wife earned. The collapse of the tax shelter market, it turned out, actually produced a tax windfall for Katz.

He also held on to his lucrative ventures, and started others. He owns The Boulderado, Incorporated, the holding company for a 160-room luxury hotel in downtown Boulder; Comtel Debit Technologies, a New Jersey telecommunications company that sells prepaid phone cards; and Astarte Fiber Networks, a Boulder manufacturer of fiber optic communications equipment. Astarte has contracts with Bell-South, NASA, and the United Nations.

But that doesn't mean that he, or his family, is making much in the way of taxable income. In 1986, Aron and Phyllis Katz filed a joint return claiming they had lost $3.6 million. In 1987, their losses were $1.8 million. In 1988, they were $1.1 million in the red. The pattern continued through the 1990s. In 1992, they claimed losses of more than $18 million; in 1993, $17 million; in 1994, $15 million.

The IRS disagreed. The Service charged the couple with millions of dollars in back taxes and penalties, claiming that the Katzes had improperly calculated their income from their S corporations and their C corporations; that they had claimed losses from previous tax years to which they were not entitled; that they had investment income, self-employment income, and capital gains that they hadn't properly declared.

After all, it's not as if the couple wasn't making money. In 1987, Phyllis Katz sold $103,000 worth of securities. She and her husband were paid more than $321,000 in fees by various companies, including publisher Simon & Schuster. In 1988, Phyllis sold off another $900,000 worth of assets. The IRS claimed the couple had over $26 million in income from their various S corporations—which for tax purposes are treated like partnerships. The companies themselves pay no taxes, but pass on their losses or gains to their shareholders, who report them on their Form 1040s.

The IRS audits involved the dozens of companies that the Katzes ran, along with their tax returns and their children's. "The twelve related cases involving the Katz family include adjustments . . . flowing between family members and flow-through entities," Ungerman wrote in the September 1999 Tax Court filing. "The settlement of many issues results in items being reclassified to a different place on the return, to a different year, or to another taxpayer's return."

He neglected to add that the reclassified items always seem to work to the further advantage of the Katz family, who in negotiations with the IRS have always managed to prevail. The Service sought over $1 million in back taxes from Aron and Phyllis Katz for 1986; the final assessment was reduced to less than $56,000. The Katzes didn't write out a check; they filed an amended petition requesting that their accumulated tax losses cover the bill. The request was granted. In 1987, the Service sought more than $9.1 million in back taxes, and settled for just over $403,000. Again, the Katzes applied their losses to that figure, and ended up paying about $34,600, less than four-tenths of 1 percent of what the IRS originally sought. It followed the well-established pattern described by their lawyer: the IRS seeks millions, and the Katzes end up with little or no liability.

Much of the dispute between the Katzes and the IRS involved "matters which required substantiation from a factual standpoint." An attorney in the chief counsel's office of the IRS, who has litigated complex cases (but has no knowledge of the cases involving the Katzes), described his experiences substantiating facts with the attorneys for a sophisticated, wealthy taxpayer.

"They confuse issues," he said. "They spend hours arguing that a document is not what the IRS says it is. First they'll spend days claiming the item isn't genuine. Then they'll agree that it's genuine, but they'll argue it's not germane to the present case and should be excluded. Then they'll say it can be included, but it's not a record of a deposit, but instead it's a record of a transfer, which can be included only to show that the bank's records are faulty. And on and on and on. They'll argue for months over every item.

"When there are ten thousand documents, some of which are bank statements containing thousands of transactions, and the opposition argues over the significance of every single item, the process becomes extraordinarily difficult."

The attorney, who asked not to be identified, suggested this was why the IRS prefers to go after middle-income taxpayers. "Why do you think we go after the little guys?" he said. "They can't fight back."

The wealthy, of course, can—and do—fight back. They also benefit from the best tax planning strategies money can buy. Mark A. Kuller, a partner in the Washington office of McKee Nelson, Ernst & Young L.L.P., worked from 1982 to 1986 for the Treasury Department and the IRS—half of that time as a special assistant to the IRS chief counsel— before he went into private practice. He told the Center that the advice of former IRS officials is highly prized by both wealthy individuals and corporations. "That would virtually be true of every tax practitioner at the IRS," he said. "If you go back through the past twenty years, it's clear that their experience enhanced their ability to help [clients] deal with the rules that they brought to life."

A canny insider with firsthand experience of the workings of the IRS and a few wealthy clients eager to avoid their taxes can cost the Treasury hundreds of millions of dollars over the course of his career.

Item: In February 1986, Abraham N. Pritzker, who was ranked on the *Forbes* list of the 400 wealthiest individuals in America, with an estimated fortune of $500 million, passed away. The Chicago financier amassed holdings that included the Hyatt Hotel chain and Royal Caribbean Cruises, Ltd. His estate filed a return with the IRS, claiming taxable assets of a mere $3,000. The IRS claimed that the family understated the value of the estate by more than $97 million, and owed $53.2 million in taxes. Pritzker's heirs disputed the assessment in Tax Court, noting that most of the family patriarch's wealth had been transferred to a series of offshore trusts. The IRS eventually settled the case for $9.5 million.

Item: Saul Zaentz, who produced the Oscar-winning international hit films *Amadeus* and *The English Patient,* first gained prestige as a producer of *One Flew Over the Cuckoo's Nest*, which made $46.5 million in profits after it was released in 1975. Of those profits, $45.3 million flowed into a series of offshore companies. The IRS audited Zaentz and, in 1986, said he owed $26 million in taxes for the years 1976 to 1982. The Service wrote to Zaentz that the offshore companies "are shams, and that you are the true earner of the income from the motion picture, *One Flew Over the Cuckoo's Nest.*" Zaentz disputed the assessment; in 1990, he agreed to settle the dispute for $1.5 million— or 6 cents on the dollar.

Item: Charles Dolan, the founder and president of Cablevision Systems Corporation, won the exclusive right to wire Manhattan for cable in 1965, a concession that eventually earned him a fortune. He started Home Box Office (Time Incorporated bought it out in 1971), Bravo (the arts and entertainment network), and the first all-sports network. The IRS audited him and claimed that he owed $234 million in back taxes for 1984 and 1986 to 1988. The IRS and Dolan settled the case in 1996, after agreeing that not only did Dolan not owe the amount the IRS sought, he had overpaid his taxes by $2.3 million.

The common thread in all three cases was one man: Burton Wallace Kanter. Kanter was born August 12, 1930, in Jersey City, New Jersey. He received his undergraduate degree from the University of Chicago in 1951, and his law degree a year later from the same school. He worked as a teaching associate at the University of Indiana Law School for two years before clerking for Judge Morton P. Fisher of the U.S. Tax Court. In 1958, Kanter joined the David Altman law firm in Chicago as an associate. Altman worked for the IRS from 1938 to 1943, first in the chief counsel's office and later in the office of division counsel. Altman's firm specialized in federal taxation, estate planning, trusts and wills. Kanter's apprenticeship there served him well: he is recognized as an expert in all these fields.

In 1963, Kanter and another University of Chicago Law School alumnus, Milton Levenfeld, became partners of the Altman firm. A year later, they struck out on their own and formed Levenfeld & Kanter, which became one of the most high-powered tax-law firms in the country. By the 1970s, the firm had added two more name partners— Roger S. Baskes and Charles S. Lippitz—and eleven other attorneys specializing in tax law. In the 1970s, the firm was embroiled in various controversial tax cases, all of which involved, in one way or another, offshore trusts and an offshore bank that Burton Kanter set up in the 1960s in the Bahamas. One of his partners, Roger Baskes, was convicted of tax fraud and jailed for two years on charges related to Levenfeld & Kanter's offshore activities. (Upon his release, Baskes successfully petitioned the Illinois Bar Association for reinstatement. Despite his conviction for criminal violations of the tax code, Baskes is still a practicing tax attorney and is a trustee of several of the trusts Kanter established for the benefit of his family.)

After Milton Levenfeld's retirement in the early 1980s, the firm renamed itself Kanter & Eisenberg. Kanter went into semiretirement in 1985, but is still of counsel to the firm, now called Eisenberg &

Janger. (Calvin Eisenberg, who worked for the IRS for four years in the early 1960s, merged the firm with nineteen tax specialists from another Chicago law firm.) He serves as a senior editor of the respected publication *Journal of Taxation*. He sits on the faculty of the University of Chicago Law School, where he shares his expertise on tax law. He also lectures on the aggressive use of trusts, offshore banks, and other tax avoidance strategies, a subject on which he is a master.

Kanter was a pioneer in the world of offshore companies and banks. Unlike his modern counterparts, with their Web sites and flashy advertisements ("Live simply and easily making a tax-free fortune using the world's most exotic places," declared one recent magazine ad), Kanter never advertised his services. He was discreet—a trait that his clients no doubt appreciated. And he was wildly successful.

From its founding in 1964, Castle Trust Ltd. (as it was first called) was a shady affair. Bahamian law required a corporation to have five directors; Castle's original board included two fictitious people: A. Alipranti and G. Bebas, supposedly from Athens. Throughout the course of its fourteen-year existence, Castle Bank was primarily a vehicle for tax avoidance and evasion.

A complete list of those who made use of the bank's secret accounts was never revealed, but some of those identified as having deposits there included some of the blue chip names in American commerce. Members of the Pritzker family, owners of the Hyatt Hotel chain and Royal Caribbean Cruise Lines, Ltd., had accounts there, as did Hugh Hefner, of *Playboy* fame, who was involved in casino deals with the Pritzkers. Tony Curtis, the actor, had an account. Henry Ford II, his wife, Christina, and several top Ford Motor Company executives, including Lee A. Iacocca, used the bank to hold their shares of a land development project on what was then the sleepy Caribbean island of St. Martin.

James Moran also had an account at Castle Bank. Moran was a member of the *Forbes* 400; a very successful Chicago auto dealer, he retired in the mid-1960s when he was diagnosed with cancer. But Moran made a miraculous recovery, and in the late sixties decided to reenter the world of auto dealing, this time in South Florida. He started buying up Toyota dealerships when gas sold for 30 cents a gallon; at the peak of the energy crisis, when Americans were trading in their gas guzzlers for fuel-efficient Japanese cars, Moran's dealerships accounted for one out of every five Toyotas sold in the United States. Moran was involved in a scheme that diverted "royalties" from every car he sold to an offshore trust maintained by Castle Bank.

Castle Bank came to the attention of the IRS in 1972, when federal narcotics agents working in California requested information on the institution. They had arrested one Allan George Palmer after watching him unload 900 pounds of marijuana from a plane. Palmer had cashed three checks for $22,500 that had been drawn from commercial accounts that Castle Bank maintained at the American National Bank and Trust Company of Chicago. IRS officials found that the signature cards for Castle Bank listed nine names, including its president, A. Goodling, the fictitious A. Alipranti, Florida attorney Paul Helliwell, and Burton Kanter.

IRS agents interviewed Kanter, who claimed to know almost nothing about the affairs of Castle Bank. Later investigation would prove that he lied about the extent of his knowledge, yet he never suffered any consequences either for misleading federal investigators or for operating what the IRS came to believe was a money-laundering scheme and a tax-evasion scheme.

The ensuing IRS investigation of Castle Bank was begun under the aegis of Operation Tradewinds, an investigation of offshore tax havens led by IRS Special Agent Richard Jaffe, and lasted nearly nine years. Jaffe used informants, undercover agents, and a variety of investigative techniques to break the veil of secrecy that the Bahamas granted to the bank's depositors. Eventually, he and his operatives managed to obtain the secret master list of Castle Bank depositors.

Mike Wolstencroft, an officer of the bank, made regular trips from the Bahamas to Miami to Chicago, ferrying documents to Kanter. On one trip, he asked Norman Casper, an IRS operative who'd been working undercover to get close to Castle officials, to arrange some extramarital female companionship for him. Casper complied, and while

Wolstencroft was wining and dining his "date," Casper used the key to her apartment to retrieve the bank officer's briefcase. Inside was the list of Castle depositors. The Service had its first solid documentation of those who were using the bank to avoid their taxes.

In the first Castle-related trial, in April 1977, Jack Payner, a Cleveland businessman, was charged with hiding $440,000 from the IRS in his Castle account. Payner's lawyer argued that any information derived from the briefcase affair was tainted, and, thus, so was the entire case against him. Federal judge John M. Manos suppressed all the evidence the IRS had gathered, on the grounds that the illegal search of Wolstencroft's briefcase tainted it.

The Supreme Court overturned Manos's ruling in a 6–3 decision. Justice Warren Burger wrote, "Payner—whose guilt is not in doubt—cannot take advantage of the Government's violation of the constitutional rights of Wolstencroft, for he is not party to this case." The court's ruling on the admissibility of evidence from the briefcase affair seemed to remove all roadblocks from using the Castle Bank depositor list in other trials.

When the entire Castle matter was referred to the Justice Department, several criminal cases were pursued against Castle conspirators. James Moran pleaded guilty to charges of tax evasion; he was given a suspended sentence, but was ordered to pay a heavy fine and $12 million in back taxes. Roger Baskes was found to have diverted some $700,000 of profit from the sale of a Reno, Nevada, apartment complex to his account in the Bahamas, and was sentenced to two years in a minimum security federal prison. Burton Kanter was tried on the same charges, but acquitted.

Special Agent Jaffe, who ran the operation that successfully cracked Castle Bank, left the IRS in 1979. More than two decades later, he still maintains that Kanter sidestepped justice. "He's a very brilliant attorney, and he thinks that he's above the law, and basically he took advantage of that in setting up the offshore bank and using it to get around U.S. tax laws," Jaffe told the Center. For his part, Kanter said in an interview with the Center that there was nothing improper about Castle Bank, which had its license revoked by the government of the

Bahamas in May 1977. He called Operation Tradewinds "very pecu-
liar," but declined to elaborate.

Kanter used more than just his offshore bank. He was the longtime
tax adviser for the Chicago Pritzker family; he set up a series of trusts
in the Bahamas for them in the 1960s, and helped them move much of
their wealth offshore. The IRS alleged that the Pritzkers had used the
trusts to avoid taxes on their U.S.–earned income of some $100 mil-
lion. That was in addition to the $53 million that the Service claimed
was owed on the Abraham Pritzker estate.

Kanter did not represent the Pritzkers, but he did help in the negotiations with the Service, appearing as an expert witness on trust issues.
When the estate case was settled for $9.5 million, the IRS agreed to
drop any future claim against the Pritzkers related to their offshore
trusts, designated the T-1740 trusts. For the $9.5 million in taxes they
agreed to pay, the Pritzker clan got a guarantee that the IRS would
never again trouble them about their offshore trusts. Said one dis-
gusted IRS insider familiar with the case, "We settled for nothing, or
next to nothing."

"All the trusts have been sustained; if they were examined, there
were no changes made to them," Kanter noted to the Center. "The
trusts are legitimate entities." He added that "some people think my
tax planning is aggressive," but insisted that there was nothing
improper about any of the trusts he has created over the years.

Kanter set up a far more complex series of trusts and offshore
companies to hide the profits from Saul Zaentz's film *One Flew Over
the Cuckoo's Nest*. While Zaentz settled his case years ago, some of the
other participants in the scheme are still fighting the IRS in Tax
Court. Among them are partners of Kanter's old firm, Levenfeld &
Kanter.

An IRS brief from one of the cases spells out how the scheme
worked: "From a date unknown to the present date, Mr. Roger Baskes
and other members of the Levenfeld & Kanter law firm were involved
in an activity that had as its purpose the movement of their income to
off-shore entities in the Netherlands Antilles to be secreted from the

United States government, in order to prevent the government from being aware of the source of income," the filing read. "A further part of the scheme and artifice herein was the return of the money to the United States in the guise of loans to be used in causing monies to be diverted to trusts for their or their families' benefit. The purpose of the scheme herein was to evade the payment of taxes on said income moved off-shore until the Levenfeld and Kanter attorneys returned the funds to the United States at some later date, and to evade payment of taxes on the monies diverted to their trusts."

Baskes, who served two years for his part in the Castle Bank affair, was one of the beneficiaries. The IRS claims that he evaded $570,000 in taxes in 1989. Calvin Eisenberg, who worked for the IRS in the 1960s, was another—he evaded $378,000 in taxes, according to the Service. Another participant was none other than Burton Kanter, who the IRS said evaded $390,000 in taxes. Five other attorneys from the firm were alleged by the IRS to be participants; Baskes, Eisenberg, and Kanter have all challenged the Service in Tax Court.

In October 1975, Levenfeld & Kanter agreed to forgo its customary fees and instead provide legal services to Saul Zaentz in exchange for 4 percent of the film's gross profits. Kanter and his partners then designed a complex scheme that involved shifting income from the film through various foreign entities and trusts in twenty-six separate steps before it was repatriated to the United States. The money was funneled through companies with names like Zwaluw N.V., Leeuwirik N.V., Nellthrope Cayman, Campobello Panamanian, and Inversiones Mixtas.

Payments back and forth were disguised as loans, investments in other films, or repayments of loans, until what was income for whom was thoroughly confused. Consider step fifteen from the IRS's brief in the case: "After Delta repaid its 'loan' to CMS by the end of 1979, CMS did not repay its 'loans' from the foreign entities: Zwaluw, Houtsende, Gelderse and Zeeuwse. Instead it 'renewed' said loans and used the money to fund another tax shelter transaction involving Century Associates."

The IRS claims that Kanter and his firm weren't forthcoming with information about their trusts. The Service sent summonses to all the Levenfeld & Kanter attorneys believed to be beneficiaries of the scheme, the trustees of their trusts, and the firm itself, requesting documents related to the transactions. In Tax Court filings, the Service contended that none of its summonses was complied with. Little wonder then that a quarter century after the Oscar-winning film premiered, the IRS is still attempting to collect the taxes due on its profits.

Using offshore havens is just one of the tax avoidance strategies in Kanter's arsenal. He served as an adviser to Cablevision, the company that won the exclusive rights to wire Manhattan in 1965. Today, the company, headquartered in Bethpage, New York, serves more than 3.4 million cable TV customers primarily in three core markets: New York City, Boston, and Cleveland. In addition to Bravo, Cablevision also owns American Movie Classics, the Independent Film Channel, and Romance Classics. The New York Rangers hockey team and the New York Knicks basketball team are also Cablevision properties.

Charles Dolan's rise to riches wasn't entirely smooth. In the early 1970s, he ran into financial troubles and brought in Time Incorporated as a partner. By 1971, Time owned 80 percent of the company; the media giant decided to take over Home Box Office and the Manhattan cable business and spin off the rest. Dolan used his remaining 20 percent stake to acquire what was left of the company, and turned to Kanter for help in restructuring his business.

The Chicago tax lawyer devised a unique corporate structure for the company: rather than a single corporate entity, Cablevision is a series of limited partnerships that shift any investment losses—which can be turned into tax write-offs—to their investors. Kanter then helped Dolan out by bringing in several investors, all of whom were his clients.

It was this ingenious structure that allowed Dolan to pay minimal taxes—or even none at all—in the 1980s. Like the Katzes, he was able to offset his income with losses generated by the various partnerships. The partnerships, however, weren't actually losing money. They only appeared to do so while paying off their debt, for which they received generous deductions. The whole corporate structure of the company acted like one gigantic tax shelter. And like Dolan, Cablevision's other investors were able to reap the same tax windfalls.

Kanter has always liked to blend business with tax avoidance. In the 1970s, for example, he became part of a massive kickback scheme with two executives from the Prudential Insurance Company, Claude Ballard and Robert Lisle.

Ballard and Lisle managed Prudential's real estate investments, and could choose companies that the insurer hired. Ballard was senior vice president of equities; Lisle was president of PIC Realty Corporation, Prudential's real estate subsidiary. Their company controlled upward of $20 billion worth of properties across the United States, and Ballard and Lisle decided who developed and managed those assets. As a result, an introduction to the two could be worth millions of dollars in business.

Kanter met them sometime in the late sixties or early seventies, when the Hyatt Corporation was involved in negotiations with Prudential over the management of the hotel. The three concocted a scheme to get kickbacks from contractors and management companies in exchange for the lucrative Prudential business. Kanter found some of the willing participants in the scheme and hid the payments using yet another elaborate series of companies and trusts. In exchange for his services, he got 10 percent of the kickbacks. Ballard and Lisle split the rest evenly.

Kanter turned to some of his old clients for business. The Hyatt Corporation, owned by the Pritzker family, got Prudential business. So did Bruce Frey, who ran BJF Development, Incorporated, a large real estate developer based in Illinois. (In 1993, Frey and Kanter tried to buy the Miami Dolphins.) The other participants in the kickback scheme were John Eulich, whom Kanter met through Abraham Pritzker sometime in the late sixties or early seventies; William Schaffel, who ran W. D. Schaffel & Company, a New York real estate developer and mortgage broker; J. D. Weaver, who managed Hyatt properties; and Kenneth Schnitzer, a Houston-based real estate developer.

The five individuals and their companies earned millions of dollars' worth of contracts, thanks to their connections to Ballard, Lisle, and Kanter. In return, over a period starting sometime in the 1970s and lasting until 1989, they paid $13 million to four companies controlled by Kanter—Investment Research Associates and its subsidiaries, KWJ Company, Zeus Ventures, and The Holding Company.

Lisle left Prudential for Travelers Insurance Company in 1982, where he did virtually the same type of work. He also continued to participate in the kickback scheme until his retirement in 1988. He died on September 17, 1993.

The IRS, which, Kanter once said, had audited him every year but one since 1961, discovered the scheme. Agents audited Investment Research Associates' 1987 tax returns, and obtained financial records, billings, invoices, expense items, and various accounting and corporate records. The records indicated that the shareholders of Investment Research Associates were trusts set up for the benefit of Ballard, Lisle, and Kanter. Agents interviewed Ballard, and soon were auditing his tax returns and those of Lisle.

The investigation expanded. The IRS interviewed more and more witnesses. It requested documents from Ballard, Lisle, and Kanter, but received incomplete records. The Service went to court to enforce summonses issued to the three and to various companies Kanter created. Many of the relevant records were not produced. In some cases, Kanter claimed that he had no control over them; in others, he said they had already been destroyed.

Agents spent years unraveling the scheme, covering office walls with ad hoc flow charts showing the participants, the transactions, bank deposits, loans back and forth between related parties, and the other minutiae of the scheme. The Service issued more than twenty-eight Notices of Deficiency to Lisle and his estate, as well as to Ballard,

Kanter, and the companies Kanter used to hide the kickbacks. The IRS brief in the case filled more than two thousand pages; the *Wall Street Journal* joked at the time that it was hardly brief.

Ballard, Kanter, and Lisle vigorously disputed the deficiencies and claimed there was no scheme whatsoever. The case went to trial on June 14, 1994, before Special Trial Judge Irving D. Couvillion. There were nearly five weeks of testimony, producing a transcript of more than 5,400 pages. The briefs ran to more than 4,600 pages, and the exhibits totaled hundreds of thousands of pages. Couvillion then weighed the evidence.

For five years.

On December 15, 1999, he issued his ruling—adding another 606 pages to the case file. He noted the complexity of the case, which involved forty separate issues. "Not surprisingly, our task of finding the facts has been laborious and frequently frustrating," he wrote.

He went into great detail about various projects for which "the Five"—the companies to which Lisle and Ballard steered business— won contracts. He wrote at length on the alleged kickbacks they paid to the three conspirators, as the IRS called Kanter, Lisle, and Ballard. "At trial, all the witnesses associated with the Five explicitly denied that the payments described were 'kickbacks' or 'payoffs' for Ballard and/or Lisle's help in steering business to them," Couvillion wrote. "Those witnesses did confirm, however, that they entered into these arrangements in exchange for Kanter's influence in obtaining business. Furthermore, it is clear from the record that Kanter, Ballard, and Lisle agreed to share and did share the money from the Prudential transactions in a 45–45–10 split."

He described the evidence presented on the complicated scheme to cover up the payments. "Kanter routinely created various corporations, partnerships, and trusts with similar names; for example, Cedilla Co., Cedilla Investment Co., Investment Research Associates, Ltd. (formerly Cedilla Co.), Cedilla Co. (formerly Arba Investments Inc.), and Cedilla Trust; KWJ Corp. and KWJ Co. partnership; Essex Corp.

and Essex Partnership. As a result of the intended confusion created by similar names, Kanter could substitute one entity for another," he wrote.

Couvillion was not confused. "We find the various entities to be pure tax avoidance vehicles. The corporations were nothing more than a few incorporating papers of no significance except when a tax return was due. Petitioners diverted millions of dollars of income. The make-believe corporations were shams and too transparent to accept for tax purposes."

His conclusion was unmistakable.

"The facts, as we have found in detail, clearly show that Kanter, Ballard, and Lisle, through the use of various conduit entities, devised a multifaceted scheme to shield kickback payments they received from transactions involving the Five," he wrote. "Their fraud resulted in the Federal Government not being paid several millions in income taxes due and owing."

Couvillion's ruling contained several harsh rebukes for the Chicago tax attorney. The judge found his testimony to be less than credible. "Kanter's explanations are mere platitudes and rationalized rhetoric intended to obfuscate the true character of the transactions and his wrongdoing," he wrote.

Couvillion faulted the attorney for his failure to provide the records the IRS requested. "Kanter, a tax professional who represents clients before the IRS and this Court, is aware of the need for documentation and records to support the items reported on tax returns," he wrote. "In light of that knowledge, coupled with other evidence, we find that his discarding of his supporting income documentation was an intentional act designed to conceal and evade the reporting and payment of Federal income tax."

Kanter disputed the judge's ruling. "For reasons unbeknownst to us, the evidence in the case was largely ignored," he said. "The shock of this case is that the government called all the witnesses, except for me, and all the testimony was against the government position."

As of this writing, Couvillion had yet to determine Kanter's tax liability. Whatever the amount, if Kanter agrees to pay it, it will represent one of the few times in his life he's written a big check to the Treasury. Kanter, who helped his well-heeled clients avoid their income taxes, is a master of avoiding his own. He paid nothing from 1979 to 1990.

3

Gimme Shelter

 By almost any definition, Macauley Taylor is a successful man. A graduate of Dartmouth College and the Harvard Business School, where he earned a master of business administration, Taylor went to work for Merrill Lynch & Company, the giant brokerage and securities firm, in 1986. Within three years, he was named managing director of the Structured Derivative Financing Group, where he designed complex financial trades for corporate clients. He had a team of three highly trained professionals working for him who held advanced degrees in law, economics, and business administration.

Taylor's job was, in its essentials, not much different from any other stockbroker's. He networked within his firm for leads on existing clients who might be interested in what he was selling. He dealt with a roster of clients, some of them long-standing customers of Merrill Lynch, some of them drawn to the firm by word of mouth or sales pitches. He used his expertise and that of his staff to recommend investments that would suit the needs of his clients. But Taylor wasn't just any other broker recommending blue chip stocks to small investors. His clients were the blue chips themselves. Among them were the *Fortune* 500 giants Colgate-Palmolive Company, the global consumer-products maker; AlliedSignal, Incorporated, the aerospace and automotive firm; and Schering-Plough Corporation, the pharmaceutical manufacturer. And catering to their needs was more than a matter of making a phone call and touting a hot stock.

Taylor and his group made sales pitches to boards of directors and skeptical top executives. They used flip charts and slide shows to explain complicated transactions involving offshore partners, foreign currencies and bonds, and corporate debt. Like all good salesmen, they listened to their customers' concerns and tried to accommodate them. It wasn't always easy.

Steve Belasco, a vice president of Colgate, explained his reaction to a Merrill Lynch proposal made on May 15, 1989. "Well, after looking at it for a while, I decided that while technically it seemed to work and had some merit, it just wasn't something I was interested in pursuing." Hans Pohlschroeder, Colgate's assistant treasurer, said of the same investment opportunity, "I turned it down, and I told them that we wouldn't do anything like this."

Those reactions were not altogether surprising, given what the men from Merrill Lynch were selling: a surefire way for a corporation to lose tens or even hundreds of millions of dollars in an offshore partnership. But Taylor was a very good salesman; Colgate, despite its initial rejection of the plan, eventually signed on, as did at least a dozen other large corporations. The head of Merrill Lynch's Structured Derivative Financing Group arranged everything. He found a foreign bank that would be part of the deals; he jetted to various Caribbean destinations to take part in partnership meetings; he arranged all the swaps—the complicated, hedged sales and buybacks of bonds—that produced those multimillion-dollar losses. For his efforts, he was well rewarded. "I could tell you from the period 1988 through '91," he said, "my compensation went up, on average, 20 to 30 percent a year."

During those years, Merrill Lynch didn't fare too shabbily either. The brokerage firm made over $20 million in fees alone, just by selling those investment partnerships that Taylor explained to Merrill Lynch's clients. It made $1.75 million by producing losses for the Brunswick Corporation, the sporting goods manufacturer best known for its bowling balls. It made $1.75 million in fees and another $2 million in commissions by losing millions for Colgate. It made $7 million in fees from AlliedSignal.

The losses were worth every penny the companies paid for them. When AlliedSignal sold off its shares in Union Texas Petroleum Holdings, Incorporated, in 1990, the company had a capital gain of $447 million. The taxes due on such a gain amounted to roughly $149 million. But AlliedSignal's management had no intention of paying taxes on their gain. G. Peter D'Aloia, AlliedSignal's vice president and treasurer, explained that one of the company's directors pointed out that, "There were ways of avoiding the tax if we were willing to enter into certain types of transactions and make certain types of investments."

Among those certain types of transactions and investments were the sorts that Macauley Taylor and Merrill Lynch had developed. Through an offshore partnership, a corporation could appear to lose, on paper, millions of dollars that would offset the very real capital gains that that company had earned. And Merrill Lynch wasn't the only firm pitching such transactions and investments. Corporate tax shelters have proliferated over the past decade; some have estimated they cost the government over $10 billion a year in lost tax revenue. In a 1999 report prepared by the Treasury Department's Office of Tax Policy, that cost was put into perspective: "Corporate tax shelters reduce the corporate tax base, raising the tax burden on other taxpayers."

"Other taxpayers," of course, means you.

And so it goes in the world of corporate income taxes, where top executives ask not how they can pay their company's taxes but how they can avoid them. Need to offset a capital gain? Sophisticated financial firms have designed the perfect tax shelter. Upset about the latest tax legislation coming out of Congress? A friendly member will write a special exemption into the bill that applies to just your company. Perturbed by the latest Treasury regulations? Hire a former congressional staff member who will persuade his old bosses to pass a bill gutting them. Fed up with U.S. tax laws altogether? Move to an offshore tax haven. Unhappy with the offshore tax havens? There are plenty of developing countries eager to rewrite their tax laws to attract U.S. businesses.

All of which helps to explain why, in the 1990s, the federal corporate income tax accounted for just over one-tenth of federal revenues. By contrast, in the 1950s, corporate taxes provided more than 27 percent of federal revenues.

As the corporate contribution to the treasury declined, so did the rate at which their profits were taxed. In the 1960s, the average effective corporate tax rate—total corporate income taxes divided by total corporate profits—was 35.4 percent. That rate fell every decade, to a low in the 1990s of 23.5 percent. And, as the corporate tax base shrank, that burden was shifted to individuals.

The revenue from the corporate income tax did not dwindle overnight. Presidential administrations and lawmakers of both parties slashed the tax rates for corporations. The Revenue Act of 1964, first championed by President John F. Kennedy and strong-armed into law by his successor, Lyndon Johnson, cut the corporate tax rate from 52 percent to 48 percent. In 1978, Jimmy Carter and Congress cut the rate another two percentage points. In 1986, the Reagan administration pushed through another cut, this time to 34 percent, as part of the sweeping Tax Reform Act of 1986. President Bill Clinton barely persuaded Congress to raise the rate to 35 percent (the measure passed the House of Representatives by one vote), the first time in forty-one years that the corporate tax rate had been increased.

The declining tax rate for corporations doesn't tell the whole story. The Internal Revenue Code grants them generous deductions that ordinary taxpayers can only dream of. If a corporation buys a fleet of limousines to ferry its top managers to and from work, it's a deductible business expense. The car that you buy for your commute isn't. A corporation that goes into debt to expand can write off the interest it pays on the loans. Run up a huge credit card bill, and the interest you pay can't be deducted. While various administrations and Congresses cut the corporate tax rate, they expanded some loopholes in the code that shrank the amount of corporate income subject to the tax. Those loopholes cost the government billions of dollars each year. All of which helps explain why a series of bad business decisions by the management of a department store chain in the second half of the 1980s translates to hundreds of millions of dollars of write-offs through the year 2009.

In 1986, when corporate raiders and junk bond dealers like Michael Milken, Ivan Boesky, and Carl Icahn were flying high, the senior management of R. H. Macy & Co., led by chairman and chief executive officer Edward S. Finkelstein, decided to beat the raiders to the punch. Rather than be bought out by a corporate raider, Finkelstein arranged an insider's leveraged buyout; he and his managers and a few outside investors borrowed $3.5 billion to buy the company. At a party to celebrate the successful conclusion of the deal, held at the Metropolitan Museum of Art, Finkelstein raised his glass to toast, quoting Shakespeare's *Henry V*, "We few, we happy few, we band of brothers."

The brothers seemed to have made a good gamble at the time. R. H. Macy & Co. owned one of the most profitable and storied department store chains in America: Macy's. Its Herald Square store in New York City was featured in the classic Christmas film *A Miracle on 34th Street*. Over the course of its 140-odd years, the chain has sold everything from liquor to linen. In 1960, it became the first retailer to sell Teflon-coated cookware; customer demand was so great that the chain quickly sold out.

Finkelstein was a marketing whiz who rose to the top of the company after turning around the chain's California stores and revitalizing its Herald Square flagship store. He and his fellow investors gambled that the economy would remain strong, allowing their stores to generate enough cash to pay off the interest and principal on their debt. They projected that the payoff for a $75,000 investment would be $1.5 million—a profit of 1,900 percent. Those projections failed to take into account the possibility of a recession, or that management might not always make the right decision.

With his company already deeply in debt thanks to the buyout, Finkelstein, over the objection of some of his fellow investors, saddled Macy's with another $1.1 billion of loans in 1988 to acquire a pair of department store chains based in California. Year after year, he overestimated the strength of the economy; each Christmas, the stores in his empire had disappointing sales largely because he had overloaded them with inventory that consumers, leery of the layoffs and plant closings that made headlines with depressing regularity, were unwilling to buy. In 1992, R. H. Macy & Co. was forced to declare bankruptcy. Finkelstein and his group of senior managers lost most of their investment. But the venerable department store did not just disappear. The Macy's name still adorns stores all over the country, thanks to the chain's new owner, Federated Department Stores, Inc., which completed its acquisition of Macy's in December 1994. Macy's had a new president, a new CEO, a new board of directors. And the old management left it with a tax windfall.

Thanks to the bad management of Finkelstein, Federated Department Stores ended up with some $950 million worth of tax write-offs. Every dollar of profit that Macy's earns can, for federal income tax purposes, be canceled out by the huge losses that forced the chain into bankruptcy in 1992, thanks to the Internal Revenue Code and what it calls a net operating loss. Those net operating losses can be carried forward by Federated until 2009.

It wasn't always that way. For most of its history, the net operating loss could be carried forward for just one or two years. The provision was originally passed as a temporary tax measure in 1918 to help companies adjust to a peacetime economy after World War I. It was eliminated for five years in the 1930s, brought back in 1939, lengthened and shortened to two years, one year, three years in the 1940s and 1950s. In 1976, the Ford administration and a Democrat-controlled Congress extended to seven years the length of time companies could claim net operating losses. In 1981, the Reagan administration requested that the carryover period be extended to ten years; a Democratic House and Republican Senate decided that fifteen would be better.

The result has been a billion-dollar windfall for corporations. In 1995, the most recent year for which complete statistics are available, net operating losses shrank the corporate tax base by some $57 billion. Total revenues from corporate income taxes that year were $198 billion; the write-off was $19.9 billion, or a 10 percent tax cut.

Some of the most profitable companies in America have been able to claim net operating losses, reducing their taxable income. The Dow Jones Industrial Average, which trebled in the 1990s, is an index of the value of thirty top industrial firms. According to their 1999 Form 10K filed with the Securities and Exchange Commission, ten of those companies carried some $3.6 billion in net operating losses. AT&T had federal net operating losses worth $267 million. Coca-Cola had $49 million worth of the write-offs. Exxon had $962 million worth; the company it merged with, Mobil, had $722 million.

Of course, some have complained about the fifteen-year carryover period. In a June 5, 1997, letter to then Treasury secretary Robert Rubin, Curtis H. Barnette, the chairman and chief executive officer of Bethlehem Steel Corporation, wrote, "Annual net operating losses . . . generated by corporations may be carried forward as a deduction against future income for a period of 15 years. But for many companies, particularly those in mature industries that have experienced major restructuring such as steel, the fifteen year loss carryforward period is insufficient." Insufficient, according to Barnette, because companies like Bethlehem Steel, which emerged from the 1980s considerably smaller, and thus able to make a correspondingly smaller amount of profit, weren't able to realize the full benefits of their net operating losses. Bethlehem Steel had some $1.8 billion worth of such losses on its books at the end of 1997.

"Your leadership in helping to obtain a five year extension of the [net operating loss] carryforward period for existing and newly incurred losses will be deeply appreciated," Barnette closed his letter. That year, Congress passed the Taxpayer Relief Act; among its provisions, the bill extended the time a company could claim a net operating loss from fifteen years to twenty. A grateful Bethlehem Steel noted in its 1998 Form 10K, filed with the Securities and Exchange Commission, "The tax law currently provides for a 20-year carryforward of that loss against future taxable income. We, therefore, have sufficient time to realize these future tax benefits."

Most corporations don't have to wait twenty years for their loopholes to kick in. Some of them are set up so that every step in their production process is designed to minimize the tax burden they face. Like Apple Computer Inc., the plucky underdog that for a time outstripped its big rival, IBM, in the race to develop a user-friendly home computer.

In 1984, upstart Apple crashed into the public consciousness with a thirty-second ad that aired just once—during Super Bowl XVIII. A colorfully clad woman raced through a crowd of gray-hued, zombielike spectators and flung a sledgehammer at a monitor beaming an Orwellian, Big Brother–like visage to the assembled audience. The powerful commercial cemented Apple's image as a different kind of high-tech company that produced a different kind of product—the user-friendly Macintosh.

While Apple's technical innovations may have set it apart from other companies in the personal computer industry, its corporate structure was nearly as complex and sophisticated as that of its mammoth rival IBM. Among Apple's subsidiaries were Apple Computer Limited, an Ireland-based manufacturing company; Apple Computer Inc., Limited, an Irish holding company that owned the Irish manufacturing company; Apple Netherlands B.V., an investment company; Apple Computer Foreign Sales Corporation, a Virgin Islands corporation set up to sell to overseas markets; Apple Computer Cayman Finance Ltd., a Cayman Islands investment company; and Apple Computer International Ltd., which Apple once described as "a Cayman Islands corporation incorporated on March 24, 1981, whose function is to conduct manufacturing operations in Singapore." For the record, the Cayman Islands are a mere 10,969 miles from Singapore. Cupertino, California, where the company was headquartered, is 2,486 miles closer.

Apple's complicated structure of subsidiaries is hardly unusual. A multinational firm might have manufacturing, finance, marketing, and insurance subsidiaries scattered in dozens of countries around the world. A car company might make engine parts in a Chinese factory financed through a Dutch subsidiary. Those engine parts are transferred to a Mexican plant for assembly. Meanwhile, the car's body parts—the fenders, doors, hood, and so on—are made in Canada, but the chassis and drive train in the United States. Which government gets to tax the profits from the sale of the car—say, in Wichita, Kansas—is determined largely by how much the corporation says it pays each of its subsidiaries for the parts it buys from them.

Apple manufactured computers in Singapore. Say the cost to produce the completed Macintosh was $200. The Singapore company transfers the machine to the Cayman Islands corporation, which sells it to the American company for $900. Apple in turn sells it to its dealers for $1,000. Total U.S. profit: $100. Total profit in the Cayman Islands: $700. Because the Cayman Islands has a corporate income tax rate that is just a fraction of that in the United States, the company would save hundreds of dollars in taxes on each computer sold here.

Which is precisely what the IRS accused Apple of doing in 1992.

The practice is known as transfer pricing, and it costs the federal government billions of dollars each year. Ernst & Young, the Big Five accounting firm that provides a wide range of international corporate clients with bookkeeping and tax advice, conducts an annual survey of the tax departments of some of the largest multinationals. In 1999, it found that "Tax and finance executives believe the up-front involvement of transfer pricing in strategic decisions could help maximize operating performance and reduce the global tax burden."

Ernst & Young cited an estimate made by the Organization for Economic Cooperation and Development, an international organization that provides economic data and recommendations to its twenty-nine member nations, that some 60 percent of global trade consists of transfers made within multinationals. Companies have wide latitude to set the prices they charge themselves to take advantage of differences in various tax systems. Singapore offers foreign corporations low tax rates; the Cayman Islands charges companies a nominal fee for operating there—income derived from foreign sources isn't taxed at all. By inflating the costs of manufacturing anything from shoes to circuit boards offshore, a U.S. corporation can save hundreds of millions in taxes.

For its part, Apple vigorously denied that its decision to manufacture in Singapore, or manage that manufacturing operation from the Cayman Islands, was made to avoid U.S. taxes. That Apple wanted to manufacture in Singapore isn't surprising. The tiny country on the tip of the Malaysian peninsula had the advantage of cheap, skilled labor and generous financing provisions for companies setting up shop there. Apple's Singapore manufacturing unit handled virtually every aspect of production, according to the company, from finding materials to the final assembly of the computer; from designing the manufacturing process to designing the boxes that the Macintoshes were shipped in.

And when it paid its Singapore subsidiary for that work, Apple included various costs that might seem surprising. The company multiplied the number of man-hours needed for production by a U.S. wage rate, rather than the much lower Singapore wage rate. The company included a U.S. overhead cost per unit, rather than the lower Singapore overhead cost. "Under the transfer pricing method used by [Apple] and Apple Singapore," the IRS charged, "all additional profit earned because of lower labor and overhead costs . . . inured to Apple Singapore." Singapore profits are immune to U.S. taxation.

In 1990, the IRS charged that Apple used its offshore subsidiaries to avoid some $311 million in taxes for 1984, 1985, and 1986. In 1992, the IRS claimed the company had avoided another $275 million in taxes in 1987 and 1988. Apple disagreed with the IRS's conclusions, and in 1993 opted to settle the transfer pricing issue in secret, binding arbitration. The ultimate resolution of Apple's battle with the IRS was never made public; some matters from the two cases are still pending in Tax Court.

At least Apple actually manufactured something in Singapore. Halliburton Company, an oil field services company, maintained a subsidiary in the Cayman Islands, Halliburton Global Limited. The Cayman Islands has no oil industry; the IRS contended that Halliburton used the subsidiary to avoid $38 million in taxes in 1990 and 1991. The company disagreed; it argued that its Caribbean subsidiary was "a corporation duly constituted and in good standing under the laws of the Cayman Islands. Global possessed economic substance. It was established to serve as the entity performing the function of centralized purchasing and distribution of chemicals." That case is still pending.

The triumphs of the pioneers of the automobile industry—like Henry Ford's assembly line and the first workingman's car, the Model T— have attained an almost mythical quality in American history. Part marketing chutzpah, part technological innovation, the stories are as old as the country's love affair with the car.

Chrysler has been one of the blue chip names in that storied history. Walter P. Chrysler unveiled the first car to bear his name, the Chrysler Six, at the Commodore Hotel in New York City in 1924. The story goes that Chrysler wanted his innovative car—powered by a high-compression, six-cylinder engine and the first to use hydraulic brakes on all four wheels—to debut at the New York Automobile Show. Organizers of the exhibition barred the car because it wasn't yet in production. So Chrysler rented space in the lobby of the hotel where wealthy investors attending the exhibition were staying. The gamble paid off. A banker with Chase Securities liked the looks of the first Chrysler and arranged to underwrite $5 million for Chrysler's company, then known as Maxwell Motor Company, to mass-produce the car.

The company introduced the first aerodynamic car, the Airflow, in 1934 (Orville Wright, the aviation pioneer, helped design it), the first car with power steering in 1951, and one of the first muscle cars, the 300-C, in 1955. During World War II, the company ceased production of automobiles and made everything from Pershing tanks and engines for the B-29 bomber to 40 mm antiaircraft guns. In all, the company handled sixty-six military projects, valued at some $3.4 billion, between 1940 and 1945.

Chrysler remained a defense contractor for years after the war, but its close relationship with the government didn't end there. Struggling against Japanese imports, its own bad management practices, and new fuel economy standards mandated by the federal government, Chrysler was tottering on the verge of bankruptcy in 1979. It lost $1.1 billion that year, and $1.7 billion the next—at the time a record for corporate ineptitude. The company was bailed out by Congress and the Carter administration, which put together the Chrysler Corporation Loan Guarantee Act of 1979, a $1.5 billion package of aid that kept the struggling car maker afloat.

Lee Iacocca, the brash, straight-talking CEO, took the government aid package and turned the company around. Chrysler put out the world's first minivan in 1980; the company bought out AMC Corporation, maker of the Jeep line of vehicles; and added the grandfather of the sports utility vehicle to its product line. By 1984, the company that had lost billions in the late seventies and first few years of the eighties turned a profit of $2.4 billion. Iacocca gained fame for his company's resurrection and his attacks on what he considered unfair competition by the foreign carmakers, particularly the Japanese. He starred in more than sixty commercials for Chrysler, many of which hammered home a "Made in America" theme, arguing that the domestically manufactured K-cars and LeBarons were superior to their Japanese rivals.

In 1998, six years after Iacocca left the helm of the company, Chrysler merged with Daimler-Benz A.G., the German manufacturer of Mercedes-Benz cars and trucks. The inherent patriotism of the "Made in America" advertising campaign became as obsolete as the Chrysler Six, at least as far as the company's willingness to continue playing by America's rules.

"The U.S. tax system puts global companies at a decisive disadvantage," John Loffredo, the vice president and chief tax counsel for Chrysler and its successor, DaimlerChrysler, told a hearing of the House Ways and Means Committee on June 30, 1999, just twenty years after his predecessors had gone, hat in hand, to beg Congress for a bailout. "This issue became a major concern and when the time came to choose whether the new company should be a U.S. company or a foreign company, management chose a company organized under the laws of Germany."

So Chrysler, one of the Big Three American carmakers, opted out of the U.S. tax system and ceased to be an American business.

For the record, Chrysler's effective federal tax rate under that disadvantageous U.S. tax system through the 1990s was a mere 18 percent—slightly more than half of the statutory rate of 35 percent. The huge net operating losses that Chrysler incurred helped the company avoid paying taxes altogether some years, and steeply reduced its tax bill other years. Adding insult to injury, Chrysler filed a petition in U.S. Tax Court in 1997 claiming it was owed a refund of $49.8 million from 1983 to 1985. The bulk of write-offs the car manufacturer claimed were related to costs associated with the government bailout of 1979. In effect, Chrysler was asking other taxpayers to subsidize the bailout a second time. That case is still pending.

By choosing to become a German corporation, Chrysler will no longer owe U.S. taxes on its overseas profits. From 1990 until it merged with Daimler-Benz A.G., Chrysler had taxable overseas income of $3.5 billion. After adjusting for foreign taxes paid, Chrysler still would have owed $590 million on those profits to the U.S. Treasury, assuming that the company paid at the statutory rate set by Congress. Thanks to its choice to be a German company, all the company's future foreign profits—earned by selling Jeeps and Chrysler minivans overseas—will escape U.S. taxation.

According to Loffredo, the companies considered choosing the United States as their home, but rejected the notion of forming "Chrysler-Daimler." "Daimler being a subsidiary of Chrysler would have opened up for review all of Daimler's operations worldwide to the IRS," he told the Center. "That's something no one should volunteer."

Chrysler will still owe some U.S. taxes. The carmaker will join the nearly 60,000 other corporations with 50 percent or more foreign ownership doing business in the greatest consumer market on earth. In 1995, the last year for which statistics were available, there were some 60,157 returns filed by such corporations. Of those, 19,962—or slightly more than 33 percent—owed some federal income tax.

"I want to make it clear that the former Daimler-Benz has been a good corporate citizen in the U.S. and has paid all taxes believed legally due on its U.S. operations," Loffredo testified before Congress. "The same is true for the former Chrysler Corporation. In addition, Daimler and Chrysler will continue to be subject to the U.S. tax laws on their U.S. operations and will continue to pay their fair share of U.S. taxes." The key word in his statement is "believed."

In 1994, Daimler-Benz filed a petition in U.S. Tax Court claiming that the fines it paid to the National Highway Traffic Safety Administration for selling cars that failed to meet minimum standards for fuel efficiency should be deductible as "ordinary and necessary business expenses." Throughout much of the 1980s, most of the Mercedes-Benz luxury sedans that the company sold guzzled more gas than federal regulations permitted. Rather than meet the fuel economy standards, which have both reduced air pollution and helped to reduce demand for gasoline—thus helping to make it cheaper—Daimler-Benz chose to pay a fine to the government. That is an option the company had under the Energy Policy and Conservation Act of 1975, which required manufacturers to meet certain mile-per-gallon averages. But nowhere does the act say that a company that chooses not to meet the standards should be able to pass along the costs of that failure to other taxpayers—something that Daimler-Benz argued in its court petition. Think of it this way: Daimler-Benz was arguing that ordinary taxpayers should foot part of the bill for those wealthy enough to afford a Mercedes-Benz.

In 1988 and 1989, Daimler-Benz's U.S. subsidiary, Mercedes-Benz

of North America Inc., made payments to the National Highway Traffic Safety Administration totaling $65 million; the company deducted
those payments on its federal income tax returns. "The amounts
MBNA paid to NHTSA in 1988 and 1989 are ordinary expenses
incurred by MBNA in carrying on its trade or business," the company
argued. "The amounts MBNA paid to NHTSA in 1988 and 1989 are
necessary expenses incurred by MBNA in carrying on its trade or business. . . . The amounts MBNA paid to NHTSA in 1988 and 1989 are
deductible under section 162 as ordinary and necessary business
expenses." The company lost its case in Tax Court, and was unable to
deduct the fines paid to NHTSA from its taxes. Even without the
questionable deductions, the company, taking advantage of legitimate
deductions allowed by the Internal Revenue Code, found other ways
to reduce its taxable income from year to year, as the documents in the
case revealed.

Mercedes-Benz of North America "engaged exclusively in the
importation and distribution of Mercedes-Benz passenger automobiles
and parts in the United States," according to the company's petition in
Tax Court. Those cars, of course, are beyond the means of the average
American; in the 1980s, the price for one of those finely engineered
German automobiles ranged between $30,000 and $70,000. In 1984,
Mercedes-Benz of North America sold more than 79,200 cars in the
United States. That year, Mercedes paid $156 million in U.S. taxes.
The next year, 1985, Mercedes sold more cars in the United States—
just over 86,900 of them. It paid about a third less in taxes—just $99
million. The following year, 1986, Mercedes had its best year in the
1980s, with more than 99,300 new-car sales in the United States. The
company's taxes totaled a mere $5.4 million.

Even with all these advantages over the average individual taxpayer,
corporations are not satisfied. Top executives view taxes as one more
line item on the balance sheet that cuts into profits. In an age when corporations routinely ship jobs offshore and lay off long-term employees

without a second thought, it's not surprising that they've come to view their tax burdens as just another line item, another cost, to be reduced as much as possible. And a growing industry in developing and selling corporate tax shelters has emerged to accommodate them.

Joseph Bankman, a professor of law and business at Stanford Law School, noted the difficulty of determining how large the market for shelters is. "Companies and counsel shown the shelters are often required to sign confidentiality agreements; these agreements, together with concerns about attorney-client privilege, prevent many lawyers from discussing tax shelters in print or public," he wrote in a June 21, 1999, article in the respected publication *Tax Notes*. "It is virtually certain though, that annual investments in corporate tax shelters aggregate to tens of billions of dollars, and that the tax shelter market is growing at a breakneck speed."

In 1998, *Forbes* magazine reported that Deloitte & Touche, one of the Big Five accounting firms, sent out confidential letters to corporations that began, "As we discussed, set forth below are the details of our proposal to recommend and implement our tax strategy to eliminate the Federal and state income taxes associated with [your] income for up to five years." For the service, Deloitte & Touche charged a fee of 30 percent of the tax savings.

On May 4, 1999, PricewaterhouseCoopers L.L.P. sent out a confidential letter, some 22,000 words in length, to invite corporations to take part in its Bond and Option Sales Strategy, or BOSS shelter, which, like the shelter Merrill Lynch sold, involved investment vehicles with foreign partners created solely to provide a paper tax loss. *Tax Notes* obtained a copy and published it. On December 9, 1999, the Treasury Department issued notice 99–59, warning companies that if they made use of BOSS, the IRS would challenge any losses they claimed. Representative Lloyd Doggett, Democrat of Texas and a member of the House Ways and Means Committee, who drew attention to the shelter in a hearing a month before Treasury acted, issued a statement welcoming the notice. "While encouraged that Treasury has quickly shut down an obviously abusive tax shelter," he said, "I am reminded that one Big Five accounting firm requires staff to cook up a new shelter every week."

And for the IRS, discovering, unraveling, and denying them can take years. Tax shelters are designed to follow the form of the tax law—every "t" is crossed, every "i" is dotted. Agreements are signed, transactions take place, money changes hands, and tax benefits are produced. The shelters Merrill Lynch designed and marketed to corporate clients in 1989 mimicked countless transactions that corporations engage in every day for legitimate purposes. Ten years later, some companies that bought Merrill shelters—the entertainment conglomerate Paramount Communications, Incorporated, among them—are still battling the IRS in U.S. Tax Court.

Taken together, the eleven foreign partnerships that the IRS discovered give an inside view into the thinking of corporate tax departments, shelter promoters, and offshore trust companies. Paying their fair share of taxes is not high on their priorities. Not surprisingly, key participants in the Merrill Lynch shelters were not willing to discuss, on the record, their roles in the schemes. What follows, then, is pieced together from Tax Court documents, transcripts, and other public records.

In October 1988, Colgate sold off a subsidiary, Kendall Incorporated, a manufacturer of medical supplies, for $952 million. Instead of rejoicing over the windfall, which included a profit of $105 million, Steven Belasco, the company's vice president for taxation, began to worry. "Once we realized the magnitude of the gain on the sale," he said, "we began to look at alternative kinds of structures or other kinds of transactions we might do to either reduce the gain or defer it." Reducing or deferring the profit would have lowered the taxes due on the profit. Unfortunately for Belasco, others at Colgate didn't share his view. "In my meetings with the investment bankers and our senior management, they indicated to me they were more interested in maximizing the cash for the transaction and getting it done quickly rather than doing some other kinds of things that might reduce the tax."

Given that publicly held corporations are supposed to make as much profit as possible, that's not surprising. Hans Pohlschroeder, the company's assistant treasurer, said that he sees Colgate as a "growth company." "We want to be growing at 15 percent earnings per share after tax," he said. Fortunately for Belasco and Pohlschroeder, another company driven to succeed, one that takes pride in its ability to deliver on its promises to clients, was trying to solve just the sort of dilemma that companies like Colgate encountered. Merrill Lynch devised a tax shelter that wouldn't interfere with getting the Kendall transaction done quickly or limit the cash that Colgate wanted. The shelter would produce losses to offset those profits, but only on paper. And best of all, because of the way the partnership was structured, shareholders would never discover it on the corporation's financial statements.

"I'm not an expert in accounting," Pohlschroeder said, "but I know that much, that when you have less than 50 percent ownership and do not control an entity, that it is deconsolidated and is off balance sheet. . . ."

In late 1987 or early 1988, Macauley Taylor, who oversaw the Structured Derivative Financing Group at Merrill Lynch, began arranging installment sales of foreign currency for cash or LIBOR notes for Merrill's corporate clients. (LIBOR stands for London Interbank Offering Rate; the notes are a financial instrument traded internationally to offset the effects of interest rate changes.) Multinational companies that do business in dozens of countries will, naturally enough, earn money in dozens of different currencies—German marks, British pounds, or Japanese yen. They also borrow in all these currencies, all of which have their own interest rates. Since the values of these currencies and the interest rates charged by the central banks that manage them all fluctuate, multinationals hedge their bets by exchanging some of that foreign currency for international bonds. One of the things that Taylor noticed while arranging such hedges is that the transactions also provided a tax benefit for the corporation using them.

In 1988, Taylor hired James R. Fields, who had worked for the IRS from 1984 to 1986 as an attorney adviser and later as a principal technical assistant to then chief counsel Fred T. Goldberg Jr. Taylor wanted Fields to work with his Structured Derivative Financing Group because of his tax expertise; the two of them were the architects of the tax shelter that Merrill Lynch would earn millions selling. Taylor had the initial idea; Fields fleshed out the concept, and together they came up with a scheme in which a corporation would form a partnership with a foreign entity in an offshore location. The foreign entity—called "the tax neutral" partner since it would owe no U.S. income taxes on any profits it made—would drop out of the partnership after a certain amount of time, appearing to receive the lion's share of the income that the partnership produced. The corporation, conversely, would appear to be left holding the bag—with only the costs, or the losses, of the partnership on its books.

Taylor and Fields drew up a schematic with various boxes representing the partners; they played around with the figures to fine-tune the deal. In 1989, they were ready to go, and began looking for companies that had large capital gains they might want to offset. Fields proved to have more talents than devising tax shelters; he was also adept at selling the scheme.

"I would say this is about an investment partnership where you combine with a sophisticated partner," Fields testified in Tax Court on February 14, 1996, recalling the sales pitch he made to potential clients. "The nature of the buying and selling transactions that that partnership can do as part of its investment activities can produce a significant tax advantage." Fields went on to describe the specific IRS regulations that the partnership would take advantage of to produce the huge loss—the contingent installment sale regulations. But, like any good salesman, he quickly got back to the bottom line. "After doing that, I'd say, now, why would that be an advantage to you?" The advantage, of course, was the millions in taxes that a company could save. When asked whether this were the case—if the investment partnership would "accomplish certain tax objectives"—Fields answered unequivocally. "Absolutely," he said.

In 1988 and 1989, Taylor and Fields and others from Merrill Lynch sold the shelter to one company after another. E. S. P. Das, the firm's managing director of investment banking, who had relationships with many of the companies, approached them initially. He broached the subject of the shelter with top managers at Dun & Bradstreet Corporation, the 160-year-old provider of global business and financial information services, and with Schering-Plough, AlliedSignal, Brunswick Corporation, American Home Products Corporation, and Borden, Incorporated. Robert Luciano, Schering-Plough's chairman and chief executive officer, made his company an early participant. He served as a director on Merrill's board; his son Richard worked for Merrill Lynch in Das's investment banking department. The elder Luciano, an attorney who had specialized in taxes, also served on AlliedSignal's board of directors. He was so enthusiastic about the shelter, he recommended it to that company as well.

Judith P. Zelisko, an attorney and the assistant vice president, director of taxes, for Brunswick Corporation, attended a Merrill Lynch sales pitch on December 8, 1989. At the time, Brunswick was in the process of selling its 36 percent stake in Nireco Corporation, a Japanese company that makes precision instruments. "Set forth below is a bullet point summary of a transaction proposed by Merrill Lynch to Brunswick Corporation," she wrote in a January 26, 1990, memo to her superiors, the controller and the vice president of finance, "to generate sufficient capital losses to offset the capital gain which will be generated on the sale of the Nireco shares. The specific dollar amounts can be adjusted to increase or decrease the capital loss required."

Some had reservations about the scheme. Belasco, Colgate's vice president for taxation, who thought that while "technically it seemed to work and had some merit," was nonetheless dubious about the shelter's having any reasonable business purpose. "In looking at this kind of transaction in its just-tax outline," he said, "it's naked. It doesn't do anything in terms of accomplishing something that the company would have wanted to do."

Wanted to do beyond avoiding taxes, that is. On July 18, 1989, after Colgate had made it clear that it wasn't interested in pursuing the

Merrill Lynch shelter, Taylor called Hans Pohlschroeder, the company's assistant treasurer, to try to persuade him to change his mind. Court records do not indicate which of the two men came up with the fig leaf that covered the shelter's nakedness, but Pohlschroeder's hand-written notes of the conversation indicate what it was: "invest in your own debt." In addition to buying LIBOR bonds, Colgate's foreign partnership would also retire some of the company's debt, thus giving it the appearance of having a business purpose beyond the tax savings.

Not all companies that bought in shared Colgate's desire to dress up the shelter. Edward L. Hennessy, AlliedSignal's chairman and chief executive officer until his retirement in 1991, testified that throughout the discussions of his company's decision to invest in Merrill's tax shelter, the idea of possibly making a profit on the deal never came up. "Well, the primary focus was [that] . . . it would help our tax situation considerably," he said. Indeed. To the tune of $151 million.

In all, the profits that Merrill offered to shelter from tax are staggering. In 1990, American Home Products sold off its household and depilatory divisions for a pre-tax profit of $1 billion. The same year, Schering sold its Maybelline cosmetics business and a pair of European cosmetic companies for a pre-tax profit of $220 million. In 1988, Dun & Bradstreet sold its Official Airline Guides subsidiary for a pre-tax profit of $752 million. Two years later, it sold three other subsidiaries for a pre-tax gain of approximately $84 million. In May 1988, Brunswick sold its filtration technology business for a $42 million pre-tax gain. Two years later, it sold two more divisions for an $84 million pre-tax gain. In October 1989, Paramount sold Associates First Capital Corporation, its consumer and commercial finance business, for a gain of approximately $1.2 billion. Those pre-tax profits amount to $3.4 billion; taxes on them would have totaled as much as $1.1 billion. The shelter that Taylor and Fields had devised would keep all that money away from the federal treasury and in corporate treasuries instead.

Zelisko, Brunswick's director of taxes, noted the price for turning the trick: "Merrill Lynch's fee is 5–10 percent of the tax savings.

Assuming a capital loss of $82 million, the tax savings would be around $28 million and a 10 percent fee on such savings results in a fee of $2.8 million. This 10 percent fee is negotiable." Five percent of $1.1 billion is the tidy sum of $55 million. And, as the Treasury Department made clear in its report on corporate tax shelters, all of that money comes out of the pockets of other taxpayers, like you, who have to pay more because corporations pay less.

As Das fed willing clients to Taylor, Fields set about arranging the legal cover for the shelter. Under the Internal Revenue Code, specifically Section 6662(a), a taxpayer who substantially understates his income tax liability—or its liability, in the case of a corporation—must pay a penalty of 20 percent of the tax due. But Section 6664(c) allows for an exception. It waives the penalties if a taxpayer acted on a good-faith opinion that there was a better than fifty-fifty chance that, if challenged by the IRS, a court would rule in the taxpayer's favor. Joseph Bankman, in assessing the market for corporate tax shelters, wrote that, "In theory, such opinions ought not to serve as protection from the substantial understatement penalty. In practice, any run-of-the-mill opinion letter is thought to insulate the taxpayer from the substantial understatement penalty; there do not appear to be any recent cases in which a taxpayer's reliance on an opinion letter has been held to be unreasonable."

For the Colgate shelter, Fields turned to Mark A. Kuller, at the time a partner in the Washington office of King & Spalding. The two had served together at the Internal Revenue Service in the chief counsel's office. Kuller ended up writing four separate opinion letters, concluding in each, after detailed recitations of prior precedents and congressional intent in writing tax law, that while the shelter might be successfully challenged by the IRS, in his opinion it would probably survive such scrutiny.

With the favorable legal opinion in hand, all that remained to do was to find the foreign partner. In the summer of 1989, Taylor contacted Johannes Willem den Baas, a financial engineer with Algemene Bank Nederland N.V., a Dutch bank that at the time had $85 billion in assets, with roughly 29,000 employees in some 950 offices in 43 countries. Taylor had worked with den Baas before, structuring very complicated derivative transactions with the Dutch banker. He figured that ABN and den Baas would be the perfect offshore partner. "ABN has a big balance sheet and he's a pretty smart guy and he can understand the stuff," Taylor said. He told den Baas what he needed in a foreign partner: someone with a lot of money to invest who was offshore, immune from U.S. taxes.

The Dutch banker, eager to develop relationships with some of America's wealthiest corporations, agreed to participate. So he referred Taylor to Peter de Beer, a trust officer and the head of the legal department of one of the bank's many subsidiaries, ABN Trust Co., Curaçao N.V., located in the Netherlands Antilles, an established tax haven. De Beer's four-lawyer staff helped corporate clients set up and manage Netherlands Antilles companies to participate in offshore transactions. He certainly grasped the concept that Taylor and Fields told him about. "My understanding was that the partnership would enter into transactions that would create a capital gain and in a later stage a capital loss, and that, depending on the percentage of your participation, you would either take part in the gain or the loss," he said. "So by having us being the majority partner at the start, we would take the majority of the gain, while in a later stage one of the other partners would take the loss."

While de Beer understood the mechanics of the shelter, den Baas later claimed he didn't. "We knew that there was a tax angle to these transactions since, during the partnership meetings—or the formation meeting, I should say—a disproportionate number of tax lawyers were present," he said, "and the fact that at the request of Merrill Lynch, but also, Peter de Beer, these meetings were held offshore and, in particular, a foreign partner was requested."

ABN became the foreign partner of choice for Merrill Lynch; in late 1989, a plethora of offshore partnerships sprung up between subsidiaries of ABN and the corporations who'd bought into Merrill Lynch's shelter. There was ACM Partnership, formed with Colgate,

Nieuw Willemstad Partnership with Dun & Bradstreet, Kralendijk Partnership with Schering-Plough, Saba Partnership with Brunswick, Maarten Investerings Partnership with Paramount, and ASA Investerings Partnership with AlliedSignal, to name a few. All were formed from late September 1989 to late June 1990.

Taylor was a busy man. He attended many of the offshore partnership meetings to update his clients on the progress of the transactions Merrill made on their behalf. For Colgate, he made six trips to the Netherlands Antilles and Bermuda in a ten-month period between October 1989 and August 1990. The first meeting for Colgate's shelter, the ACM Partnership, was held on October 27, 1989, at the Southampton Princess Beach Hotel, a 600-room hotel that stands atop the highest point in Bermuda. In addition to spectacular views of the Great Sound and the South Shore, the Princess offers guests an eighteen-hole golf course, eleven tennis courts, two pools, water sports, and a beautiful club on a private pink sand beach. Three weeks later, on November 17, ACM held its second meeting, at the Marriott Castle Harbour Resort in Bermuda, which at the time featured 400 richly furnished rooms. The hotel also boasted three pools, Jacuzzis, a sauna, an eighteen-hole championship golf course, six tennis courts, water sports, cycle rentals, exercise room, three restaurants (including the only Japanese restaurant on the island), and a disco. The third meeting took place on December 12, 1989, in Curaçao, the Netherlands Antilles, in the offices of the partnership (which happened to be the offices of ABN Trust Curaçao); so did the fourth, on February 28, 1990. Six days earlier, Taylor had been in Bermuda for the first meeting of the Saba Partnership, a tax shelter for the Brunswick Corporation.

Beyond the beaches, tennis courts, and golf courses, there was a more important reason that the partnership meetings for the various shelters Merrill arranged were held offshore. "We wanted to keep the transaction out of the United States as much as possible," de Beer, ABN's man in Curaçao, explained. "It was our preference also not to discuss or do anything with regard to this deal in the United States." De Beer spoke from experience. "Well, working in Curaçao for a number of years, we did a lot of transactions with United States corporations, and we know how sensitive that can be, and that's to avoid any risk in that respect. Better safe than sorry." The risk was taxation. "Tax risk, yeah. To avoid any risk there, to have all meetings and filings and all the documentation outside the United States."

Of course, Taylor's life wasn't all just travel for meetings in exotic Caribbean locales to avoid tax risks. He oversaw a series of mind-numbingly complex transactions involving the foreign partnerships. Taylor and the members of his Structured Derivative Financing Group at Merrill Lynch purchased—and then sold—the financial instruments for the offshore partnerships. He was the point man who interacted with Merrill's brokers to arrange all the sales, which took place in the span of a year. The amounts of money invested were staggering—Kralendijk, the Schering-Plough shelter, purchased $1 billion of private placement notes on January 18, 19, and 25, 1990, all of which it sold, on March 12 and 16, 1990. On February 28, 1990, Saba Partnership, Brunswick's shelter, purchased $200 million of bonds from Chase Manhattan that it sold three weeks later. ASA Investerings Partnership, AlliedSignal's shelter, purchased $850 million in floating-rate private placement certificates of deposit on April 25, 1990; on May 17 and 24, 1990, it dumped the CDs. When Merrill was unable to find a buyer for the private placements for the Nieuw Willemstad partnership, Dun & Bradstreet's shelter, the brokerage firm issued the LIBOR note itself and paid $42.5 million in cash. Taylor was involved in each transaction.

In the end, the offshore partnerships, the carefully crafted sales of LIBOR notes, the private placements and hedged transactions, all worked perfectly. Neither market fluctuations in interest rates nor falling or rising values of foreign currencies had any effect on the performance of the partnerships. ABN earned profits, and, on paper, the American corporations all ended up with losses. It was too good to be true. So good, in fact, that the IRS began to challenge every Merrill Lynch shelter it discovered.

On March 12, 1993, the IRS denied the losses that Colgate, Merrill's corporate client in the deal, had claimed to offset its capital gain.

On April 13, 1995, the IRS denied the losses Borden claimed. On September 27, 1996, the IRS denied the losses AlliedSignal claimed. One by one, as the Service discovered on audit that corporations had made use of Merrill's shelter, it denied the tax losses.

But the companies themselves weren't ready to surrender their paper losses without a fight. Colgate's case, *ACM Partnership, Southampton-Hamilton Company, Tax Matters Partner v. Commissioner of Internal Revenue*, was the first to go to trial, on February 12, 1996, nearly seven years after Merrill Lynch first approached Colgate with its shelter proposal. Fred T. Goldberg Jr., the former IRS commissioner who once worked with Fields at the Service in the chief counsel's office, was one of five lawyers from two law firms that represented ACM, and ultimately Colgate, in court. Thirty witnesses testified, and some 1,200 documents were entered into evidence, ranging from the original charts that Taylor and Fields had drawn up when planning the shelter to the minutes of the final meeting of the partnership.

In its final brief in the case, ACM's lawyers argued that "The ACM transactions had practical economic effects apart from the creation of tax benefits. . . . Each transaction engaged in by ACM had a reasonable prospect for profit or loss. Each transaction had economic substance." They cited Colgate's desire to reduce its debt as the legitimate business purpose for the company's participation in ACM.

In the end, however, it was all for naught. On March 5, 1997, Tax Court Judge David Laro ruled that the ACM partnership had engaged in a sham transaction. "We do not suggest that a taxpayer refrain from using the tax laws to the taxpayer's advantage," he wrote in his opinion. "In this case, however, the taxpayer desired to take advantage of a loss that was not economically inherent in the object of the sale, but which the taxpayer created artificially through the manipulation and abuse of the tax laws. A taxpayer is not entitled to recognize a phantom loss from a transaction that lacks economic substance." Colgate would have to pay its taxes on its capital gains after all. (An appellate court allowed the company to deduct some of the costs of participating in the shelter.)

On August 20, 1998, Tax Court Judge Maurice B. Foley ruled that AlliedSignal and ABN were not partners at all, but a debtor and creditor, and that AlliedSignal was not entitled to any of the losses that its shelter, ASA Investerings, had generated. That ruling was upheld on appeal; U.S. Circuit Judge Stephen F. Williams wrote that "AlliedSignal's interest in any potential gain from the partnership's investments was in its view at all times dwarfed by its interest in the tax benefit."

On October 27, 1999, Tax Court Judge Arthur L. Nims III ruled against Brunswick and the Saba Partnership. "At the end of the day, Brunswick's involvement in the [contingent installment] transactions, with their attendant intricate investments in the [private placement notes], CDs, LIBOR notes, money market accounts, hedges, swaps, etc., all carefully masterminded by Merrill Lynch, did not meaningfully change Brunswick's economic position, and it therefore lacked the requisite economic substance necessary to validate Brunswick's targeted capital losses."

The shelters he sold collapsed, but Macauley Taylor didn't. He's still at Merrill Lynch, arranging complex derivative transactions for corporate clients, solving their various accounting, financial, and tax problems. James Fields left Merrill in 1992; he went to work for the Treasury Department as deputy tax legislative counsel in the Office of Tax Policy. (The Office of Tax Policy would later issue the study on corporate tax shelters in 1999.)

While working for the Office of Tax Policy, Fields wrote a number of letters on tax policy that were made public, on topics ranging from the marriage penalty to Section 936 of the Internal Revenue Code, which gives U.S. corporations a tax break if they locate factories in Puerto Rico. Fields also wrote about transition rules (often called "rifle shots," because they're aimed at giving preferential treatment to a single taxpayer), the taxation of international shipping, and the rules on foreign income earned by U.S. corporations. He left Treasury in September 1993, around the time that the IRS began investigating the various players in the Merrill Lynch shelter, and went on to be a vice president at Citibank. As the various Merrill Lynch partnerships wended their way through Tax Court and appellate courts, Congress and the Treasury Department grappled with the issue of corporate shelters. Bill Bradley, the former senator from New Jersey, made shutting them down the centerpiece of his tax reforms when he sought the Democratic nomination for president in 2000. Periodically, Treasury makes headlines announcing new initiatives to crack down on them. Congress has considered legislation that would force corporations to reveal on their tax returns any shelter they had participated in; considering the lengths to which corporations go to secure legal opinions that the tax avoidance strategies they engage in are not tax avoidance strategies at all, that seems to be an impractical approach to the problem.

Kenneth J. Kies, the former chief of staff of the Joint Committee on Taxation—Congress's in-house policy think tank on tax matters—has testified several times before the Senate Finance Committee and the House Ways and Means Committee arguing that there is no corporate tax shelter problem. Kies is now a managing partner in PricewaterhouseCoopers's Washington office, the same firm that promoted the BOSS shelter.

Kies's view carried some weight with Republican members of the House. Dick Armey, the House majority leader, reacted angrily to any suggestion that shelters deserve legislative attention. On February 15, 2000, at his weekly press briefing, he declared, "Since tax is a very large part of [a corporation's] costs, anything they can do to minimize that share of their costs would be a legitimate thing. . . . The fact of the matter is that we write the tax code, and any corporation ought to do what they can to minimize that cost [to] their shareholders."

Indeed. There's no doubt that corporations do so every day.

4

Special Effects

"The whole world was talking about this one," Mario Kassar, the chairman of Carolco Pictures Inc., said of his days-long bash at the 1990 Cannes Film Festival, and he wasn't exaggerating. Arnold Schwarzenegger was among his guests, as was Michael Douglas. Kassar had flown them in from Hollywood on Carolco's corporate jet, and then, with much pomp and the wail of sirens from a police escort, driven them around Cannes in a fleet of Mercedes-Benz limousines. Sylvester Stallone, Clint Eastwood, and Mick Jagger were among the entertainment elite who attended Kassar's bash.

From the deck of his 203-foot yacht, Kassar and his celebrity guests watched a fireworks display that lit up the sky of Côte d'Azur with the names of upcoming Carolco films and their stars. At the Grand Hotel du Cap, where F. Scott Fitzgerald and his expatriate friends once held sway, Kassar staged another party, flying in his favorite band, the Gypsy Kings, to provide the music. As the flashbulbs of the paparazzi exploded, Stallone and Schwarzenegger—Rambo and the Terminator—danced together. The pictures were beamed around the world.

Kassar was beaming too. He ran the most successful independent movie studio in the world. He had turned "the house that Rambo built" into a diversified entertainment company that traded its shares on the New York Stock Exchange. LeStudio Canal Plus of France and Pioneer Electronics of Japan had just made a $90 million investment in his company. *Total Recall* was scheduled for release that summer—a blockbuster that would go on to earn $262 million. And, unbeknownst to the Hollywood stars and directors who praised him and the bankers and investors who backed him, Kassar had managed to deposit nearly $180 million of profits from his company in a series of offshore trusts, without paying a dime in taxes on the money.

Welcome to Hollywood, where, in the $30-billion-a-year movie industry, income taxes are largely optional.

Mario F. Kassar is hardly a household name, but the string of hit movies he made should ring some bells. He produced all three Rambo movies, the Schwarzenegger action hits *Red Heat* and *Terminator 2: Judgment Day*, and *Basic Instinct*, a stylish thriller that starred Michael Douglas.

Kassar and his company changed the way Hollywood did business by designing motion pictures to appeal as much to foreign audiences as to American ones. To guarantee large foreign sales, he offered multi-million-dollar contracts to lure Hollywood's biggest names to his projects. He paid Stallone $16 million to star in the third Rambo movie, which was $2 million more than the entire cost of the first film. He paid Arnold Schwarzenegger $10 million to star in *Total Recall*. In 1989, director Renny Harlin, at the time best known for *A Nightmare on Elm Street IV*, got $3 million from Carolco—an unprecedented sum for a director without a blockbuster on his list of credits—to direct *Gale Force*. Writer Joe Eszterhas, who penned the screenplay for *Jagged Edge*, got $3 million to work on *Basic Instinct*.

Kassar's largesse didn't end with stars, directors, and writers. He was very generous to himself as well. In 1989, for example, Kassar paid himself a salary of $1.25 million. He and his partner, Andrew Vajna—the two founded Carolco in 1976—split $148,000 for "nonaccount-able" travel expenses, and $189,128 for "financial planning services."

Kassar's lifestyle was as big budget as his movies. He bought a five-bedroom, Spanish-style mansion in Beverly Hills worth more than $4 million. The two acres of gated property featured a racquetball court, a tennis court, a swimming pool, and two guesthouses. He tooled around Los Angeles in a chauffeur-driven stretch limousine or in a Rolls-Royce that sported RAMBO vanity plates. When he attended the Cannes Film Festival, he preferred to spend $200,000 renting a yacht rather than stay in a hotel room—a far cry from the days when, as a teenager, he slept on the Riviera's beaches to be near the movie industry's biggest movers and shakers.

Kassar was dubbed the Billion-Dollar Man by the Hollywood press, but the nickname was only half accurate. The films he made had earned well over $2 billion worldwide by 1993. Yet despite the block-buster earnings, Kassar's company, Carolco Pictures, Inc., showed lackluster profits.

In 1985, *Rambo: First Blood Part II* grossed more than $150 million in U.S. theaters. That year, Carolco declared its U.S. income to be $2.9 million. In 1986, a year in which Carolco released no new films, the company reported that its revenue from feature films was $27.7 million. Nonetheless, the company declared a loss of $1.8 million. In 1987, Carolco grossed $33 million from *Angel Heart* and *Extreme Prejudice*. The company declared a U.S. profit that year of $9.7 million.

Carolco's lackluster profits from blockbuster revenues weren't the only oddity. Consider the taxes the company paid.

The tax rate on corporate profits in 1985 was 46 percent. That year, Carolco's effective federal income tax rate was 3.7 percent. In 1986, Carolco paid taxes at a rate of 6.8 percent. In 1987, when the corporate tax rate was cut to 40 percent by the Tax Reform Act of 1986, Carolco's effective tax rate dropped to a mere 0.7 percent.

There are other countries where a 1 percent corporate tax rate isn't anything out of the ordinary. The Bahamas, the Cayman Islands, and other tax havens allow corporations to shelter their profits from the IRS. Carolco had a Netherlands Antilles subsidiary, and frankly explained in its annual reports filed with the Securities and Exchange

Commission the tax benefits it provided. Consider this statement from Carolco's 1988 annual report:

> The Company's predecessors have in prior years paid little or no federal or state income taxes since a significant amount of the Company's revenues was received by Carolco International N.V. ("CINV"), a Netherlands Antilles subsidiary of the Company. . . . CINV is subject to substantially lower rates than United States statutory tax rates. Since it is management's intention to permanently reinvest the undistributed earnings of this foreign subsidiary, no provision has been made on the Company's financial statements for federal income taxes on these earnings. At December 31, 1987, the Company had approximately $97,000,000 of retained earnings in CINV.

In other words, Carolco diverted, by its own account, $97 million in profits from such films as *Rambo: First Blood Part II* and *Angel Heart* to a subsidiary in the Netherlands Antilles. Although all the costs associated with making the movies were charged to the U.S. company, the offshore subsidiary collected all the profits. "CINV, as distinguished from other subsidiaries responsible for distribution, incurs only minimum distribution expenses and is responsible for only a small portion of general overhead expenses," the company explained in its SEC filing. Carolco's executives had no intention of bringing the money back to the United States, where the Internal Revenue Service would take its cut. Total taxes paid to the U.S. Treasury on those profits: zero.

Which is really par for the course in Hollywood, where offshore trusts, tax shelters, and blockbusters that generate millions but end up with no profits are the norm. In the motion picture industry, tax avoidance and evasion are older than the sign on the Hollywood Hills. Ever since the silent era, some of the biggest stars, directors, and money men in the studios were creating accounting illusions as masterful as the ones they put up on the big screen:

- In the late 1920s, the Internal Revenue Service's Intelligence Unit, now known as the Criminal Investigation Division, went after twenty-five Hollywood bigwigs and celebrities who dodged their taxes. The IRS eventually recovered more than $2 million.

- Producer Jesse L. Lasky earned more than $1 million when he brought *Sergeant York* to the screen in 1941. The film, based on the true story of a Tennessee pacifist who became a hero in World War I, struck a chord with Americans who looked on anxiously at another European war. The film garnered nine Academy Award nominations, and Gary Cooper, who played Alvin York, won an Oscar for best actor. A year later, when the United States entered the war and Congress extended the income tax to cover every worker to pay for it, Lasky tried to disguise his income from the film as capital gains, which were taxed at a much lower rate than income. Twelve years later, the IRS finally caught up with Lasky, winning a case against him and his wife in Tax Court for nearly $450,000.

- In the 1970s, Burton Kanter, the Chicago tax lawyer who helped structure the offshore trusts that enabled producer Saul Zaentz (*One Flew Over the Cuckoo's Nest*) to avoid millions in taxes, devised a movie shelter to enable well-to-do investors to realize up to $40,000 in tax write-offs for each $10,000 of investment. The shelters, known as "service company partnerships," were used to finance such films as *The Great Gatsby, Shampoo*, and *Funny Lady*.

- In the 1980s, dozens of Hollywood stars and producers ended up owing hundreds of thousands of dollars in back taxes for investments they made in bogus tax shelters. Among those stung: Michael Landon, Lorne Greene, Bill Cosby, Norman Lear, and Woody Allen. Some of the architects of the scam shelters ended up in jail, including New York lawyers Michael Oshatz and Leonard Messinger, who created some $225 million worth of phony tax losses for their clients.

- Hollywood studios regularly cook their books to turn block-busters into busts. *Batman*, which grossed more money for Warner Brothers when it was released than any other film in the company's history—some $253 million in the first year—ended up, according to the studio, losing $36 million. Eddie Murphy's *Coming to America* grossed more than $350 million, but when humor columnist Art Buchwald, who claimed that the plot of the film was stolen from him, sued Paramount Pictures for royalties, the company claimed that the film had lost $18 million. In a 1992 decision, a California superior court judge called Paramount's accounting practices "unconscionable." Buchwald got a share of the profits.

Unconscionable is a word that could well be used to describe Kassar's stewardship of Carolco Pictures—a company that rose out of nowhere to dominate Hollywood, only to collapse from self-dealing, shady transactions, and a mountain of debt.

The Lebanese-born Kassar was working on the margins of the film industry when he met Andrew Vajna, a native of Hungary, in 1975. Kassar had followed in the footsteps of his father, a film distributor, and eked out a living earning 5 percent commissions on the sales of European films to Middle Eastern and Asian markets. Vajna, a graduate of UCLA, manufactured wigs in Hong Kong before he decided to get into the film distribution business. The two joined forces to sell the foreign rights to second-rate American films. In 1976, they formed Carolco Pictures and branched out to produce a few low-budget films of their own in Canada.

Their partnership, while successful, still left them on the margins of the glitzy world of Hollywood, far from the big stars and bright lights and blockbuster profits. And then, in 1981, Kassar and Vajna bought the rights to a 1972 bestselling novel by David Morrell that had languished at Warner Brothers for nearly a decade.

Although several directors had been interested in Morrell's book about a deranged Vietnam veteran who shoots up an Oregon town, production had never begun, despite the interest of stars like Al Pacino, Robert De Niro, and George C. Scott in the lead role. Kassar and Vajna gambled on the novel and on the talents of Sylvester Stallone, whose career at the time was foundering.

The result was *First Blood*, the 1982 action film that earned an astonishing $9 million in its first weekend of release, despite a near total absence of promotion. Stallone resuscitated his career with his portrayal of John Rambo, the rampaging Green Beret. Film critics, social scientists, and other commentators spilled rivers of ink debating whether the film's box-office success signaled a return of healthy patriotism or a new strain of ugly jingoism. And the $120 million that the movie earned put Kassar and Vajna and Carolco on the Hollywood map.

In 1985, Carolco released the sequel to *First Blood*, titled *Rambo: First Blood Part II*. Unlike most sequels, the second film did even better than the first, earning a worldwide total of $300 million. The company dubbed Stallone the "world's number one box-office champion" and trumpeted itself as "the most prominent provider of independent U.S. film to the international marketplace." Carolco, nicknamed "the House that Rambo built" by the Hollywood press, was on its way to grandeur.

In 1986, Carolco Pictures went public, selling 3.6 million shares on the New York Stock Exchange. Eighty percent of the company's stock was owned by Carolco Investments B.V., a Netherlands corporation. Carolco Investments B.V., in turn, was owned by Kassar, Vajna, and two trusts—the Kassar Family Trust, a legal entity of the Isle of Jersey, and the Mong Family Trust, located in Hong Kong and named for Vajna's father-in-law, which benefited members of Vajna's family.

In 1986, Carolco announced its intention to produce two to four "event" movies a year—films with big stars, action, adventure, mass appeal, and, of course, big budgets. That same year, Kassar and Vajna, who named themselves cochairmen of Carolco, hired Peter Hoffman, the company's tax attorney, as their president and chief executive officer.

Hoffman might not have known much about gaffers or best boys or special effects, but he was expert in creating the complex structures that allow Hollywood's movers and shakers to avoid taxes. Alexander Salkind, who produced *Superman*, turned to Hoffman in 1979 when the revenues from the film were tied up in lawsuits with Marlon Brando, director Richard Donner, Warner Brothers, and Salkind's own company. Like *Coming to America*, how much profit *Superman* earned was hotly disputed. While the courts tried to unravel exactly who was to get what from the film's profits, Salkind was unable to repay a $45 million loan he had gotten from a Dutch bank to make the film. Hoffman set up a complicated scheme using British and American tax shelters to raise capital, promising investors tax benefits in return for their money. Hoffman's shelters proved a godsend for Salkind. He used the proceeds to produce *Superman II, Superman III,* and *Supergirl,* and, in the process, managed to pay off Slavensburg's Bank, N.V., which delighted Frans Afman, the banker who had made the loans to Salkind.

Hoffman and Afman were soon arranging financing and tax shelters for other movie producers—notably the Cannon Group, best known for its action movies, which starred the likes of Chuck Norris and Charles Bronson. By 1986, the debt-ridden company was under investigation by the Securities and Exchange Commission for making fraudulent statements, raising $339 million under false pretenses, and failing to disclose that it had paid Afman a $75,000 consulting fee. By that time, Credit Lyonnais, the venerable French bank that was founded in 1863, had bought out Slavensburg's Bank, and Afman was its senior vice president and manager of the entertainment business division, which made hefty loans to Hollywood producers. At the same time he was determining the creditworthiness of Cannon, Afman served on the company's board of directors and received a salary of $75,000 a year.

After the two left Cannon, Kassar and Vajna reunited them in 1986 at Carolco. Hoffman became the company's president and chief executive officer; Afman served as a consultant and a director. The two had already set up the financing and tax shelters used to make the first Rambo film; over the years, Afman would ensure a steady stream of loans from Credit Lyonnais to make movies and Hoffman would shield the millions those movies made from taxes.

The money flowing into the company allowed Hoffman to embark on an acquisition spree. Like the larger motion picture studios with which it competed, Carolco diversified and bought International Video Entertainment, Incorporated, a videocassette distribution company; Orbis Communications, Incorporated, a syndicator of television programming; and the film library of Hemdale Communications, Incorporated, which included such movies as *Platoon, The Last Emperor*, and *Kiss of the Spider Woman*. Carolco even made an animated series for Saturday morning viewing based on its Rambo films.

Hoffman designed the acquisitions to provide Carolco with a steady stream of revenue apart from the new films it made, which were growing ever more lavish. Consider the third installment in the Rambo series. Sylvester Stallone, as already noted, was paid $16 million to star in the film—a sum that exceeded by $2 million the entire budget of the original Rambo film. Stallone, blistered by critics over his previous film, *Over the Top*, delayed shooting for months to rewrite the script. He wanted the third Rambo installment to be more cerebral, along the lines of Oliver Stone's Oscar-winning *Platoon*. Kassar and Vajna threw cold water on the idea; Vajna told *Forbes* in June 1987, "Rambo is an action/adventure film, so if you take out the action, you don't have a film."

After spending $5 million to build sets in Mexico, Stallone decided to film in Israel instead. And Thailand. And Arizona. The first film had been shot entirely in Canada, the second in Mexico. In Israel, eighty crew members spent five and a half weeks building a single set for the film: a seven-acre Russian military base. As the production grew to epic proportions, and the budget spiraled to $40 million to match it, Vajna fumed and attempted to fire Stallone. Instead, Stallone stayed, and two years later it was Vajna who left Carolco.

Vajna and Kassar hadn't seen eye-to-eye about the company's rapid expansion. Kassar was fond of telling Hoffman, "You find the money, I spend it." He hired directors, gave them office space and staff, and set them loose to come up with projects. Vajna wandered the halls of Carolco's seven-story Sunset Boulevard headquarters, stared at all the new faces brought in by Hoffman's acquisitions and Kassar's free spending, and quipped, "Who are these people?" In November 1989, the company announced that Vajna, worn out by the day-to-day responsibilities of the movie business, was leaving the company.

Kassar and his trusts bought out the stake Vajna and his trusts owned in Carolco Investments B.V., the Netherlands corporation that owned most of Carolco's stock. The details of the transaction, as outlined in documents filed with the SEC, were incredibly complex. New entities were created to own the shares of the old company, with names like Trust-en Administratickantoor Nestor B.V. and New Carolco Investments B.V.

Companies in Aruba, the Netherlands Antilles, and Panama swapped millions of dollars and shares of stock with one another. To finance the deal, Credit Lyonnais; Bear, Stearns & Company; and AIG Capital Corporation made loans totaling $33 million to Kassar's New Carolco Investments B.V. In the end, Kassar ended up owning 62 percent of the company's stock.

As for Vajna, the deal he struck with Carolco and his old partner was quite generous. For example, he was given a lump sum payment of $2 million for a three-year nonexclusive consulting agreement with the company. Life insurance policies the company held on him were turned over to him. He was allowed to keep the company car he'd been using. He was even promised "such personal, legal, and tax planning as required to consummate the transactions."

The personal, legal, and tax planning certainly paid off. Vajna didn't pay a dime of taxes on the money he received from Carolco. The company did not disclose the price Kassar paid to buy Vajna out of the company, but documents filed in U.S. Tax Court show that in 1989, Vajna received $98 million from Carolco Investments B.V. Thanks to the complex shifting of shares and assets and offshore companies and foreign trusts, Vajna claimed that none of the money he received from Carolco was taxable under the Internal Revenue Code.

In November 1989, Vajna started another independent studio, Cinergi Pictures Entertainment, Incorporated. Like Carolco, it made big-budget films like Bruce Willis's *Die Hard with a Vengeance* and Oliver Stone's *Nixon*. And like Carolco, according to SEC reports, the company paid little or no income taxes after it went public.

While Vajna's departure from Carolco Pictures left him a much wealthier man, it was Kassar who went on a spending binge. He shelled out $43 million to make Oliver Stone's film *The Doors*, which grossed only $65 million. Kassar paid Michael Douglas $15 million to appear in *Basic Instinct*. His biggest gamble of all was the special effects–laden thriller *Terminator 2: Judgment Day*. When Arnold Schwarzenegger asked to be paid with a jet rather than cash, Kassar bought him a Gulfstream G-III, valued at roughly $14 million. Overall, he spent upward of $90 million on the film, which at one point employed 2,000 people.

The gamble, of course, paid off. The second Terminator movie, released in July 1991, earned the staggering worldwide total of $490 million—more than the first two Rambo movies combined. Kassar, however, was less than elated. According to *Newsweek*, he was heard to remark, "The picture is making millions, and I'm struggling to stay alive." Kassar's struggle was with banks and creditors; his penchant for raiding the company's till for his own benefit didn't help matters either. Despite the success of *Terminator 2*, Carolco was lunging toward bankruptcy.

In the eighteen months between Vajna's departure and the premiere of its most successful film, Carolco had taken on hundreds of millions of dollars of debt. As of June 1991, a few weeks before the sci-fi saga hit the screens, the company disclosed in filings with the SEC that it owed Credit Lyonnais alone more than $188 million, and $340 million overall.

Adding to the red ink were the losses from some of Kassar's event movies. For each Rambo or Terminator, there were two films that didn't pan out. Remember *The Music Box*, with Jessica Lange? Or how about *Mountains of the Moon*? Both were favorites of the critics, both were Carolco films, and both flopped.

"They want crap," Peter Hoffman told a reporter for the *Los Angeles Times* in a 1990 interview, reflecting on the failure of the two films. "Every time people tell you they don't, it's bull. They want crap." Hoffman's aesthetic judgment of Carolco's successful movies landed him in some hot water with Kassar, who had to soothe the wounded egos of Stallone and Schwarzenegger, both of whom reportedly felt insulted by the remark.

Kassar and Hoffman, however, had more pressing problems than the ruffled feathers of their multimillion-dollar stars. The two had worked out a way to cancel out the $33 million in debt that Kassar's Netherlands corporation, New Carolco Investments B.V., had incurred when Kassar bought out Vajna. Carolco would buy $45 million of Kassar's stock for $13 a share, Kassar would use the money to pay off the debt, and he'd still have enough shares under his control to continue running the company. There was only one problem with the deal: when it was announced on September 24, 1990, a share of Carolco stock sold for about $8 on the New York Stock Exchange.

Outraged shareholders sued Kassar and Carolco in California, arguing that the sale enriched Kassar at their expense. In December, State Superior Court Judge John Zebrowski agreed, ruling that there was "no remotely plausible justification" for the inflated purchase price, which he characterized as a "case of self-dealing" and a "breach of fiduciary duty." The judge froze 2.2 million shares of stock in Kassar's control and ordered him to either find another buyer for his shares of stock or return the money to the company. Noting the offshore structure of the company's ownership, Zebrowski said in his ruling, "We need to get a sufficient amount of Carolco stock into the United States, held by someone we can trust."

Kassar had no intention of complying with that part of Zebrowski's decision. He sold his shares, at the inflated price, to third parties, with the largest bloc going to RCS Video International Services B.V. of Italy. A federal magistrate signed off on the arrangement in November 1991.

By that time, however, Carolco was falling apart. The company announced that it had lost $91 million in the first nine months of the year. Credit Lyonnais, which had severed its ties for good with Frans Afman (a move hailed by Dutch banking authorities because, in their words, it ended "this double function which, in our opinion, is undesirable"), began to call in its loans. To protect their investments, Carolco's foreign partners, RCS Video International, Pioneer LDCA Inc., and LeStudio Canal Plus, pumped hundreds of millions into the company to keep it afloat in return for a bigger stake in the filmmaker.

For his part, Kassar did his best to cut costs. He fired forty-nine employees and notified his remaining staff that the company would no longer pay for milk at the coffee machines. He didn't, however, see fit to trim his own hefty salary. Instead, Carolco announced in SEC filings that his pay would increase to $1.5 million in 1992, to $1.75 million in 1993, and to $2 million in 1994. He granted himself a $500,000 bonus for the success of *Terminator 2,* and continued to give himself a $7,500 monthly allowance for "non-accountable" business expenses.

Cutting out the milk wasn't enough to win back the confidence of Carolco's shareholders. The stock price plummeted to just over $2, wiping out much of the value of Kassar's $200 million stake in the company. Hoffman announced that he would be leaving the company when his contract expired in March 1992. The company spelled out the first of many reorganization plans to forestall bankruptcy in 1992. In September 1993, in a filing with the SEC, it warned investors that it had run up some $207 million in debt. The unrepatriated profits of its Netherlands Antilles subsidiary, Carolco Investments N.V., which at its peak had accumulated $163 million in profits, had, according to its stateside parent, dwindled to a mere $30 million.

Kassar, meanwhile, was undeterred by his company's poor financial condition. In 1993, he announced plans for another slate of big-ticket pictures, including a remake of *Lolita*, starring Jeremy Irons; *Cutthroat*

Island, a pirate film; and *Showgirls*. He entertained reporters in his mansion, telling them that *Showgirls* would be the definitive film on Las Vegas lap dancing, or outlining his plans for a film biography of the Marquis de Sade, all while his five-year-old daughter played by his feet.

Unfortunately for Kassar, his overseas creditors had lost patience with him. In 1994, Carolco's annual report noted that Credit Lyonnais would no longer loan any money to the company. Repaying the old loans without finding a new source of credit, the annual report said, would have "a severe adverse effect on the operations and financial viability of Carolco."

In 1995, Carolco released the last of its big-budget event movies, *Cutthroat Island*, which starred Geena Davis and Matthew Modine. The film was a bomb, and later that year Carolco filed for bankruptcy.

During the bankruptcy proceedings, it was revealed that the Internal Revenue Service had been auditing the company for five years. IRS agents, in fact, even maintained an office at Carolco's Sunset Boulevard headquarters while going through the company's books. Shortly after the company filed Chapter 11, the IRS issued a claim against the company for $229 million in unpaid back taxes. Ten months later, in September 1996, a bankruptcy court judge approved a final settlement between the IRS and the insolvent company—for $6.3 million, a little less than 3 percent of what the Service had sought. But the IRS, it turned out, was just getting started; the audit of Carolco pointed to a massive tax avoidance scheme by Kassar and Vajna.

On December 22, 1995, just after it had sent its bill to Carolco, the IRS sent a Notice of Deficiency to Vajna, claiming that he had understated his income by $121 million in 1988 and 1989. The IRS said that Vajna owed $41 million in back taxes and penalties. On the same day, the IRS notified Kassar that it had determined that he had failed to report $199 million in income on his returns from 1988 through 1990. Kassar got a bill for $68.6 million.

By far, the largest amounts of income the IRS said that Kassar and Vajna omitted from their tax returns came from the series of offshore corporations that owned Carolco. The two producers argued that they didn't owe any taxes on their foreign earnings because family trusts had received the income, and that the trusts were legally residents of Hong Kong and the Isle of Jersey, and thus owed no U.S. taxes.

Remember the $98 million that Vajna received when Kassar bought him out of the company? In a document filed with the U.S. Tax Court, Vajna argued that none of the money was taxable because it came from a foreign corporation and, "at all relevant times in 1989, 50 percent or more of the outstanding stock of [Carolco Investments B.V.] was owned by foreign persons." And who were the foreign persons? Well, one was the Mong Family Trust, of Hong Kong, set up by the father of Vajna's wife, Cecilia. Another was the Kassar Family Trust—legally, a citizen of the Isle of Jersey. Together, the two trusts owned 50.1 percent of Carolco Investments B.V. Vajna personally owned 24.95 percent; "a non-U.S. corporation owned and controlled by Mario Kassar" owned the other 24.95 percent. The millions in income from that foreign-owned corporation went to those same foreigners—the trusts in Hong Kong and the Isle of Jersey.

As for the non-U.S. corporation owned by Kassar, it was called Canora S.A. Canora was incorporated in Panama in 1975; it didn't, however, stay there. "Effective as of March 4, 1988, Canora S.A. transferred its assets to Cordelia Corporation N.V., a Netherlands Antilles Corporation," Kassar declared in a filing in U.S. Tax Court. "In July of 1988, Cordelia Corporation N.V. changed its name to Canora Corporation N.V., which ultimately transferred all its assets to Canora A.V.V., an Aruban corporation." That year, according to the IRS, Kassar's offshore company, bouncing from tax haven to tax haven, along with his family trust on the Isle of Jersey, had income of $4.5 million from Carolco Investments B.V.—income that the IRS claimed was ultimately earned by Kassar. Overall, the IRS alleges that Kassar had more than $17 million in undeclared income from a series of offshore entities with names like Twinfalls A.V.V. and Beheer-en Belegging-maatschappij Petina in 1988, a year in which Kassar declared his taxable income to be just over $26,000.

In 1988, according to Carolco's annual report filed with the SEC,

Kassar's salary was $750,000. Carolco also spent more than $260,000 for a security system for Kassar's Beverly Hills mansion. The IRS determined that the company paid more than $342,000 for the producer's personal expenses, $356,000 in additional salary (paid to Clorenda N.V., yet another offshore company owned by Kassar), and $11 million in dividends from Carolco and other corporations under his control that he had characterized as loans. In all, IRS auditors determined that Kassar's total taxable income in 1988 was more than $30 million—a far cry from the $26,000 figure Kassar claimed on his 1040.

Kassar disputed all of the IRS's assessments; in May 1997, he was scheduled to have his day in court. Like many large, complex Tax Court cases, the trial was delayed. Unlike others, the reason was that the Justice Department informed Kassar, and his ex-partner Vajna, that they were the subjects of a criminal tax fraud investigation. The Service and attorneys for Kassar and Vajna agreed to continue the trial until the criminal investigation and any subsequent prosecution was completed.

The joint motion for continuance filed by the IRS and attorneys for Kassar indicated that the Justice Department was interested in many of the same offshore transactions that had caught the eye of the IRS. Unlike the IRS, Justice could send Kassar and Vajna to jail. Thus, the two producers, who would certainly have been called to testify in their Tax Court trials, might have had to plead the Fifth Amendment to protect themselves from criminal liability. Indeed, many individuals whom either the IRS or Kassar and Vajna's attorneys intended to call might have found themselves in the same situation. "Other witnesses who are important to the resolution of this case are also potentially implicated in the criminal investigation of the matters relating to this case," the joint motion stated. "Consequently, their Fifth Amendment rights are also implicated in this proceeding."

Among the other witnesses was the architect of Carolco's offshore tax structure, Peter Hoffman. In 1996, Hoffman was indicted on two counts of felony tax fraud. The Justice Department charged that Hoffman, to avoid paying taxes, had used a complex deferred compensation scheme while he was the company's chief executive officer. Instead of receiving his full salary, Carolco held part of it in an account for him. Hoffman paid no income taxes on the money deposited in the account maintained for his benefit. Each year, Hoffman borrowed money from Carolco, using the deferred compensation account as collateral. The government charged that Hoffman "did not intend to repay this money to Carolco and that his description of the payments as loans was a sham to justify his receipt of over $1 million in tax-free income."

Deferred compensation plans are one of the typical means by which those with high incomes avoid paying taxes. The IRS says that they're perfectly legal, provided that when an individual receives the deferred portion of his salary, he pays taxes on it. In Hoffman's case, the government argued that he was having his cake and eating it too— that is, the payments he took from Carolco and described as loans were actually salary. To bolster its claims, the government pointed out that Hoffman had never signed a promissory note for the loans. Moreover, Hoffman had never disclosed in Carolco's annual reports—as he was required to do by securities laws—that he had borrowed money from the company; when Kassar and Vajna borrowed from the company, they always did so. When Hoffman closed out the account in 1990, Carolco had credited it with $1 million. He'd borrowed $800,000 against the plan, leaving him with a balance of $200,000. Rather than report the full million as income, he reported the balance instead, and avoided paying taxes on some $800,000 in income.

Hoffman's attorneys blamed Carolco's accounting department for omitting the loans from the company's annual reports, and for failing to include them on Hoffman's 1990 W-2 Form. Their star witness, Andrew Vajna, testified that the payments to Hoffman were indeed loans, and not income. "Peter was an important part of this exciting venture," Vajna told the jury, "so if he needed money, we were happy to lend it to him."

Long after the exciting venture was over, he continued to be Hoffman's banker. Vajna admitted on the stand that he personally had loaned Hoffman $400,000 to pay for his team of defense attorneys.

The loan was a good investment; speculation was rampant that the government was trying to convict Hoffman to ensure his cooperation in the criminal investigation of Vajna and Kassar's offshore dealings.

For his part, Hoffman testified that of his $750,000 salary, he set aside $450,000 in the deferred account. He said that he arranged for loans so that he would have "flexibility" in his financial affairs. "There was never a dispute with Carolco about whether I would pay back the loans," he told the jury. There was no promissory note, Hoffman said, because "we were friends, we trusted each other."

Hoffman's wife, however, apparently didn't share that trust. Hoffman also told the jury that he closed his deferred compensation account because, "My wife said, 'I love Mario, but I don't trust him. I want my money.' "

On September 8, 1997—the day before his trial began—Hoffman paid the taxes due on the $800,000 in income from 1990; while the payments settled his tax bill from the IRS, he still faced the criminal charges for tax evasion. He claimed that the fault lay, once again, with Carolco's accounting department, and that he wasn't aware that his 1990 W-2 Form was in error. "We're all here because of the 1990 mistake," he told the jury.

In closing arguments, Assistant U.S. Attorney Monica Bachner called Hoffman "a brilliant tax lawyer who believed that he was entitled to play by a different set of rules than everyone else." She told the jury, "You've heard the saying that if it walks like a duck and quacks like a duck, well, these payments walked and quacked like income."

In the end, the jury sided with Hoffman. They acquitted him of two charges, added to the indictment in 1997 and unrelated to his days at Carolco, and deadlocked on the two others. U.S. District Judge John Davies declared a mistrial. When the government announced it would retry the case, Hoffman pleaded guilty in March 1998 to a misdemeanor tax evasion charge and paid a $5,000 fine plus back taxes from his 1989 and 1990 returns. There was no agreement in his plea bargain to cooperate with the investigations of Kassar and Vajna.

A few weeks after Hoffman's plea, at the Cannes Film Festival, Kassar and Vajna put in a joint appearance. While rallying to defend their old president—and themselves—against the IRS and the Justice Department, the men who made Rambo decided to renew their partnership. While they hadn't yet resurrected the famous office they shared in the heyday of Carolco, when their desks faced each other's in an office of their Sunset Boulevard headquarters, they'd already started lining up writers, directors, actors, and financing for their next slew of blockbuster films. The still-pending Tax Court case hasn't slowed them down at all.

The reunion was a natural, according to *Variety*, the entertainment industry journal, which had noted as early as 1995, "There's little question they did their best work together."

5

Well-to-Do

George B. Kaiser was already a wealthy man when he did the deal that made him a billionaire.

Tall and lean, now in his fifties, the Harvard-educated native of Tulsa made his first fortune in Oklahoma's oil and gas business. It's an industry whose giddy booms, followed by brutal busts, have ruined any number of entrepreneurs. Kaiser, however, managed to prosper through both good times and bad.

And it's no wonder. The impatient Sooner, who can't seem to get his words out fast enough, gets straight down to business and sticks to it. If a meeting strays from the matter at hand, Kaiser will get up and leave. He lives at a pace his friends call "Kaiser Time"—a breakneck pace in which everything must go according to his schedule and needs. Pity the executive whose arrival doesn't coincide with the keeper of Kaiser Time.

The shrewd and thrifty oilman doesn't look like a multimillionaire. He's not showy or ostentatious, and he doesn't stand out in a crowd. He doesn't own mansions in offshore locales. He certainly doesn't flaunt his wealth. Though he could afford the sleekest of sports cars or a fleet of limousines, he prefers driving beat-up company cars. "I just want reliable transportation to get from point A to point B," he told the Center in an interview. Still, some who know him best could see him for what he is.

"He always looked like a winner," said Wayne Swearingen, a one-time oilman, now a semiretired consultant, who knows and admires Kaiser. "He doesn't participate even in some of the oil and gas advocacy organizations that his father was quite active in. I guess he considers it a waste of his time and money."

That may be because Kaiser has made a practice of not following the conventional wisdom of his colleagues and competitors in the energy business. When everyone is buying, he sells. When everyone is selling, he buys. And when he sees an opportunity to make a fortune, he pounces.

In 1990, Kaiser forwent the "black gold" that had so enriched him for an altogether different endeavor: he bought the Bank of Oklahoma, N.A., from the Federal Deposit Insurance Corporation, the government agency that guarantees the soundness of the nation's major savings institutions. At the time, Oklahoma was reeling from the worst financial crisis in its history. But Kaiser saw the potential for profit in the state's largest savings institution, which only a few years earlier had nearly collapsed in a sea of red ink. And that potential was realized soon thereafter: buying the bank landed him on *Forbes* magazine's list of the 400 wealthiest Americans, and ultimately pushed his net worth to well over $1 billion.

What's more, Kaiser pulled it all off at a time when he claimed he had no income, and paid almost nothing in federal income taxes. He didn't need offshore trusts, controlled foreign corporations, or a passport from Belize to make his tax-free billion. With his shrewdness, his eye for a deal, and his adept handling of the Internal Revenue Code, he was able to turn Oklahoma into his own personal tax haven.

Oklahoma's economy rises and falls with the price of oil. In the 1970s, while the rest of the nation suffered through an energy crisis that led to gas lines, high unemployment, recession, and the twin double-digit inflation and interest rates, the demand for oil caused a boom in the state. Wells that had been unprofitable to drill in the days of $10-a-barrel oil suddenly became gold mines when the OPEC cartel pushed the price upward of $40. A bumper sticker of the time captured the mood of Sooners: "If you don't have an oil well, get one."

Thanks to his father, Kaiser had several. Herman Kaiser fled Nazi Germany in 1938 and settled his family in Tulsa. After the war, he arranged sales of oil field pipe between German firms and American companies. In 1949, the elder Kaiser got into oil and gas production, drilling wells in western Kansas. He had relatives in the business who ran a firm called Francis Oil & Gas, Inc.; by the time George was ready to work for his father, the name had been changed to Kaiser-Francis Oil Company, and Herman Kaiser was the owner.

George was born in 1942, attended Tulsa public schools, and went on to earn a bachelor's degree and a master's in business administration at Harvard University. He briefly considered joining the U.S. foreign service, but instead returned to his hometown in 1966 to work for his father. In 1969, George took over management of the business.

At that time, Kaiser-Francis Oil was a company with all of ten employees, just another of the many small, independent oil and gas producers. But in the years that followed, Kaiser turned the firm into the largest privately held producer of natural gas in the state. Like many of his fellow Sooners, Kaiser rode the boom brought on by the 1970s energy crisis. He drilled for oil in western Kansas, he bought natural gas properties in Louisiana and Texas, and he greatly expanded his holdings in his home state. But in 1979, he decided to ride the boom in a different direction.

From 1979 to 1982, when everyone wanted a well of his own, Kaiser made millions by selling off many of his oil and gas properties at peak prices. "We have no pride of ownership," he told *Forbes* in a 1991 interview, explaining the sales. "You can't be emotional." The strategy fit in with Kaiser's business philosophy, which is to go against the conventional wisdom. "I love deals when people on the other side are using rules of thumb," he said in the interview. "That means they're not doing the analysis."

Kaiser's analysis pointed him to banking, so he bought 2.7 percent of BancOklahoma Corporation, the parent company of Tulsa-based Bank of Oklahoma. With his purchase of the stock came a seat on the bank's board of directors, a position he assumed in 1980.

Banks in Oklahoma had made a fortune loaning billions during the boom, on the premise that oil prices would keep climbing; some experts predicted $100-a-barrel crude in a matter of years. As a result, investing in drilling seemed like a sure thing, even as interest rates shot upward in the late 1970s and early 1980s. "The oil and gas industries were one of the few areas where people thought you could borrow at 21.5 percent interest rates and still make a profit," Charles Cheatham, the general counsel of the Oklahoma Bank Association, told the Center. "Money came pouring into the state from all over the country. That had an effect on the whole state. Apartments and office buildings had 99 percent occupancy rates. This was an incredible bubble."

But as OPEC's pricing regime began to collapse, the bubble burst. The price of oil did what had been unthinkable to those who were confidently predicting that crude oil would soar: it declined. The first big drop occurred in April 1981; the price spiraled downward until, by 1986, it had reached levels not seen since the early 1970s. Suddenly, all those Oklahoma wells were unprofitable again. The same banks that had loaned billions during the boom found themselves holding mountains of bad debt. And that debt, it turned out, was backed by devalued assets, as oil producers went bankrupt, apartment and office buildings stood empty, and the state's energy-dependent economy collapsed along with the price of crude.

The Bank of Oklahoma might have weathered the storm, since it had largely avoided the lending binge. But in 1984, the bank had gone on an acquisition spree, buying nine banks in the Tulsa area and a tenth, Fidelity Bank, N.A., in Oklahoma City. Fidelity's books were dripping red ink from the energy sector loans it had made in the boom days. "I think perhaps the company did not do an adequate job of determining how serious the problems at Fidelity were," Kaiser told the *Tulsa World* in an October 1990 interview.

Even though the management at the Bank of Oklahoma understood the depth of the problems at Fidelity, they nonetheless went ahead with the merger. As a board member, Kaiser favored the deal, and even defended it six years later. "It was very important for Bank of Oklahoma to have a franchise in Oklahoma City," he told the *Tulsa World*. "It was the only franchise realistically available without starting from scratch and I think the idea was fine."

That fine idea nearly ruined the bank. After posting a $51 million loss in the second quarter of 1986, the Bank of Oklahoma turned to the Federal Deposit Insurance Corporation for a bailout. Rather than close the bank, the FDIC kept it afloat through a program called Open Bank Assistance; only those banks deemed "essential" to their communities qualified. In exchange for 55 percent of the stock of the bank's holding company, the FDIC pumped $130 million into the institution. Stockholders like Kaiser lost most of their investment in Fidelity. But the FDIC left the board and management in place to administer the bailout.

Other Oklahoma institutions weren't so lucky. No one considered them "essential" to the community. By 1994, more than a dozen years after the bust began, 162 of the state's banks and savings and loans had closed their doors—a financial debacle that cost taxpayers, who bailed out depositors, more than $4 billion. Oil and gas producers laid off workers or went bankrupt, as did the companies dependent on their business. For them, there was no taxpayer-financed bailout.

In March and April 1986, Demco, Incorporated, an Oklahoma City–based manufacturer of oil and gas drilling equipment, laid off 98 of its 400 workers. Halliburton Company cut 550 jobs in the first six months of that year at its Duncan, Oklahoma, factories; overall, the oil field services company's employment in Duncan declined from 4,000 in early 1982 to 2,200 in 1986. Philips Petroleum Company, a worldwide oil producer headquartered in Bartlesville, Oklahoma, slashed its workforce there by a sixth; 1,000 of the 6,000 employees who worked in the company's hometown were left without paychecks.

There were record numbers of bankruptcies as well: Seneca Oil Company; Waterford Energy, Incorporated; and MGF Oil Corporation, to name a few. Kaiser picked up all three from various bankruptcy courts and added them to Kaiser-Francis Oil's empire. Just as he had sold off oil properties at peak prices during the boom, Kaiser was acquiring them at bargain-basement prices during the bust.

Other companies disappeared entirely. Colin Schmidt worked for eighteen years as a systems analyst for the Tulsa-based Bovaird Supply Company, another oil field services supplier. The company, founded in 1871, weathered over a century of ups and downs in the oil industry. At its peak in 1982, Bovaird Supply employed 820 workers. Then the bust came. Schmidt still remembers the day in June 1983 when the first job cuts were announced. "They went from department to department, reading a list of names and laying people off," Schmidt recalled. "In my department, we thought, 'They can't lay us off. They need this new system so they can do their job better.' But they came in and laid off people in my department too."

By the end of 1994, Bovaird's payroll had dropped to 250. Oil production in Oklahoma had fallen off so much that the company tried to survive by selling its wares in Russia. "They had the same problem everyone else in Russia did," Schmidt said. "Getting paid."

In January 1996, after 124 years and five generations of Bovairds running the company, the family sold what little remained of the failing business to Continental Emsco Company, another oil field supplier. The new owners promptly closed the doors of Bovaird Supply's Tulsa headquarters, a move that put the last sixteen employees—including Colin Schmidt—out of work.

The job losses at Bovaird Supply were hardly unique. In 1998, State Representative Russ Roach, a Democrat from Tulsa, reported that 108,000 jobs disappeared in Oklahoma from 1982 to 1988. Those jobs were primarily in the high-paying oil and gas industries; they were replaced, for the most part, by low-paying service jobs. Oklahoma's per capita income in 1982 was slightly below the national average, but has since plummeted. In 1998, the finance office of Republican governor Frank Keating noted that "Oklahomans receive an average of 80 cents for every $1 received nationally. Regrettably, this is only half the story. These numbers conceal the fact that the average is even worse in the state's rural areas."

"There was terrible pain for a long time," recalled Charles Cheatham, of the Oklahoma Bank Association. "We had a deflationary economy. Our gross state product decreased, tax revenues decreased, and the value of real estate decreased. The average home decreased in value by 30 percent. There are still people after fifteen years of this with negative equity in their homes."

The Bank of Oklahoma, however, did fairly well. In 1987, thanks to the FDIC bailout, it was able to acquire two more banks, one in Yukon and the other in Norman, expanding its reach through the state. By 1989, the FDIC had the Bank of Oklahoma back on its feet: it recorded a modest profit that year of $3.8 million. The FDIC was ready to return the bank to private hands, and put it up for sale.

All but one of the bidders came from out of state: Kaiser, who held the inside track. Not only did the native son serve on the bank's board of directors but on the audit committee as well, and therefore was intimately familiar with the bank's loans—both good and bad. Kaiser's bid wasn't the highest, but unlike his competitors, he didn't ask the FDIC to bail out any of the bad loans still on the bank's books. In the end, Kaiser's inside track proved fruitful: he paid just under $61 million for a bank that the FDIC had bought four years earlier for $130 million. What's more, the Bank of Oklahoma was losing millions when the FDIC stepped in, but was now turning a profit.

"I never wanted to be a banker," Kaiser told the Center. "Oklahoma is a state that can't be banked by Chase Manhattan. We need relationship banking or community banking. I was concerned that that style of banking would disappear with all the bank consolidation. And really it has, except for us."

Following his successful bid, Kaiser immediately pledged to aggressively finance local business expansion, to provide loans and capital to his fellow Sooners, and to raise the bank's profile in charitable events and community causes. He was proclaimed a "favorite son" for rescuing the Tulsa-based bank and keeping it in hometown hands. "Really, my consideration here is, first of all, the critical necessity for Oklahoma to have a home-owned, home-controlled financial institution," he told the *Tulsa World* in an October 1990 interview. "That sounds a bit holy, but generally, that's the personal motivation. But it will be a profitable transaction as well."

That was putting it lightly. By the end of 1998, Kaiser's shares of BOK Financial (the holding company that owns the bank) were worth nearly $917 million, fifteen times what he paid for them. Kaiser's strike is even more phenomenal considering that, when he bought the shares, he claimed he had no income. At the same time Kaiser was buying the Bank of Oklahoma from one part of the federal government, the FDIC, he was telling another part, the Internal Revenue Service, that he wasn't paying any income taxes because he had lost money that year.

Kaiser paid for the bank in 1991—a year in which he filed a federal income tax return declaring a total taxable income of negative $2,328,639. The previous year, when Kaiser made his successful $61 million bid to buy the bank, he declared a loss of $115,561. Kaiser's total income tax payments those years: zero.

In 1989, Kaiser actually had some earnings. He filed a tax return showing total taxable income of $11,699—equal to an hourly wage of $5.62. For the record, the average hourly wage for nonsupervisory bank employees—tellers, security guards, janitors, and the like—was $8.13 in 1989, or $2.51 more an hour than Kaiser, the future bank owner, claimed he earned. Kaiser paid $2,688 in federal income taxes that year.

In the three prior years, from 1986 to 1988, Kaiser declared losses as well. Over the six years from 1986 to 1991, Kaiser's average annual income was negative $860,000. But before taking up a collection for the George B. Kaiser Relief Fund, remember that in 1992, his net worth landed him on the *Forbes* list of the 400 wealthiest Americans, where he has remained ever since.

His purchase of the Bank of Oklahoma the year before had a lot to do with his landing on the list. In 1991, the Tulsa oilman received more than $100 million from an entity known as GBK Corporation. Following an audit, the IRS suggested that the entire amount was dividend income. On the heels of the audit, the Service questioned the validity of various deductions and losses Kaiser and his wife claimed. In fact, the IRS sent the couple a Notice of Deficiency in 1997 for $48.6 million for back taxes, interest, and penalties.

The Kaisers, maintaining that they owed no additional taxes, contested the IRS's findings in U.S. Tax Court. Kaiser told the IRS that the $100 million he received from GBK was not a dividend, but a loan. He had paid interest on the amount, he noted—a staggering $3.3 million in 1991 alone. "They dropped it immediately," Kaiser said of the IRS's position on the loan. "There was no issue. The Internal Revenue Service on occasion will raise spurious issues to increase its leverage." After negotiating with IRS attorneys, the Kaisers settled the case for substantially less than the government initially sought: they sent the government a check for $11,891.

From 1989 to 1991, Kaiser's average annual tax burden rose— thanks to the settlement with the IRS—to $4,860 a year. That's less than the amount that a married couple with an income of $41,140 would pay. If that couple saved every penny of their annual income, it would take them more than 22,000 years to accumulate the $917 million that Kaiser made from his investment in the Bank of Oklahoma.

That couple could afford to borrow $151,000 to buy a home. Kaiser was able to persuade GBK to loan more than 650 times that amount to buy the Bank of Oklahoma. That's because GBK stands for George B. Kaiser.

GBK Corporation is a holding company whose principal asset is Kaiser-Francis Oil. In his role as president, chairman, and sole director of GBK, Kaiser loaned himself the $100 million to buy the Bank of Oklahoma. Kaiser was able to satisfy the IRS that the money was indeed borrowed, and not a dividend from his company, as the Service initially contended. "There are about eleven things you have to show to disprove that, and the only one I didn't have was the corporate minutes," he told the Center. "I'm the only director and I hold all the directors' meetings in the shower. I don't take minutes because the ink runs."

Because Kaiser is paying back the money he borrowed from his company, he can even deduct the $3.3 million he paid in interest to GBK from his personal income taxes. It's called investment interest expense, and it's fully deductible under the Internal Revenue Code.

As for GBK, which had enough spare cash to make a $100 million loan, its returns showed losses almost as prodigious as Kaiser's. From 1986 to 1992, GBK filed returns claiming $507,000 in red ink. Some years the company had income and paid taxes; other years, it claimed losses and paid nothing. And some of those losses came from firms that had nothing to do with GBK, Kaiser-Francis Oil, or George Kaiser. Instead, the losses were attributed to those bankrupt companies that Kaiser bought up during the bust—firms like MGF Oil and Waterford Energy, which had more to offer Kaiser than a chance to boost his gas production.

Waterford Energy operated roughly 150 gas wells in Beaver County, Oklahoma. Like many other independent oil and gas companies, it borrowed heavily during the boom and suffered huge losses during the bust. When it ended up in bankruptcy court in 1990, it had about $7 million in assets, and something far more valuable on paper. Waterford possessed $151 million in losses the company had racked up over the years. Those huge losses that Waterford suffered in the 1980s wound up as huge write-offs on the tax returns of GBK Corporation in the 1990s.

In 1992, Kaiser erased a $40 million profit made by his GBK Corporation because Waterford Energy lost millions in the 1980s. GBK can continue to apply those Waterford losses to its tax returns until 2005. By using the net operating losses of bankrupt companies like Waterford or MGF Oil, another company whose tax benefits Kaiser enjoyed, he turned the profits of Kaiser-Francis Oil into paper losses on his tax returns.

The oil bust, with all its business failures and bankrupted energy producers, provided Kaiser the perfect opportunity to use net operating losses to lower his tax burden. In 1997, the IRS challenged the Waterford write-off, arguing that "losses resulting from acquisitions made to evade or avoid income tax are prohibited." Like Kaiser, GBK received a large bill from the IRS—this one for more than $24 million including interest and penalties—covering 1989 to 1992. And like Kaiser, GBK contested the charges. The company argued, for example, that it "acquired Waterford for sound business reasons; the acquisition was not made for the principal purpose of evading or avoiding federal income taxes."

"We acquire oil and gas companies and properties all the time because we're in the business of acquiring hydrocarbon reserves," Kaiser said of the Waterford purchase. "During the desperate depression of the 1980s, there were no oil and gas companies without net operating losses. Any company you'd buy had them. There was no indication that we didn't comply with the Internal Revenue rules."

Kaiser carefully complied with the rules, in part to preserve the net operating losses he used so shrewdly. Waterford filed a plan of reorganization in the U.S. Bankruptcy Court for the Southern District of Texas on November 7, 1990. The filing laid out the steps that the company, which was soon to be managed by Kaiser and a group of his executives, would take to get the company out of debt and satisfy creditors. "The principal motivations of the plan are to reorganize the debtor . . . to meet its obligations as they mature and to preserve the tax attributes of the debtor in order to allow the debtor to realize the benefits of the tax attributes, including net operating losses." Once Kaiser took control of Waterford, his company would enjoy the "benefits of the tax attributes" of the debtor.

A November 27, 1989, letter that D. Joseph Graham, the chief financial officer of Kaiser-Francis Oil, wrote to Steven Ensz, then president of Waterford Energy, was even more specific about the company's interest in the acquisition. "I apologize for taking so long to get back to you on the Waterford Energy, Inc. offer," the letter began. "I have been spending almost all of my time on the purchase of another oil and gas company, which, coincidentally, also has very significant tax attributes, and have just now been able to return my attention to Waterford. Although our appetite for an acquisition of this nature is somewhat relieved by the other opportunity, we are still interested in trying to reach an agreement on Waterford. . . ."

Kaiser's appetite for acquisitions with "significant tax attributes" wasn't entirely relieved by the purchase of that other oil and gas company: in 1990, he took over Waterford; in 1991, he merged Waterford with Kaiser-Francis Oil and claimed Waterford's net operating losses on GBK's tax return.

In 1998, the IRS finally settled the case with GBK Corporation, without going to trial, for $3.7 million—or roughly 15 cents on the dollar. The IRS refused comment on the settlement, citing the confidentiality of taxpayer information. The Service allowed the deductions for the Waterford losses to stand.

George Kaiser once remarked to *Forbes*, in a comment he would probably like to take back, that "Gas is the only commodity you can legally steal." A class action suit filed in Oklahoma state court accused Waterford and its new owner, Kaiser-Francis Oil, of doing just that. The suit charges that Kaiser's companies participated in "a scheme which resulted in the systematic underpayment of royalties to royalty owners" of the wells that Waterford, and later Kaiser-Francis, operated.

Two years before Kaiser's company took over Waterford, a royalty owner, Robert A. Funk, had sued the company for $3.4 million. Funk claimed that Waterford was paying him less than he was owed for the gas the company was pumping out of his land. Funk was familiar with the oil and gas business; as president of Funk Exploration, Inc., he was another Sooner who rode the energy boom. His company built the Beaver Gathering System, a pipeline that transported gas in the panhandle of Oklahoma. Funk Exploration got huge loans from banks in the early 1980s: $20 million from Wells Fargo Bank, a $200 million line of credit from Marine Midland Bank, and a $500 million line of credit from Chemical Bank. He saddled his company with so much debt that, when the bust came, he couldn't repay his loans. In 1985, Chemical Bank forced him out, reorganized the company, and renamed it Waterford Energy.

When Funk set up the Beaver Gathering System, he also instituted a scheme to secretly charge royalty owners an inflated "transportation fee" for pumping gas from their land. Funk didn't mind paying the fee himself, because much of that money ended up in his own pocket (part of the profits Funk Exploration earned). But after he turned over control of the company to Chemical Bank, he was getting cheated just like the other royalty owners in Beaver County. So Funk sued Waterford in 1988.

"I am not being paid as a lease instructs to be paid," Funk told attorneys for Waterford in a 1989 deposition. "I should get gross proceeds, [there] should not be any transportation deducted." Funk further complained that his royalty check did not indicate that Waterford had deducted any fee from it. When asked by Waterford's attorneys whether he knew of the fee because he was the one who instituted it, Funk answered yes.

Kaiser told the Center that "We prefer picking up bankrupt companies because you know all the liabilities." Yet he wasn't aware of Funk's scheme until after he had filed the bankruptcy reorganization plan. He didn't schedule the claims of other royalty owners. He discovered Funk's transportation fees when Jack and Verdeen Slatten, two other royalty owners in the Beaver Gathering System, sued Kaiser-Francis Oil. Kaiser settled with them out of court for $25,000 and a promise that they wouldn't disclose the terms of the settlement to anyone else.

Eventually, other royalty owners—some 1,300 of them—found out about the fees. In 1995, they filed a class action suit in Beaver County District Court, alleging that they'd been underpaid some $35 million by Waterford Energy and its successor, Kaiser-Francis Oil. The suit alleges that Kaiser-Francis Oil continued to collect the transportation fee, year after year, long after the Slattens' lawsuit exposed the scheme. The average claim was $17,750; Galen Bridenstine, the royalty owner chosen to represent the class, claimed he was out a little less than $9,000.

Attorneys for Kaiser-Francis Oil argued that Kaiser was not aware of Funk's scheme, and in any case, those claims were barred by the statute of limitations. They filed a motion in bankruptcy court, arguing that Waterford's bankruptcy eliminated any claims prior to Kaiser-Francis Oil's taking over the company. They vigorously denied that the company engaged in any scheme that paid royalty owners less than they were owed. And they attempted to prevent the royalty owners from suing as a class. After five years of litigation, the royalty owners, as of this writing, have yet to get their day in Oklahoma's courts. The trial, scheduled for May 1999, was pushed back to March 2000, then delayed again.

Kaiser told the Center that the suit is groundless. "We were disadvantaged as well," he said. "If the fee for the pipeline is excessive, then we are hurt too. If the pipeline's overcharging, we're overcharged. I don't think anybody is an appropriate plaintiff in this case."

The Waterford royalty owners aren't the only Oklahomans who have claimed that Kaiser's companies have legally stolen from them. A group of landowners in Grady County, in the south-central part of the state, have also alleged that Kaiser-Francis Oil has paid them less than they're owed for the gas the company drains from their property.

Glenn Mayo, whose elderly mother, Murlene, is one of the plaintiffs, told the Center, "When the price of gas was up to $3.50 per thousand cubic feet, they paid 16 to 22 cents on it." Royalty owners are supposed to get one-eighth of the sale price on the gas—almost 44 cents at a price of $3.50. "You can see how much money you're losing," Mayo said.

Over the years, that lost money has added up to about $10,000. Not a fortune by any means, but as Glenn Mayo says of his mother,

"When you're old, and you depend on Social Security, every little bit helps."

Mayo isn't optimistic that his mother will ever recover the money, despite being a participant in a lawsuit that was filed in 1993. "My mom's eighty-six, and it's unlikely she'll see any benefit out of it. My grandpa didn't see any, my dad didn't see any, so I guess it's an ongoing thing."

"I've probably been around the oil and gas business for about twenty years and have never heard of anything like this," Richard Allen, the attorney representing Mayo, said. He filed the 1993 lawsuit on behalf of her and thirty other landowners in Grady County. The attorney spent hundreds of hours in the arduous task of unraveling Kaiser's empire, studying leases and sales records and royalty payments.

"Kaiser-Francis owns a few buildings up in Tulsa and you walk in and there's 500 different corporations in those buildings," said Allen. "Those people that I deposed might be the vice president of twenty different companies, all of them owned by Kaiser and his family."

One of those companies, Texas Southwest Gas Corporation, buys gas from Kaiser-Francis Oil for far less than the market price, the suit alleged. The gas is pumped from land owned by Murlene Mayo and the other Grady County royalty owners, who receive their percentage on those Kaiser-Francis sales. Texas Southwest Gas then resells the gas for full price on the open market. The difference in price ends up in George Kaiser's pocket.

"We've run the records and we know what Kaiser-Francis made out of these wells," Allen said. "We've got how much they paid the royalty owners. They admit that they're selling to themselves. They're saying, 'We can get around the law and do this.' "

Kaiser and his lawyers aren't eager to find out if a judge would agree with them. Instead, they challenged the right of Allen's clients to sue as a class of similarly aggrieved plaintiffs. They won the first round in a trial court, and in February 1998, the civil appeals court of Oklahoma upheld the trial court's refusal to certify Allen's clients as a class. The majority held that because Kaiser-Francis Oil had different types of agreements with the various royalty owners, the plaintiffs did not have enough in common to be considered a class. The majority noted, however, that the plaintiffs could pursue their cases individually.

Should Allen's clients sue separately, each would have to pay attorney fees and court costs to recover amounts in some cases as little as a few thousand dollars. "These are people that don't have much income and I'm finding out they've only been paid a tenth of what they're due," Allen said. "The problem is, how can a person getting a hundred-dollar royalty check challenge a person like Kaiser and his lawyers?"

Kaiser, after all, is one of the 400 wealthiest Americans. In 1995, he used some of that money to push the Oklahoma legislature to pass a bill that would limit punitive damages to $100,000. Kaiser wanted to make it harder for ordinary Oklahomans to sue powerful companies. When the legislature balked, Kaiser helped raise $2 million to get tort reform passed as a ballot initiative. Governor Frank Keating threatened to veto a banking bill if it didn't include Kaiser's tort-reform package. Oklahoma's elected representatives bowed to the pressure. Keating remarked at the time that the bill passed thanks to "a very real fear of my veto and George Kaiser's money."

The oilman believes he did the state a service. "The U.S. civil legal system is fatally flawed," he said.

Tort reform isn't the only business-friendly measure to come from the Oklahoma statehouse. As elected officials have struggled with the implications of the oil bust, they've crafted a number of programs to attract businesses to the state. Keating has called for right-to-work laws, aimed at restricting the activities of labor unions, and reform of the state's worker compensation system.

And in 1993, the legislature passed the Quality Jobs Program Act, aimed at attracting companies to the state by offering to pay 5 percent of the wages for new jobs created there for up to ten years. The purpose of the bill was to help Oklahoma recover from the oil bust. The list of companies that have taken advantage of the program reads like a who's who of the *Fortune* 500—Boeing, AT&T, Mutual of Omaha, Hertz Corporation, Amoco Corporation, and Seagate Technology, to name a few. Some of the wealthiest corporations in the country get a rebate from ordinary Oklahoma taxpayers, whose incomes are already, on average, among the lowest in the country. Or, as the state's finance office put it, "[T]he Quality Jobs program, an economic development incentive, is placing an increasing demand on income tax revenues."

While ordinary taxpayers might be footing the bill for the Quality Jobs program, to date it hasn't made much of a difference for the average Sooner. Six years after it was enacted, the state's per capita income remained among the lowest in the nation. "The problem in our state," the finance office reported in 1998, "is that we have plenty of jobs, they just pay relatively low wages." Layoffs are still common in the oil industry. In January 1999, Governor Keating called for an emergency session of the legislature to address the plight of Oklahoma's oil and gas producers.

One business, however, has done very well. The same month Keating called for the emergency session, the Bank of Oklahoma announced that it had record earnings in the previous year. George Kaiser believes that the profits he earns from the bank are all to the good of his fellow Sooners. "I guess the image we're seeking as a bank is an Oklahoma-based company which wants to be deeply involved in the restoration of the Oklahoma economy," Kaiser told the *Sunday Oklahoman* in June 1992. While that restoration for the rest of the state has been slow in coming, it hasn't prevented Kaiser's bank from enjoying a boom of its own.

He doubled its profitability in his first year as chairman and boosted commercial, real estate, and consumer loan business by 20 percent or more in each category. He expanded in the Tulsa area by buying nineteen branches of the Sooner Federal Savings & Loan in 1992. He bought a mortgage company from the Resolution Trust Corporation, the government entity charged with cleaning up the savings and loan mess, to further expand the bank's presence in real estate lending. "We've been one of the most dynamic banks in the marketplace," Kaiser boasted to *American Banker*, the trade magazine for savings institutions, in a September 1992 interview.

Year after year, the bank has issued glowing earnings reports. By the time it issued its 1998 annual report, Kaiser decided to extend the bank's reach beyond his home state. "Over the past several years, we have succeeded in building the Bank of Oklahoma into a position of dominance in our home state," the report read. "The challenge we face is strengthening that position while expanding into surrounding states. . . ." Those states include Texas, New Mexico, and Arkansas. Kaiser's BOK Financial has acquired banks in all three.

There was just one dark cloud hanging over the Bank of Oklahoma's sunny future. The IRS was auditing the bank, a fact also disclosed in the company's annual reports. Unlike other parts of Kaiser's empire, the bank paid taxes—although its effective tax rate ranged between 20 percent and 33 percent in the years after Kaiser bought it, always less than the 34 percent corporate tax rate.

In 1999, the company announced the result of the audits. "During 1998, Internal Revenue Service examinations for 1994 and 1995 were closed with no significant adjustments. During 1997, the Internal Revenue Service closed its examination of [the Bank of Oklahoma] and BOK Financial for 1992 and 1993, respectively. As a result of the outcome of these examinations, BOK Financial realized a $9.0 million tax allowance that was no longer needed."

Like Kaiser and his company, the bank had complied with the Internal Revenue Code and satisfied the auditors. Once again, the IRS cleared Kaiser.

6

Shore Leave

 From the Pilgrims who founded Plymouth Plantation to the scientists, technicians, and engineers who sent the astronauts to the heavens, America has always been a country of pioneers. Since the last lunar module left the surface of the moon, that pioneer spirit has been redirected toward cyberspace. The new economy, driven by computer software and hardware, instantaneous transactions over the Internet, and countless other innovations, has changed the way Americans—and the world—work, shop, and communicate.

Seagate Technology, Incorporated, based in Scotts Valley, California, was one of the companies that blazed the trail. Founded in 1979, Seagate built the first 5.25-inch hard drive, the internal mechanism that stores the programs and information that make a computer run. The company dominates the market for disk drives, and today remains the world's largest manufacturer of the devices.

Alan Shugart, Seagate's founder, served as chairman and chief executive officer until he was fired in 1998. If a true maverick ever headed a *Fortune* 500 firm, it was Shugart. In 1996, he tried to get his Bernese mountain dog, Ernest, on the ballot for Congress to protest what he saw as the poor choices the parties were offering voters. He managed to raise $3,000 for the canine candidate, but failed to secure him a chance to run for the House.

Shugart began his career with IBM in 1951, moved to Memorex in 1969 (taking with him 200 of Big Blue's top engineers), and then struck out on his own with Shugart Associates. He tried to develop the first floppy disk, but in 1974, with his venture in the red, he gave up corporate life for a fishing boat and a bar that he co-owned with some friends. In 1979, he returned to the computer business and formed Seagate.

"Every time you send an email, log on to your favorite website, use an ATM machine or buy something using the Internet, you create information," Seagate's company fact sheet says. "Seagate Technology is a leading provider of technology and products enabling people to store, access, and manage the world's information." It makes disk drives for the lower-priced personal computers and the high-end network servers that link tens or hundreds of PCs together. It makes tape drives and other devices to back up those networks. It plans to make even more powerful disk drives that will allow computer users to watch television live over the World Wide Web and store hundreds of digitized films, shows, and even home movies on a PC.

In 1999, the company had revenues of $6.8 billion, of which nearly $1.2 billion was profit. According to its annual report, it paid $20 million in taxes to the federal government that year—an effective tax rate of less than 2 percent. Seagate achieved its low tax rate, in part, because in 1982 it became a pioneer of a different sort. That year, David "Tommy" Mitchell, then the company's vice president of operations, toured the Pacific Rim in search of new, cheaper sources of raw materials and a place to set up a purchasing office. He went to Hong Kong first, but didn't like what he saw there.

"Hong Kong is a very confusing place to get established," he said in November 1991, recalling his foreign travel in testimony before the U.S. Tax Court. "And so, when we spent the two days in Hong Kong that we were looking around, it didn't really seem like anybody wanted us in Hong Kong, or was willing to help us out."

So Mitchell continued his tour of Southeast Asia. "I went on to Singapore, where I was given a great reception by the EDB, or the Economic Development Board," Mitchell said. "The EDB met us at the airplane. So automatically we felt good about it, and the infrastructure seemed to be in Singapore." Officials of the country's Economic Development Board, whose purpose was to attract foreign jobs, made sure Mitchell knew that the infrastructure could support the kind of manufacturing Seagate wanted to do. "They took me to see a whole bunch of different companies that were in the electronic assembly business, and told me that what would be the chance that maybe you could do the assemblies here."

Mitchell warmed to the idea of manufacturing in the tiny nation on the southern tip of the Malaysian peninsula, in part because Singapore offered the company "pioneer status." Mitchell explained what it meant: "Well, pioneer status, to me, meant one of the first guys to be in Singapore," adding that the company would get "favored treatment" from the government of the country. "There are a lot of things that went with it," he said. The government offered to help the company find suitable buildings for its manufacturing operations and hire local workers to staff them. Mitchell and the company took the government up on its offer and became pioneers. They incorporated Seagate Singapore on July 30, 1982, and opened their first factory there just four months later. The facility had all of fifty employees.

By 1987, Seagate employed more than 8,000 workers in Singapore, making it the country's second-largest employer. And from that modest overseas beginning, Seagate's global manufacturing operations have expanded to neighboring Malaysia and Thailand, to Northern Ireland and Mexico, even to the People's Republic of China. In fact, the worldwide leader in disk drive manufacturing is also a worldwide manufacturer, with some 82,000 employees scattered across the globe, 65,000 of them in Asia. That first pioneering step to Singapore provided Seagate with other benefits as well. "One was a tax holiday," Mitchell explained.

And the advantages of that are amply documented in the company's 1999 annual report, filed with the Securities and Exchange Commission.

A substantial portion of the Company's Far East manufacturing operations . . . in Singapore, Thailand, Malaysia and China operate under various tax holidays which expire in whole or in part during fiscal years 2001 through 2009. The net impact of these tax holidays was to increase net income by approximately $35 million in 1999. . . . Cumulative undistributed earnings of the Company's Far East subsidiaries for which no income taxes have been provided aggregated approximately $1.634 billion at July 2, 1999. These earnings are considered to be permanently invested in non-U.S. operations. Additional federal and state taxes of approximately $585 million would have to be provided if these earnings were repatriated to the U.S.

Welcome to the new economy.

Singapore is just one of the countries offering tax incentives to attract U.S. firms' manufacturing operations. Indonesia offers twelve-year tax holidays to new businesses. The Philippine Economic Zone Authority, a government body similar to Singapore's Economic Development Board, grants foreign firms up to eight years of tax-free income. Malaysia has set up a Multimedia Super Corridor south of the capital of Kuala Lumpur. High-tech corporations establishing new businesses there will enjoy a ten-year tax holiday, duty-free imports, and unlimited visas for foreign "knowledge workers" to staff their operations. Software makers Microsoft, Oracle, and Sun Microsystems all have agreements to set up shop there.

American companies are moving more than just their manufacturing operations offshore. They're also moving large amounts of profit out of the United States, beyond the reach of the Internal Revenue Service. Foreign governments, eager to attract jobs, are helping them out by exempting them from local taxes. In the global world of corporate welfare, the average taxpayer ends up holding the bag.

Seagate is not alone in pooling income offshore. *Fortune* 500 companies have long made it a favored practice to avoid taxes. Citigroup Incorporated, the giant global banker, reported it had $1.3 billion invested overseas. "At December 31, 1999, $1.3 billion of accumulated undistributed earnings of non-U.S. subsidiaries was indefinitely invested. At the existing U.S. federal income tax rate, additional taxes of $399 million would have to be provided if such earnings were remitted."

MBNA Corporation, the giant credit card company, stated in its 1999 annual report that it had $198 million in offshore earnings. "It is not practicable to determine the amount of any additional U.S. income taxes that might be payable in the event that these earnings are repatriated," the company said.

In 1999, Apple Computer had $520 million stashed away offshore; CSX Corporation, the railroad freight operator, had $290 million in 1997 alone, plus $205 million more in 1998. United Technologies, Incorporated, the conglomerate that makes Otis elevators, Carrier air conditioners and heaters, and aircraft engines under the Pratt & Whitney name, did not say how much money it had accumulated offshore in its annual report, but it was very clear about its plans for the cash. "The corporation's intention is to reinvest these earnings permanently or to repatriate the earnings only when it is tax effective to do so," it announced. United Technologies' effective tax rate in 1999 was 25.9 percent—a fact the company celebrated. "The corporation has continued to reduce its effective income tax rate by implementing tax reduction strategies," it said.

The ability of multinationals to pool profits overseas without paying tax on them is nothing new. An individual must report income derived from any source, including foreign earnings, on his or her tax returns. By contrast, corporations that set up subsidiaries in Singapore, China, or the Cayman Islands have created, for the purposes of the Internal Revenue Code, foreign corporations. Income those corporations earn is not subject to U.S. tax unless it's sent back to the parent company in the United States. And a multinational corporation can use those offshore subsidiaries to lower its U.S. income taxes.

The practice is known as transfer pricing, and it costs the treasury billions of dollars each year. The tax code requires that a corporation deal with its subsidiaries at arm's length; that is, it must deal with them as it would with any other unrelated company. If a U.S. corporation imports a product made by its offshore subsidiary, it can't pay an unreasonably high price for the product. Doing so would allow it to shift taxable income from the United States to its offshore subsidiary. The foreign subsidiary would earn a greater percentage of the profit than its American parent, and could invest that money overseas tax free.

Like Seagate Technology, with its $1.6 billion worth of profit stashed away in foreign countries. The IRS audited Seagate's returns from 1983 to 1987, and sent the company a Notice of Deficiency for some $112 million. It audited the company's returns from 1988 to 1990 and charged it with another $79 million in taxes and penalties due. Under Section 482 of the Internal Revenue Code, the Service has the authority to reallocate income of corporations and their offshore subsidiaries to prevent avoidance of taxes. It did just that with Seagate, charging that the company improperly inflated the price its Singapore subsidiary charged for its disk drives by shifting research and development and other costs from its U.S. operations to the foreign manufacturer. Seagate filed petitions in U.S. Tax Court, disputing all the deficiencies.

The IRS has had limited success recovering taxes from corporations under Section 482. On September 21, 1999, Tax Court Chief Judge Mary Ann Cohen sent the community of tax professionals into an uproar when she ruled that Compaq Computer Corporation, one of the leading makers of personal computers, was not entitled to a $3.4 million foreign tax credit.

Compaq claimed the credit as part of a tax shelter scheme known as dividend stripping. On September 16, 1992, the company purchased 10 million shares of Royal Dutch Petroleum Company, a Netherlands-based oil producer, on the New York Stock Exchange. Shareholders who owned the petroleum company's stock on that day were paid a dividend. Compaq held the shares just long enough to qualify for the dividend, then sold them for a loss. Compaq received dividend income of $22.5 million. Royal Dutch Petroleum withheld 15 percent—the $3.4 million in question—for withholding taxes, which were paid to the government of the Netherlands.

On its tax returns, Compaq reported the $22.5 million as income. At the corporate tax rate of 35 percent, the company owed about $7.9 million. It reduced its income by the loss it incurred when it sold off the stock—some $20.7 million. The loss reduced its taxes by $7.2 million. So the net effect of the scheme was that Compaq owed $700,000 on its U.S. taxes. Except that U.S. corporations get a credit for the taxes they pay to foreign governments. The $3.4 million paid to the Netherlands was subtracted from the U.S. taxes the company owed. Thus, Compaq claimed a tax benefit of $2.8 million on the transaction, at the expense of the U.S. Treasury.

The Internal Revenue Service challenged the foreign tax credit, arguing that its purpose was simply to avoid U.S. income taxes and that it had no other economic benefit. Judge Cohen agreed; she called Compaq's investment "a mere tax artifice." She noted that Compaq's financial officers signed off on the transaction—involving nearly $1 billion of the company's money—without knowing anything about Royal Dutch Petroleum. Cohen called the investment "less than businesslike." So much for due diligence.

Tax Analysts, the respected nonprofit group that studies state, federal, and international tax issues, published several commentaries on the shelter in its journal *Tax Notes Today*. Lawyers, academics, and accountants questioned the wisdom of Cohen's ruling. John F. Prusiecki, an attorney in the Chicago office of Altheimer & Gray, called Compaq's transaction both "real"—meaning it should be allowed—and, at the same time, "solely tax-motivated." Marc D. Teitelbaum, a partner at Sonnenschein, Nath and Rosenthal in New York, argued that "Compaq satisfied the only substantive requirements of the foreign tax credit regime and should be able to claim a foreign tax credit for the Netherlands withholding taxes."

The heated debate over foreign tax credits and the dividend stripping shelter overshadowed another ruling Judge Cohen made involving Compaq. On August 13, 1996, the IRS, again under Section 482 of the Internal Revenue Code, sent Compaq a Notice of Deficiency, claiming that the company had understated its U.S. income by some $214 million, and therefore owed some $76 million in taxes for 1991 and 1992. The IRS charged that the prices charged by Compaq Asia Ltd., the company's Singapore subsidiary, were higher than the arm's-length prices for its products.

In her ruling, Judge Cohen acknowledged that the Service had "broad authority to allocate gross income, deductions, credits, or allowances between two related corporations if the allocations are necessary either to prevent evasion of taxes or to reflect clearly the income of the corporations." Nonetheless, she found that, while Compaq's Asian profit margins may have been higher than those of other companies, the IRS could not substitute its "business judgment" for Compaq's. The same company that had invested hundreds of millions of dollars in a transaction designed to produce a tax benefit of $2.8 million was a better judge of how much it owed in taxes than the IRS. Compaq didn't have to pay a dime of the $75 million the IRS contended that it owed.

In its 1999 annual report, Compaq noted that Compaq Asia Ltd., which, like Seagate Singapore, is also enjoying a tax holiday, has invested its profits overseas. "These earnings would become subject to incremental foreign withholding, federal and state income tax if they were actually or deemed to be remitted to the United States," the company said. "Compaq estimates an additional tax provision of approximately $2.1 billion would be required if the full amount of approximately $6 billion in accumulated earnings were actually or deemed distributed to the United States."

The IRS also faced long odds in the Seagate cases, which, taken together, involved potential taxes owed of slightly less than $200 million. One of the issues involved the amount of research and development costs that Seagate charged to its Singapore subsidiary. Alan Shugart, the company's brash CEO, testified that R&D wasn't all that important to the company that allows the world to manage its information.

"Research and development, in our kind of business, has become a misnomer, because there really isn't—we don't do any research at all," he testified. "And as I mentioned right at the start, there haven't been any real revolutionary changes in magnetic recording since, gosh, the middle '70s, I guess, or early '70s."

"Tommy" Mitchell, the company's vice president for operations, and later its president, was asked whether Seagate's corporate strategy was to be on the "cutting edge of technology." He answered with a single word: "No."

While Seagate's top executives played down the role of research and development in its operations, they were happy to stress the need to move offshore. "We finally reached the conclusion that we absolutely had to, from a cost standpoint, take our labor-intensive disk drives offshore for assembly and test in order to compete, and even though it was risky, we had to do that," Shugart said. "And secondly, we saw the need for having the offshore operations in order to capture what looked like a growing market in east Asia, also, for disk drives. So for those two reasons we went ahead and took the gamble to commit to build disk drives in Singapore."

The risk Seagate undertook in moving offshore was actually a component the company used in determining the "arm's length" price it charged itself for the disk drives and components it manufactured there. Because Seagate Singapore faced greater uncertainties than the Scotts Valley operation, the company argued, it was entitled to charge a premium for the components it produced. The gamble paid off. Disk drives that cost $300 to produce in California cost only $145 to produce in Singapore.

Yet when the Singapore operation transferred components to its U.S. parent, it charged the company the California price. Donald L. Waite, Seagate's chief financial officer, explained that the company "wanted to give an incentive to Seagate Singapore to, you know, make certain that they became an efficient manufacturer." The California executives "felt that by giving them the benefits of any manufacturing efficiencies that they created, they would have an incentive to become an efficient manufacturer."

By contrast, there were no profit incentives for Seagate's domestic plants to become more efficient. When Seagate transferred components manufactured in the United States to Singapore, it sold them to its subsidiary at cost. "It was my understanding that Seagate Scotts Valley was not deemed to be in the business of buying and reselling components," Waite said. "Therefore, under the tax regulations, they were not required to mark up those parts sales."

The IRS discovered a transfer pricing agreement between the company and its offshore subsidiary dated 1983—that was actually drafted in 1985—calling for a "pseudo-royalty" to be paid by Singapore to the American headquarters. The Service compared the prices Seagate Singapore charged its parent company with the prices it charged third parties. It found that Seagate split research and development costs equally between the two companies, inflating the price Seagate Singapore could charge to its California parent.

In the end, Judge Thomas B. Wells ruled that Seagate hadn't dealt at arm's length with its foreign subsidiary. However, he also found the Service's adjustments to Seagate's income were "arbitrary, capricious, and unreasonable." Wells determined that Seagate had unreported income of $45 million, rather than $285 million. Instead of owing $112 million, the company ended up owing nothing. Seagate had net operating losses available that allowed it to offset the extra income.

During the course of the trial, various Seagate executives testified that the main reason for the move to Singapore had little to do with taxes, and everything to do with cutting costs. Manufacturing a disk drive—

and the various components that go into it—is an arduous task that involves threading and fastening wires and soldering the connections, all under the lens of a microscope. Gloved and hooded technicians draped in white smocks do the work in "clean rooms" that keep dust, dirt, and moisture from damaging the delicate parts. While Seagate and other companies have spent millions trying to automate the work—to have machines replace the deft fingers of tens of thousands of workers—so far the efforts have yielded little success. Labor remains one of the biggest costs for Seagate and other producers in the cost-sensitive market in which they compete.

"The disk drive market is a worldwide market and within very few seconds of a price change in Singapore the people in Munich know about it and so forth," Shugart said in his November 1991 testimony in Tax Court. "It's a worldwide market."

To compete in that market, Shugart and his executives had to lower costs. "First of all it was the cost consideration, to get labor-intensive assemblies offshore," Shugart explained, "and secondly, we thought probably that the components that required labor-intensive effort could probably be done more productively . . . than we could do in the United States." Thus, they sent Mitchell out on his Asian fact-finding tour in July 1982. Seagate shut down for the first two weeks of that month for vacation, and that was all the time Mitchell needed to set in motion the beginnings of Seagate Singapore.

"I only had two weeks," he said. "So I put an ad in the paper for somebody to find a managing director. . . . And one of the guys that came in for an interview was S. C. Tien. . . . And S.C. was from National [Semiconductor, Incorporated, another manufacturer of computer components]." Mitchell recognized that Tien had experience with the kinds of labor-intensive electronic work—some of it done under a microscope—that Seagate was looking to transfer to Singapore. "Tien and I, of course, didn't know each other, and we only had two weeks. So we began to spend every evening talking and getting to know one another, and formulating what we do. . . . At the end of the two weeks, I left, and left Tien with the reins."

Raymond Merle, an engineer who worked for the personal computer division of IBM, was the liaison between his company and Seagate. IBM was one of Seagate's biggest customers, and part of Merle's job was making sure the products met IBM's standards. He saw how the company prepared for the move to Singapore. "The philosophy was that you could go take a picture of the [Scotts Valley] manufacturing floor, and take that to Singapore, and stick it on the wall, and then make it a duplicate image, if you will, of that manufacturing process, and try to guarantee yourself that you didn't create a lot of problems. So that was the general thrust of what they went through."

Sing Cheong Tien, who became the general manager of Seagate Singapore, proved adept at managing the task. He was able to set up component manufacturing operations and run them far more cheaply than Seagate was able to do in Scotts Valley. One advantage was labor costs: it cost $55 an hour per employee to manufacture in Scotts Valley, California, but only $12 in Singapore. Which is not to say that the company's California workers were paid $55 an hour. Those costs included benefits like health insurance and pension plans. They included Seagate's portion of Social Security and Medicare taxes. And they included costs the company incurred complying with various regulations, from workplace safety to environmental protection.

"The labor cost—the manufacturing cost is probably about, in the Far East as compared to Scotts Valley, is about 20 percent," Mitchell said. "So you saved about 80 percent."

Workers in Singapore came much cheaper, especially since the company paid them wages that were low even by that country's standards. Linda Lian, who worked as training manager for Seagate Singapore, said that the company conducted a fairly comprehensive survey of wage rates in the country. "We were relatively at the lower end, and that's mainly because we were careful about not having [a] high labor cost," she said.

Recruiting workers at the low rates wasn't easy. "We did the normal advertisement, but we relied a lot on personal contacts. We had a task team force formed where members have to visit the homes of employees who left the company, [to] try to understand why they left us, coax them to rejoin the company. We even paid bonuses to operators who went around to hire their friends or people they know who'd like to join the company."

Not only was it cheaper to manufacture in Singapore, the workforce was more compliant. Mitchell said the workforce in Scotts Valley was "basically made up of surfers," who did not much impress Seagate's vice president of operations. "It's really difficult, when you have a high turnover of people. . . . And our absenteeism was really bad. And our quality was not consistent at all," he said.

"Scotts Valley is very close to Santa Cruz, and Santa Cruz is on the beach," he added. "And so the graduates of high schools in the Midwest would go to California to spend some time on the beach, and then find out they really had to work, and then they would come to work for Seagate, but they would end up looking in a microscope. And they wouldn't look in it very long. And that wasn't really their intent in life, to go to work every day and run a soldering iron under a microscope."

The company changed its hiring practices by going offshore. Kenneth Wing, a vice president whose responsibilities included the reliability of the company's disk drives, wasn't at all concerned about the change, or the inexperience of the Singaporeans who were going to be hired. "There's no difference in going to Santa Cruz and hiring 500 people whose background is surfing, and putting them in a disk drive factory and teaching them how to build disk drives," he said.

As the company moved its manufacturing to Singapore, it needed to train its Asian workers to make the components—and eventually the completed disk drives. So Seagate sent its new workers from Singapore to Scotts Valley, where they could learn the techniques from the American workers whose jobs they'd soon be taking. "The process that Seagate had was what they call a hand-holding process," Merle, the IBM engineer, recalled. "They had set up an educational facility downtown in Scotts Valley. They brought a team of manufacturing engineering people over from Singapore." And when the Singapore workers returned home, Lian, the training manager, debriefed them.

"One of the areas of concern they had was that they see some great differences in terms of the wage, the pay, the pace, and the discipline requirements to perform on a workstation. They found there was quite a difference, because our requirements were a little more stringent."

Seagate continued the practice of having its domestic workforce train foreign workers who'd be replacing them into the nineties. In October 1993, Seagate, which still has factories in Minnesota, Oklahoma, and California, brought some Asian workers to its Bloomington, Minnesota, plant. "The people from Malaysia were there training for a month," a former employee recalled. "The day after they flew off, I was out of there in an hour." There was no prior notice from the company that the layoffs were coming. "I can understand many places have to lay people off," the employee said. "But not being told wasn't a very good deal."

Two hundred other employees were shown the door as well. Seagate's director of human resources at the Bloomington plant filed an application for Trade Adjustment Assistance, a federal program established in 1974 to provide extended unemployment benefits and training for workers who lose their jobs because of imports. On the application, he wrote, "The company owns and operates production facilities overseas that are now making what these workers had been." The workers were certified for the program, which is funded by federal tax dollars.

Before Seagate began its operations in Malaysia, the company turned to Thailand. The cheap Singapore workers, laboring under the stringent pace, still weren't cheap enough, not when there were other Asian countries with even lower wage rates. Thai workers could be had for even less money. In October 1983, Seagate established another subsidiary, Seagate Thailand, to manufacture E-Blocks, one of the labor-intensive components of a disk drive. Tien set about finding a factory there and hiring workers to staff it. He then brought them to Singapore for training. "I had to crank up the Thai operation," he explained. "So, the strategy I put together was to bring enough people from Thailand into Singapore to sit on my line, to take over the production of E-Blocks. . . . Now, this was not an easy task, because I remember that I brought in 200 Thai operators into Singapore, and this was done by busing them all the way from Bangkok, and then I had to find places to house 200 Thai girls. And we were not about to rent all kinds of apartments, but fortunately, at that time, Singapore was going through a really bad recession, and I was able to negotiate with a local hotel which was not far from our factory, to house four Thai girls per room at something like forty Singapore dollars a day for a period of maybe a couple of months."

The recession helped Seagate's Asian subsidiaries in other ways. Tien found the company a new, 285,000-square-foot factory on the cheap thanks to it. "During lunchtime, I would go over there," he said. "I found out that this [building] was being held by a bank. I approached the bank and they told me that they wanted 11 million for the building—11 million Singapore dollars. . . . That building was put together at the cost of almost 30 million.

"I told Tom [Mitchell] about the building, but he continued to evade it. He didn't like the building because it had a swimming pool on the top. He told me that all I wanted the building [for] was so that I can do backstrokes up there."

But Mitchell eventually authorized the purchase of the factory. "I remember that I called him from a car phone in Korea," Tien said. "[I told him] I only got one more day. . . . So he just told me, he said, okay, Tien, go ahead and do it."

Seagate Singapore acquired the new factory at a bargain-basement rate, where it soon began manufacturing both components and completed disk drives. Over the years, the company expanded its operations wherever it could find cheap labor or a tax holiday, or, better yet, both. It opened factories in Mexico, China, and Malaysia. It transferred jobs from its facilities in Minnesota, Oklahoma, and California. And it continued to lay off workers.

In July 1984, Seagate booted 700 workers from its Scotts Valley plant after moving much of its disk drive production to Singapore. In

December 1988, it let go of roughly another 600 of its California work-ers. In October 1989, the company laid off 200 workers from the Min-nesota plant it acquired when it bought component manufacturer Imprimis, Incorporated.

Some of the Asian countries that gave the company preferential tax treatment are finding that Seagate's commitment to them isn't any stronger than it was to the "surfers" who worked in its Scotts Valley plant. In 1999, it slashed 1,600 workers in Singapore. In January 2000, it announced that 2,900 Thai workers could look for work elsewhere. It announced in September 1999 that up to 10 percent of its Malaysian workforce would be cut.

Seagate celebrated the cuts. "As a result of the company's signifi-cantly improved productivity and operating efficiencies, a smaller global workforce will be needed to meet existing and anticipated future market requirements," a press release announcing the coming layoffs declared. "A workforce reduction, approximately ten percent over the next nine months, will be managed through natural attrition, voluntary separation packages, and job elimination where required."

The best news of all, from Seagate's perspective, was what all this meant for the company's bottom line. "When fully implemented, the company expects to realize a $150 million cost savings per year from these actions."

How much of the savings will remain offshore is entirely up to the company to determine.

7

Tricks of the Trade

Joe Conforte learned about evading income taxes at the same time he became a player in the world's oldest profession. While driving a taxi in Oakland, California, in the 1950s, Conforte began arranging trysts between prostitutes and sailors hell-bent on making their shore leave memorable. The barrel-chested hack ferried the eager servicemen to the haunts of Bay Area working girls, who returned the favor by paying Conforte a "gratuity" for each trick he brought their way. Business came as regularly as the tides, and so the accidental pimp, himself an ex-GI, was flush with cash.

And Conforte could do as he pleased with that found money, whether relegate it to his mattress, load up on new possessions, or, as he did from time to time, battle Lady Luck at the casinos of Reno, Nevada. Because the extra income didn't show up on his W-2 Form, one thing he didn't have to do was report it on his tax return.

That was the first of many tricks that this son of a bootlegger learned to sidestep the taxman. Over the next four decades, in fact, Conforte evaded millions in taxes using Swiss bank accounts, foreign corporations, shell companies, and corrupt politicians. He attracted the attention of the Internal Revenue Service, which audited and investigated him repeatedly, charged him with both avoiding and evading his taxes, and finally seized what it believed to be all his assets to offset his $13 million tax bill. Even then, Conforte was unbowed. Using front men and $1.5 million that he had managed to hide from the Service, he bought back his most valuable property from an IRS auction, and kept the ruse going for nearly five years.

Conforte made his fortune running brothels, and his franchise was a prodigious cash cow: at any given time he had perhaps 100 women plying their trade, each paying him half of her earnings. Movie stars, politicians, and even one irreverent clergyman frequented Conforte's houses of ill repute—an ongoing procession that earned the former cabdriver tens of millions of dollars each year, almost all of it in hundreds, fifties, and lowly dollar bills. Cash was in fact the secret of this sexual entrepreneur's success.

The heart of Conforte's operation was the Mustang Ranch, a famous—some would say infamous—brothel that was the first legal house of prostitution in the United States. The ranch, which Conforte ran for twenty-two years, hosted as many as 200,000 customers annually. Former Mustang employees interviewed by the Center were tight-lipped about how much money the ranch actually took in, but they did disclose that, in the late 1990s, the average customer paid $300 for a "party" with a Mustang girl. Two hundred thousand customers a year paying $300 for each encounter—the potential annual revenue is staggering.

But attaching numbers to Conforte's take is ultimately only guesswork. After all, the typical "john"—loath to be saddled with a canceled check or credit card bill from a house of pleasure—happily paid cash. The paperless nature of the transaction also helped Conforte. Because cash transactions can be virtually impossible for auditors to trace or document—even in more traditional businesses—the paperless nature of the ranch's transactions helped Conforte keep his profits secret.

The IRS calls men like Conforte informal suppliers—self-employed individuals operating in cash. They include such disparate types as moonlighting professionals operating off the books, cabdrivers, baby-sitters, plumbers, and electricians. In 1994, the Service estimated that only 18.6 percent of their income is ever declared to the government. With no third-party documentation—like W-2 Forms or 1099s that report wages, salaries, dividend and interest income—it's almost impossible for the IRS to collect any of the estimated $12.3 billion in taxes that informal suppliers owe but don't pay. It's the second-largest component of the tax gap—the amount of taxes owed each year that is not paid voluntarily.

The largest portion of the tax gap—closely related to informal supplier income—is unpaid taxes from the business income of sole proprietors. The Service estimated that in 1992, such individuals, who own their own businesses, reported only about 68 percent of their income, and shortchanged the government by $16.9 billion. Neither category includes the illicit economy—the money generated by enterprises like narcotics, loan-sharking, or illegal prostitution and gambling. The most recent estimate, done in 1981, suggested that the total unpaid taxes owed by the underground economy might be as high as $15.4 billion a year. Adjusting for inflation, that climbs to $28.2 billion in 1999.

Berdji Kenadjian, a former chief economist of the IRS, believes that such taxes simply can't be collected. In testimony before the National Commission on Restructuring the IRS, a congressionally mandated panel that studied ways to improve the performance of the Service, he said, "To collect all the taxes owed—that is, to close the tax gap—is an impossible task." He noted the futility of concentrating the efforts of the IRS on the types of taxpayers with the lowest rate of compliance. "Moonlighters and other off the books people frequently operate on a small scale," he said. "Typically, they want to get paid in cash to make their incomes invisible to tax officials. In view of this, how can a practical tax official justify chasing millions of such people spread all over the country to find without the benefit of documents . . . what often may turn out to be small amounts of unreported income?"

The advantage of operating in cash wasn't lost on Conforte. But unlike the moonlighters and most other "off the books" people, he didn't earn small amounts of unreported income. He raked in millions.

Conforte is a legendary figure in Nevada, a larger-than-life character who seems a throwback to the freewheeling Nevada of the nineteenth-century silver rush. "Joe Conforte was a good ol' boy, and he owned Storey and Lyon Counties—everybody knew it," said Michelle Trusty-Murphy, an English professor at Western Nevada Community College who grew up in and near Reno. "I remember lots of stories of the Mustang—mostly about Joe Conforte, who, for the most part, was thought of well. There were always stories every Thanksgiving about how he and Sally [his wife] gave free turkeys and all the fixings to poor families in the area.

"When I was a young child, a friend of my eldest sister had gotten a singing gig at the Cabin in the Sky restaurant, just outside of Virginia City. This restaurant was owned by Joe Conforte. This friend was on her way to this singing engagement, and was quite overdressed for a Nevada highway at 5 P.M. on a Saturday. She was pulled over by one of the local cops.

" 'You know you were speeding, don't you?'

" 'Yes, Officer. I'm in a big hurry. I have an important engagement.'

"The officer looked closely at the way she was dressed, the amount of makeup she had on, and stepped away from the car for a moment. He stuck his head in the car and said in a low voice, 'You one of Joe's girls?'

"She wasn't a prostitute, but she figured being associated with Joe was not that bad. After all, she was on her way to sing for Joe's restaurant, so she answered, 'Yes.' 'Go ahead then,' he said.

"She told me that from that day on, anytime any cop wanted to know if she worked for Joe, she let them know. If it was good enough to get out of a ticket, it was good enough for her."

The casinos of Reno had first drawn Conforte to Nevada, but the cabdriver soon saw an opportunity to make money there without risking his bankroll. "Every chance he got he was off to Reno to gamble," Jim Sloan, a Reno journalist, wrote in *Nevada: True Tales from the*

Neon Wilderness, his 1993 book on the state's folklore. "He lost, but he met some people, including a dealer who helped run one of the cow counties about thirty miles outside the city limits. 'We need a man like you,' the dealer said. 'We need a house [brothel] here. It'd be good for the county. Everybody needs to get laid now and then; it keeps the heart strong and cuts down on domestic violence.' So Conforte moved, set up his trailers, and started raking in the business."

Conforte opened his first brothel in 1955. Located at the northeast edge of Storey County, near Reno, the cathouse was little more than a string of mobile homes named the Triangle River Ranch. The mobility was important: prostitution was illegal, so whenever Storey County officials put the heat on, Conforte rolled the trailers some 500 yards across one of two nearby county lines. If he went southeast, he'd be in Lyon County; northwest, he'd be in Washoe County. And when the heat was off, he'd roll the trailers back to Storey County.

Until 1971, Conforte made his money illegally. His shenanigans required that local officials turn a blind eye, and money helped that along: Conforte was fond of handing out cigars wrapped in cash to grateful local officials. Such practices were not uncommon in Storey County, a rugged area of western Nevada that gained notoriety in the 1850s because its hills held silver and gold. The twentieth century wasn't as kind, however. While nearby Reno and Lake Tahoe enjoyed economic booms, fueled in large measure by tourism, the good times never made their way to little Storey County. "I grew up most of my life here in Nevada," said Trusty-Murphy, the professor of English at Western Nevada Community College. "Before Nevada reached its current state of population growth, this was thought of as the last vestige of the old American West, including everything that made it good and made it bad. Good ol' boys were the people who ran—and still run—this state, and if you wanted to get anywhere you needed to align yourself one way or the other with one or more of them."

Bill Raggio, at the time the district attorney of Washoe, refused to play Conforte's game. He made it clear that if Conforte were ever caught in his county, he'd throw the book at him. Conforte tried his old tricks, but unlike other politicians and local officials, Raggio refused to accept the cigars wrapped in cash. So Conforte concocted a scheme to rid himself of the meddlesome D.A.: he tried to blackmail Raggio by choreographing a tryst with an attractive, underage girl.

Raggio, who is now the majority leader of the Nevada state senate, declined to be interviewed by the Center; a spokesman indicated that Raggio is now unwilling to discuss the affair with any journalist. But in 1986, he did explain Conforte's scheme to a reporter. "Conforte told me that I would be publicly accused of furnishing liquor to a minor girl and that I would be further accused of having been intimate with such a girl unless I agreed to dismiss the criminal charge pending against Conforte and make a public apology to him."

The scheme didn't work. In 1959, Conforte was found guilty of extortion and sentenced to prison. Much to Raggio's delight, the Triangle River Ranch was declared a public nuisance and burned down by order of the Storey County commissioners.

"You have to understand Conforte had flouted the law," Raggio said in the 1986 interview, "and it was necessary to do what was done. Nobody else would take the guy on."

After serving twenty-two months in a county jail, Conforte was back flouting the law. Local officials in Storey County were no more willing to take him on than they had been before his conviction. Federal officials, on the other hand, took notice of the brash and colorful pimp. An IRS audit revealed that Conforte's reported income was not nearly large enough to support either his personal lifestyle or his professional endeavors. Auditors were not particularly interested that Conforte made his money from running a brothel; even though the source of his money was illicit, the government still demanded its share of the profits. That principle was established during Prohibition, in a 1923 Supreme Court ruling involving a bootlegger accused of evading income taxes. Writing for the majority was Associate Justice Oliver Wendell Holmes Jr.: "Of course, Congress may tax what it also forbids." In 1963, Conforte pleaded guilty to tax evasion and spent two years in a federal prison. But the experience hardly diminished his enthusiasm for brothels.

In 1967, Conforte and his wife, Sally, a onetime competitor in the flesh business, bought the Mustang Ranch. This time around, Conforte acted the part of the local businessman. He gave money to charities, contributed to political campaigns, opened a trailer park for low-income retirees, and willingly paid nuisance fines to Storey County for running his brothel. Even when no fines were owed, he'd pay a few thousand dollars into the local treasury. Then, in 1971, the local board of commissioners made Storey County the first in the nation to legalize brothels. Eleven Nevada counties eventually followed suit, enticed by the tourism possibilities and the taxes and licensing fees imposed on the brothels.

It was the heyday for Conforte and the Mustang Ranch. Later that year, *60 Minutes* aired a piece about the ranch called "The House in Storey County." Mike Wallace interviewed Conforte, who gave a bravura performance. "Every walk of life comes in here, every walk of life—every businessman, everyone," he said. "It's comical to see someone make a speech in a certain club or a certain place knocking this business, and the next night, he's here as a customer. I just laugh." The media attention didn't end with the CBS newsmagazine; *Rolling Stone* followed with a cover story on the Mustang Ranch in 1972 that featured its owner surrounded by his girls. "The Crusading Pimp: Joe Conforte's Fight to Keep Nevada Clean," the headline read.

Conforte had established himself as a good citizen and a bona fide businessman, and he wasn't shy about flaunting his success. He drove expensive cars, wore expensive clothes, and was never seen without a stunning woman. He also showed a knack for finding new sources of revenue, exploiting the Mustang Ranch for its kitsch value, for instance, by opening a souvenir shop where patrons—but more often just the curious—could buy mugs, T-shirts, and other tchotchkes.

Business wasn't just booming, it was entirely legitimate—except as far as the IRS was concerned. The Service began sending the Confortes notices that they owed additional income taxes, and by 1976 the Confortes owed more than $7 million in back taxes and fines.

But putting a precise figure on what the couple really owed was a near impossible task. That's because the ranch was operated primarily in cash, leaving agents assigned to the case guessing about the brothel's annual income. Prostitutes and employees were paid in cash. Ranch expenses were paid in cash. Even the annual county licensing fee was paid in cash. The only records the brothel kept at the time were "trick sheets"—paper ledgers that reflected the earnings of a prostitute. The IRS obtained a trick sheet only after a ranch employee plucked one from trash he was asked to burn.

April 1977 marked the start of the Confortes' serious battles with the IRS. Both Joe and Sally were indicted for failure to pay withholding taxes. The ranch didn't issue the prostitutes W-2 Forms, the government alleged. They didn't withhold taxes from the girls' earnings.

The Confortes countered that they had no obligation to do so. They didn't have to withhold taxes, since their prostitutes, all of whom lived at the ranch, were not employees; instead, they maintained they were independent contractors—self-employed individuals who could largely do as they pleased. The Confortes' claim, considered audacious at the time, was in many ways visionary. *Fortune* 500 firms like Microsoft and Xerox Corporation have followed the brothel owners' lead and saved millions in Social Security taxes, health insurance payments, and pension costs by reclassifying employees as independent contractors.

A self-employed individual must file quarterly returns and pay taxes based on an estimate of her annual income. She also must pay both the employee's and the employer's share of Social Security and Medicare taxes—an extra 7.65 percent of her income that salaried employees don't have to pay.

Because of this extra tax burden, many self-employed workers are unable to come up with the money. According to the U.S. General Accounting Office, the investigative arm of Congress, 1.9 million self-employed taxpayers were delinquent in paying $6.9 billion in taxes as of 1997. Many of these individuals were not evading taxes, the GAO concluded, but were simply unable to pay what they admitted to owing the government.

In 1977, when Joe Conforte claimed his girls were self-employed, just over 7.3 million taxpayers were in that same category. In 1995, the most recent year for which statistics are available, 12.9 million taxpayers were self-employed. Among those most likely to be classified as independent contractors are electricians, construction workers, computer programmers, and taxi drivers.

And exotic dancers. "The majority of them like being independent contractors," Michael Ross, a lobbyist for the National Cabaret Association, told the Center. "You're your own business. A lot of these women know what the hell they're doing. There's a tradeoff for everything. Most of these people set the schedule they want, and do whatever they want to do." He conceded that the IRS may have reason to worry about the owners of exotic dance clubs, and the performers, paying their taxes. "I hear about tax fraud all the time," said Ross, who trade group represents some 10,000 strippers. "The upshot to the whole thing is that you've got an industry where everyone's a business and everyone's going to do whatever they can to get by."

Getting by, of course, is a relative term. Joe Conforte made millions. And prostitutes working in legal brothels sometimes have earnings that put them in the top 10 percent of all taxpayers. JenLynn Sweet, a former accountant, writer, and an occasional prostitute, worked for a time at the Moonlite Bunny Ranch, near Reno. Sweet told the Center she could earn upward of $275,000 a year. "I was making $5,500 a week on average," she said. Like the Mustang Ranch, the Moonlite Bunny was largely a cash business. "The only receipts that are generated are from credit cards, but everything is recorded on our daily card," she said, acknowledging that the cards are easily changed to underreport taxes. "There's a lot of room for fudging, because it's stuff that's just penciled in."

Prostitutes were recognized as independent contractors thanks to a court case that Joe Conforte's nephew, David Burgess, filed in 1993. Burgess ran a brothel just up the street from the Mustang Ranch. He claimed that he deserved a refund on the employment taxes he paid in the late 1980s, because the women he "employed" were actually independent contractors.

The original case ended with a hung jury, but the matter was eventually resolved when the Department of Justice agreed that the girls were independent contractors; Burgess, for his part, paid a small fine for not reporting the payments originally. Two decades ago, these kinds of independent contractor cases were uncommon. But adult-entertainment business owners are increasingly filing for employment tax refunds, and the courts uniformly find in their favor. "It is illegal for David Burgess to be, essentially, a pimp," Kevin Jackson, the attorney who represented Burgess, told the Center. "He can operate a brothel, but he can only lease the premises to the girls and the girls have to do all the negotiating. They rent the space, they pay him a small daily amount and then a percentage of their income, but they set their own price and terms." According to Jackson, Burgess got his refund.

But Burgess's uncle, Joe Conforte, was not quite so lucky. Both he and Sally were arrested on ten counts of criminal tax evasion, including charges that they failed to withhold income taxes from their employees. IRS documents indicated that the Confortes "systematically burned" all records that could establish how much tax they should have paid. Given Joe Conforte's previous conviction for tax evasion, the IRS argued that the couple's efforts to destroy business records proved their guilt. "Mr. Conforte had been convicted of tax evasion in earlier years based upon a net worth analysis," according to federal Tax Court documents. "One of the methods of preventing a net worth reconstruction of income is to operate solely in cash. We think it is proper to take into consideration a taxpayer's knowledge of the indirect effects of his actions in determining whether those acts were taken to avoid taxes."

The Service said, "After an exhaustive review of the record we are convinced that the evidence clearly establishes petitioners' understatement of income was with intent to evade tax."

The courts agreed, and the Confortes paid the price: Joe was sentenced to five years in prison, while Sally earned a suspended sentence. Both were also slapped with a $10,000 fine. The Confortes ultimately appealed the decision to the Supreme Court of the United States, which in December 1980 refused to hear the case. Conforte left his wife in charge of the ranch and fled the country. During his time abroad, he opened an account at the Discount Bank and Trust, in Geneva, Switzerland, under the name of José C. Montoya. Money from the Mustang Ranch flowed into the account, which was beyond the reach of U.S. tax authorities.

In 1983, the extortion artist and tax fugitive returned voluntarily to the United States, lured back by a Justice Department invitation to testify at the trial of U.S. District Judge Harry Claiborne. Claiborne, one of Conforte's former defense lawyers, had been charged with tax evasion and accepting bribes.

Conforte claimed that he had paid Claiborne over $80,000, in return for assurances that his conviction for tax evasion would be overturned by the Ninth Circuit Court of Appeals. But the federal appeals court refused to reverse Conforte's conviction, so the brothel operator returned home to testify about his dirty dealings with the judge. Conforte maintained, for example, that he paid Claiborne several bribes during the sixties and seventies, once even handing over loot in an underground parking garage. In early 1984, Claiborne's trial ended in a hung jury, in part because Conforte's testimony struck some jurors as completely unreliable. With three convictions and an unfavorable ruling from Claiborne's court, Conforte hardly fit the profile of an untainted party. Later that year, Claiborne was retried and convicted of the tax evasion charges—the first sitting federal judge to be found guilty of felonies. Claiborne was impeached and removed from office in 1986.

As for Conforte, he served just fifteen months of his five-year sentence—the reward for his cooperation in the Claiborne trial—and was again a free man. He returned to Nevada, seemingly undaunted, and, as was his habit, embroiled himself in a new controversy.

In 1985, Strong Point Inc. announced its plans to buy the Mustang Ranch for $18 million. The California-based firm, which was once traded over the counter, hoped to finance the deal with a public stock offering. According to *Forbes* magazine, the announcement sent the company's stock from $.25 to $3.25, an irony that didn't escape Conforte. When asked why he thought American investors would be interested in owning Mustang stock, he told the magazine, "So they can brag to everybody, 'Hey, I've got stock in the biggest whorehouse in the world!' "

Strong Point had as much luck dealing with Conforte as the IRS. In the summer of 1987, the firm announced that it was unable to raise enough money to buy the Ranch. It cited the Confortes' failure to disclose accurate financial information as a principal reason for its failure to attract enough capital. While the potential public offering generated plenty of stories in the generally staid financial press, one detail, buried in Tax Court documents, was overlooked at the time: Conforte still owed the IRS $12 million in back taxes and penalties.

Two years later, it was revealed that Conforte had lined up another deal to sell a 60 percent stake in the ranch. An investment group led by Phoenix lawyer Darrell Rippy hoped to take public a company whose assets would have included the brothel, 380 acres of surrounding land, and a nearby mobile home site owned by Conforte. Six weeks after Rippy's group announced its intentions, it had already managed to raise 77 percent of the required capital. But when the remainder of the funding proved elusive, Conforte tried to boost the Mustang's appeal by once again diversifying its product: this time, he proposed adding a special wing for male prostitutes and female customers "who just want sex without entanglements."

Rippy and his would-be investors ultimately backed out, although IRS interest in the ranch never waned. In fact, in the fall of 1990, the

Service took the extreme step of seizing the brothel in order to get the millions in back taxes Conforte owed the government. But, as a prostitute named Brandy recounted for the *San Diego Union-Tribune*, Conforte, aware that the feds were on the way, refused to go quietly: "Joe went into his office and, 15 minutes later, he came out with a huge bag of money. As he's leaving the driveway, the manager called us all in and told us all to pack up. Five minutes later, we're all running down the halls, thinking the IRS was coming in to take all our valuables." Conforte himself seemed unfazed by the whole affair. "It was time for me to retire. They just made the decision for me," he told the *Union-Tribune*.

Perhaps the strangest twist in the saga of the Mustang Ranch was the IRS's initial plans to run the brothel itself to pay off Conforte's tax debt. When late-night talk-show host Arsenio Hall joked that then President George Bush was a pimp, the Service abandoned the plan and decided instead to auction off the ranch's assets. The sale, which took place in November 1990, attracted hundreds of curiosity seekers who gathered to ogle everything from paintings pulled from an orgy room's walls to boxes of colored condoms. Rarely has the IRS sold more memorable items.

The prize item at the auction, and the final one for sale, was the ranch itself. Only one bidder appeared—a mysterious man who arrived in a gold car with Nevada vanity plates: NV LAW2. Within moments, he won the ranch for $1.5 million and rushed from the scene.

As it was later revealed, the mystery bidder was Victor Alan Perry, a local lawyer and the brother of Conforte's personal attorney. Perry, it turned out, made the bid on behalf of a company called Mustang Properties, Inc.

Altogether, the IRS raised $2 million from the auction—a far cry from the $13 million in taxes that the Service said Conforte owed. The brothel owner was present at the sale, and signed autographs. He offered one reluctant reporter a card good for a free visit to the ranch.

Asked why the new owners would honor such a card, Conforte had a ready reply: "Professional courtesy," he said. "These cards will always be good."

Indeed, when the ranch reopened a month later, Joe Conforte was back as its general manager. Conforte claimed that he was just an employee of Mustang Properties, that he no longer had a financial stake in the ranch. In fact, he had used Perry and Mustang Properties as fronts to buy back his property from under the nose of the IRS. "We all knew that Joe still owned the place," said one former ranch prostitute. "It was public knowledge at the ranch."

The auction was just another minor aggravation for Conforte, who in short order was back to his old tricks. For example, when Storey County commissioners pledged to keep the brothel closed, he offered to raise by several thousands of dollars the annual fees the ranch paid. Those fees were Conforte's carrot: in the 1990s, they accounted for as much as one-sixteenth of the county's budget. Conforte also wielded a stick. "At voting time each year, we were forced to vote," recalled one former ranch employee. "We were instructed who to vote for. And if we didn't go up and vote, we would be fired. I would be so enraged by this. I live in Oregon and was registered to vote up there, but they didn't care."

The brothel owner also developed and managed a trailer home community of mostly low-income elderly residents, giving him yet another block of captive voters. And he wasn't above trying to secure those votes for his favorite causes. "I am not going to lie to you," Conforte told a reporter in 1991. "I want to keep [the residents] happy . . . for political reasons. I go around the trailer park and tell the people, 'Look, you've got two candidates. Now I think this one is pro prostitution, this one is not, and I would like you to vote for this one.' "

Life was, once again, good for the ex-convict. Though still saddled with a multimillion-dollar tax debt, he drove around town in a Mercedes and kept a Ferrari safely parked in his driveway. The brothel operated a Web site that sold mugs, T-shirts, and even a pink collector-series phone card. In 1991, Conforte grabbed national headlines again by offering U.S. troops returning from the Desert Storm conflict in Kuwait the warmest of welcomes: a complimentary twenty-four-hour date with a Mustang girl. The going rate for such a service was $1,000, and Conforte never failed to mention his generosity when asked about the idea. One marine who took advantage of the offer told a reporter from the *San Diego Union-Tribune*, "It was all we thought about, that's all the division talked about."

And then, without warning, Conforte announced his intended retirement. He extricated himself from day-to-day operations at the ranch and took an uncharacteristically quiet role in the business.

His decision may have been prompted by the ill health of his wife, Sally. She died of diabetes-related complications in late 1992, and shortly thereafter Conforte apparently moved to Brazil, where he was believed to have lived while he was a tax fugitive in the early 1980s. News about the Mustang and its owner dwindled, as Storey County and the ranch adapted to life without the Italian-American firebrand. Only Conforte's son made headlines during this time, when he pleaded guilty to drug charges after injecting a friend's dog with methamphetamines.

Conforte's retirement wasn't merely a matter of convenience. Plagued as he was with an ever-growing tax bill (the penalties continued to accrue), Brazil was a safer place for him to hide and watch the next spectacle unfold. In 1998, a federal grand jury issued a thirty-three-count indictment against the brothel baron for orchestrating the scam to hide his ownership of the ranch. Also named in the indictment were Conforte's shell companies, A.G.E. Enterprises and A.G.E. Corp., and Shirley Colletti, a former Storey County commissioner. Colletti, one of the reliable pro-prostitution politicians, had run the ranch after Conforte fled the country.

Prosecutors had the goods on Conforte, who never showed for his day in court. They demonstrated how Conforte paid off local officials, set up Swiss bank accounts through which he funneled the millions sent to him by his collaborators at the ranch, and even threatened to kill jittery business partners. Conforte's former lawyer, Peter Perry, had turned on his client, alleging in an earlier lawsuit that Conforte was still holding the ranch's reins.

Throughout late 1998 and early 1999, jurors heard witness after witness divulge the details about Conforte's business practices. He had set up A.G.E. Corp., which bought the ranch from Mustang Properties in 1992. A.G.E. Corp. in turn set up a subsidiary, A.G.E. Enterprises, Inc., to run the brothel. A.G.E. also owned the trailer park in Lockwood, Nevada, and because of the legal action against Conforte, the elderly residents of the ninety-four trailers feared higher rents, and possible eviction.

Details about how badly the brothel's accounts had been managed were evident in A.G.E.'s Chapter 11 bankruptcy records. According to papers filed in September 1998, the company's total assets were $4.8 million (which largely consisted of the property, assessed at $4 million), while the amount owed to the IRS was a whopping $48.5 million.

Conforte may have been on another continent, but his influence was by no means diminished: the president of A.G.E. was Robert Del Carlo, a friend of Conforte's who was also, conveniently, a former Storey County sheriff. "He was amazed at how easily they could be bought, how cheaply they could be bought and what they would do for the money," Perry said of the brothel owner's attempts to control local officials.

In July 1999, U.S. District Judge Howard McKibben ordered the brothel's owners to close the ranch, most likely forever. The jury found that A.G.E. existed only to cover up Conforte's continued ownership of the brothel, and decided that the fraudulent entity and its holding company would have to forfeit a combined $40 million to the federal government.

Shirley Colletti, the former county commissioner, was found guilty of funneling money to Conforte and was ordered to pay $220,000 for her role in the scam. She requested a new trial, and her lawyer continues to proclaim her innocence. "Why doesn't the government get off its lazy butt and go arrest Conforte instead of picking the pocketbook of a 63-year-old woman?" Colletti's lawyer asked after the decision. "They know where he is. They even know his phone number."

Approximately 200 workers found themselves abruptly unemployed when the Mustang closed its doors in August 1999. Storey County officials were unhappy about the second, and possibly final, closing of the ranch, which generated an estimated $233,000 in annual tax revenue. The closure itself was anticlimactic—federal agents arrived in a gray sedan, told everyone at the ranch they had to leave, and fastened the gates of the brothel with heavy padlocks.

As for Joe Conforte, he once again gets the last laugh. In October 1999, the Brazilian supreme court ruled that the pimp-turned-brothel-owner could not be extradited to the United States to face racketeering and other charges. Unless he turns himself in, it's highly unlikely that he'll ever face responsibility for the crimes with which he's been charged.

While his colleagues, friends, and loyal workers were forced to bear the brunt of the IRS's decades-long case against the Mustang Ranch, Conforte remains a free man, comfortably ensconced in his Brazilian hideaway. "None of my former coworkers are really liking their new situation," said a former ranch prostitute who calls herself Tia. "I know I speak for many ladies when I say the government sure did a hatchet job to everyone except Joe Conforte. Thanks a lot, Uncle Sam."

8

The Market Wizard

At a time when more and more Americans have a 401(k), mutual funds, Individual Retirement Accounts, and even their own on-line stock portfolios, the Chicago commodities markets have by and large remained a playground for the few. Profits are made by correctly foreseeing the price movements of various commodities and financial instruments, everything from pork bellies to crude oil, gold to government debt. It's an arena where Wall Street powerhouses rub elbows with small-time operators, where the trillions traded each year are backed by a tiny outlay of cash and a great deal of debt—or leverage, as the traders call it—and where fortunes can be made by canny operators with strong stomachs and superior knowledge. Gary K. Bielfeldt is such a man.

Born just outside the little town of Anchor, Illinois, Bielfeldt was raised on a farm, then went off to study agriculture at the University of Illinois at Urbana-Champaign, where he met his wife, Carlotta. After earning his bachelor's degree in 1958, he stayed on another year and was awarded his master's in agricultural economics. After finishing his studies, he began his career running a small brokerage firm in Peoria, Illinois, a city whose very name is synonymous with Middle America.

"Will it play in Peoria?"—a saying coined by traveling vaudeville acts—was later made infamous by Watergate figure John Ehrlichman, who tested every bit of misinformation the Nixon administration considered releasing to the press by asking that question.

Conservative with a small *c*, hardworking, independent, and not given to boasting, Peoria is a city whose character was well suited to the modest, laconic Bielfeldt. As a broker, he earned fees and commissions for his services, but the lion's share of the profits from successful trades went to the investors themselves. Trading was where the real money was, and he wanted a piece of the action. He started an account for himself with a mere $1,000. By 1965, after a few years of speculating on fluctuations of the price of corn, he'd managed to build it up to $10,000. Then he took his first big gamble.

After evaluating the market, Bielfeldt was convinced that there was money to be made in soybeans. He asked for outside advice from Thomas A. Hieronymus, his faculty adviser at Urbana-Champaign, who agreed with his student's analysis. Bielfeldt spent his entire $10,000, so painstakingly accumulated, on soy futures contracts, betting that the price would go up. The market went down, nearly far enough to force a margin call that would have wiped out his stake completely. Sure of his reading of the market, Bielfeldt refused to fold. The market turned, the price of soy futures shot up, and by the time he sold his contracts, he had doubled the value of his account. He was on his way to becoming one of the most successful traders in the country.

"I learned how to play poker at a very young age," he confided to Jack D. Schwager, who interviewed him for the 1988 bestselling book *Market Wizards*. "You don't just play every hand and stay through every card, because if you do, you will have a much higher probability of losing." Bielfeldt doesn't consider himself a gambler, but he acknowledged that his trading and card-playing strategies have something in common. "When the percentages seem to be strongly in your favor, you should be aggressive and really try to leverage the trade similar to the way you raise on the good hands in poker."

Bielfeldt kept playing the soy futures until 1983, when he suffered a series of losses. The setbacks made him choose a different dealer: the federal government. The skilled trader positioned himself for huge profits in the Treasury bond futures market, which had hit rock bottom when he got in, and rose as the Reagan economy expanded in the go-go 1980s. Like the contracts he traded in soybeans or corn, T-bond futures are purchased at a fixed price and resold at a future date. Profit is made by correctly predicting which way interest rates will move. Unlike other commodities, Treasury notes carry a very low risk, and offer a very low margin of profit. Bielfeldt, ready to raise the ante, leveraged himself to the hilt.

He regularly bought and sold $50 billion worth of T-bond futures a year, financing them by entering into repurchasing agreements with large institutional investors like Goldman Sachs & Company, Merrill Lynch & Company, and Salomon Brothers, Incorporated. He became a major player in a field dominated by Wall Street's largest firms, all from his base in Peoria. His margin of profit was small—from 1985 to 1989, he had $154 million to show for the hundreds of billions worth of positions he'd taken in the market. But Bielfeldt wasn't complaining—his average annual profits amounted to $30.8 million.

The big money played well in Peoria, and nationally. His successes were noteworthy enough that he drew the attention of Schwager, whose book of profiles carried the subtitle "Interviews with Top Traders." As for Peoria, Bielfeldt consistently contributed to community services throughout the town and the surrounding area. In 1988, he brought Auguste Rodin's most famous work, *The Thinker,* to the Lakeview Museum of Arts and Sciences, along with forty-four other works by the French master. Bielfeldt's wife, Carlotta, was the chairwoman of the local museum, but her husband landed the exhibit.

Bielfeldt had done some trading with Cantor Fitzgerald Incorporated, an international financial holding company. The firm's founder, the late B. Gerald Cantor, and his wife, Iris, owned the largest private collection of Rodin works at the time. Cantor and Bielfeldt's dealings led to the exhibition. "They didn't even know of my wife's involvement with the museum, it was just based on our business relationship,"

Bielfeldt told the *Chicago Tribune*. "I'd helped them in the government securities market and they offered this as a way of saying thank you."

His philanthropy hasn't been limited to his hometown. In 1993, Bielfeldt donated $5 million to his alma mater, the University of Illinois at Urbana-Champaign, for the construction of an athletic administration center that now bears his name. The same year, he and Carlotta, along with their children, gave $1 million to establish the Office for Futures and Options Research at Urbana-Champaign through their charitable organization, the Bielfeldt Foundation. The gift also created a professorship in honor of Bielfeldt's former agricultural economics professor, Thomas A. Hieronymus, who helped the trader in his first big gamble.

But by and large, Bielfedt's largesse has been directed to Peoria. "I judge success by what I do with the money I accumulate," Bielfeldt said in his *Market Wizards* interview. "One of the things that my wife and I have done is to establish a foundation so that we could share some of our success with the community by supporting various programs." The Bielfeldt Foundation was formed in 1985; in 1997 alone, it paid out more than $1.8 million for education programs and community development.

One of Bielfeldt's most ambitious—although ultimately failed—hometown endeavors was a downtown redevelopment project he initiated in 1986. His partnership, Bielfeldt & Company, purchased land where he planned to build a $51.6 million, multiblock, 405,000-square-foot shopping mall and office complex. By 1988, residential housing and a 200-room hotel were discussed as possible additions to the centerpiece of the new Peoria.

Neither the millions he gave away nor the millions he earned changed Bielfeldt's lifestyle. He continued to live in a comfortable if modest two-story, Colonial-style home in the Peoria Heights neighborhood, on a street that overlooks the Country Club of Peoria golf course. The assessed value of the property was $145,480 in 1999, about $45,000 above the average value of homes in Peoria, according to the Richwoods Township property assessor's office. The house is not nearly so opulent as some of the larger houses on his block, but it is convenient. His offices are about a half-mile drive from his home.

Bielfeldt has also made it a point to keep his friends and family close, living just blocks away from his son, David, and his attorney, Edward Sutkowski, who also invested in some of Bielfeldt's projects over the years. The market wizard continued to trade heavily, working twelve hours a day, and often awakened in the middle of the night to place orders for T-bills on the London and Tokyo markets.

On July 17, 1991, Bielfeldt, who made his fortune from the debt issued by the Treasury Department, tried to swing another profitable deal with the government. He filed a series of amended tax returns with the Internal Revenue Service for the years 1985 to 1988. The amended returns were quite different from the originals: on these new filings, he claimed that he was a dealer of government debt, rather than a trader. That change led him to claim that gains and losses were ordinary, rather than capital. And that in turn entitled him to ask for a refund from the government of some $81.8 million.

What a difference a few words can make.

The third edition of *Webster's New World College Dictionary* defines a dealer, in part, as "a person who deals; specifically, . . . b) a buyer and seller; person engaged in trading." A trader, by contrast, is defined, in part, as "a stockbroker who trades esp. for his own account rather than customers' accounts."

The IRS, and the tax code it enforces, has never been known for brevity or conciseness of language. Section 1.471-5 of the code makes this distinction between dealers and traders:

[A] dealer in securities is a merchant of securities, whether an individual, partnership, or corporation, with an established place of business, regularly engaged in the purchase of securities and their resale to customers; that is, one who as a merchant buys securities and sells them to customers with a view to the gains and profits that may be derived therefrom. . . . Taxpayers who buy and sell or hold securities for investment or speculation, irrespective of whether such buying or selling constitutes the carrying on of a trade or business, and officers of corporations and members of partnerships who in their individual capacities buy and sell securities, are not dealers in securities within the meaning of this section.

The tax code agrees with *Webster's*. Dealers make money from their customers, traders make money from their investments. But Bielfeldt wasn't in the habit of making such distinctions. He argued, for example, that he and his company were indistinguishable. "I've always viewed both entities as the same," he said. "I never made a distinction."

The IRS, for its part, did. Rather than write Bielfeldt a check for his millions, IRS agents descended on his main office in Peoria and his branch office in Chicago. They audited Bielfeldt, along with his trading partnership, Bielfeldt & Company, and two of his partners in that firm—his son and one of his two daughters. They looked into his trading activities and his company's pension fund. They reviewed all of his records, some stretching back to 1972. And in the end they issued Notices of Deficiency to Bielfeldt, his company, and the company pension plan that totaled some $94 million. The market wizard saw a potential swing in the position he'd taken on his tax returns of nearly $177 million.

Bielfeldt filed eight Tax Court petitions to challenge the IRS. Unlike the commodities markets he had largely mastered over the years, he wasn't able to dump the losers. In 1991, Bielfeldt made one more gamble. The man who made his fortune from government debt claimed that he was owed more than $80 million that he had overpaid in taxes. "I made the biggest mistake of my life when I filed for a tax refund," he said in an interview with the Center.

Some of the issues involved in Bielfeldt's various disputes with the IRS were fairly complex. A motion filed jointly by the IRS and Bielfeldt's attorneys requested that the same Tax Court judge preside over all eight cases, because the "issues include complicated commodities transactions, deemed distributions from the profit sharing plan, the revocation of the tax exempt status of the partnership profit sharing plan, and prohibited transactions." One issue, however, was relatively straightforward—determining whether Bielfeldt was a trader or a dealer.

On his original 1985 tax return, Bielfeldt had included a note with the return. "During 1985 the above-named taxpayer had a very extreme change in the volume of trading activities conducted on his own behalf," it read in part. "The magnitude of trading activities now qualify the taxpayer as a 'trader' for tax purposes rather than 'investor.' " The Internal Revenue Code allows traders more generous deductions for business expenses and losses than it does for investors.

Dealers are even more favored by the tax code, although they perform a different function: performing trades for customers. Bielfeldt insisted that he had many retail customers. The records he produced to support his claim, however, showed that he traded largely for himself, and only with the "primary dealers" in Treasury notes. Primary dealers—large firms like Salomon Brothers and Goldman Sachs—buy and sell T-bonds every day. By contrast, Bielfeldt had long periods of inactivity, up to 100 days at a time, when the poker player refused to play the cards being dealt. Nonetheless, he insisted that he also had many retail customers. "These people were people that we knew as long-term clients, personal friends, employees, friends of friends of personal friends," he said, adding that "the vast majority of them" were from Peoria. The rest of his customers, he claimed, were the large primary dealers in Treasury notes themselves. He testified that he went to great lengths to remain on good terms with those customers.

"Peoria is not an easy place to get in and out of and if you're going to fly customers in, it's much more convenient for them if you pick them up, fly them in, and take them back, and this is what I did," he said. He entertained dealers from Goldman Sachs, Salomon Brothers, Cantor Fitzgerald, and a number of other firms. He testified that in 1988, he flew Paul Volcker, the former Federal Reserve chairman, and Republican Representative Bob Michel, then the House minority leader, to Peoria to discuss the markets with some of his other guests, including a pair of Goldman Sachs executives.

"I went out to New York, I picked people up. I flew them out to Peoria, I showed them my office, I bought their dinner, I paid for all their expenses." The traders flew in on Bielfeldt's own jets. "Bielfeldt & Company originally had an Aero Commander 800 and then we acquired a Learjet in 1986. We acquired the planes because of the fact that it was helpful in developing the business relationship with the people we were dealing with."

When his tax troubles began, Bielfeldt wasn't quite so confident in those relationships. Under cross-examination, he admitted to contacting eight of the individuals he had listed as customers after he had been informed that the IRS intended to depose them. "I told them I was having a dispute with the IRS," Bielfeldt explained. Asked whether he had "suggested reasons" that he might be a dealer, Bielfeldt replied, "I guess if you—if you classify the fact that you would view another primary dealer as a customer, I suppose I may have said that."

The $81 million gamble didn't pay off. Tax Court Judge David Laro ruled on November 6, 1998, that Bielfeldt was indeed a trader, and not a dealer. In his opinion, he wrote that the market wizard's "definition of the word 'customer,' to wit, any person with whom he had established business relationships and with whom he dealt regularly . . . misses the mark." Laro denied the $81 million refund request, and ordered Bielfeldt to pay $44.9 million in taxes and penalties for the years 1984 through 1988.

Bielfeldt blamed the setback on his ignorance of the tax code and the advice he had gotten from his former accountant, Jack Williams, of KPMG Peat Marwick. "When those tax returns were originally filed, did you understand the tax definition of a difference between one who reports ordinary gains and losses as opposed to one who reports capital gains and losses?" Bielfeldt's attorney, Maureen McGinnity, asked during her direct examination of her client during the Tax Court proceedings.

"No, I didn't," Bielfeldt replied.

Later, he added that he tried to explain to Williams "the activities that I was involved with, how the activities had grown and expanded, and I was relying upon him to give me the best accounting advice." When contacted by the Center, Williams said he was under a court order not to discuss the case, and added that he was not required to appear during the trial.

The "best accounting advice" had already put Bielfeldt in a $44.9 million hole, and he still had seven outstanding Tax Court cases awaiting resolution.

Some of the other cases involved smaller amounts of money. For example, the IRS billed Bielfeldt more than $1 million in taxes and penalties for 1989 and 1990. Bielfeldt had claimed depreciation and expenses for the property his firm had acquired in downtown Peoria, where it had once planned to build offices and a shopping mall. The firm spent $206,855 to conduct feasibility studies for the project, but nothing came of it. The firm considered demolishing the buildings that sat on the land, and renovating, but it made only one improvement. Bielfeldt & Company "did not raze the buildings, except for one decrepit structure that had been used for sale of pornographic material prior to its acquisition by the partnership," according to a 1996 court petition filed by Bielfeldt's attorneys.

The Service also disallowed losses that Bielfeldt claimed in connection with his sale of a condominium on Marco Island, Florida, a tropical paradise in the Gulf of Mexico with miles of white-sand beaches and no fewer than six country clubs. In 1990, the Bielfeldts sold their condo there, complete with its furnishings, and claimed a loss on the sale of the personal property.

The IRS challenged deductions that Bielfeldt & Company claimed for "professional fees," which included "several outside professional firms, including attorneys, certified public accountants, as well as employee benefit consultants, in order to verify the proper application of the Federal income tax laws," according to a petition Bielfeldt filed in Tax Court. Those fees, amounting to more than $166,000, were incurred "as a direct result of the Service's examination of tax years 1984–1989," the Bielfeldts claimed, and were "ordinary and necessary trade or business expenses." The IRS disagreed, arguing that the Bielfeldts were attempting to write off the cost of their own legal defense.

The Service disallowed deductions taken by the Bielfeldts for trading losses and for the operation of the two planes that the partnership owned, and it also charged deficiencies in self-employment tax and underreported income from a state income tax refund the Bielfeldts received. And all of that in just one of the seven remaining cases. Bielfeldt and the IRS settled the case without going to trial; he ended up paying $5.9 million, rather than the $1 million the Service originally sought. That was small potatoes compared to the tens of millions in back taxes that the IRS sought from the Bielfeldt & Company Profit Sharing Plan, a retirement fund that Bielfeldt originally set up in 1972.

The plan, which qualified for tax-exempt status under section 401(a) of the Internal Revenue Code, operated under many of the same rules that govern 401(k) accounts. Any income that the plan earned was not subject to taxes, provided that it would be saved for the beneficiary's golden years. Anyone who dips into a 401(k) or an Individual Retirement Account before reaching their late fifties pays not only taxes on the money withdrawn, but an additional 10 percent penalty. In developing the rules for personal retirement savings, Congress gave taxpayers a carrot to save—the tax-free accumulation of income—and a stick to discourage the premature raiding of retirement nest eggs. In Bielfeldt's case, the egg was more suited to a brontosaurus than a bird.

In 1983, Bielfeldt's plan account had a balance of more than $8.4 million. In 1984, the balance was just under $11.8 million. Two years later, it was $44 million. By the end of 1988, it held more than $50 million. In just six years, the worth of his retirement account had increased nearly 600 percent. During those years, the maximum tax-exempt annual contribution he could make to the plan was $15,000.

The first-rate returns were largely a product of the savvy of the retirement fund's investment manager: Bielfeldt himself.

In 1974, the predecessor to Bielfeldt & Company, called Bielfeldt, Lauritsen & Hagemeyer, directed the trustee of their pension fund to deliver its funds—less than $15,800—to the partnership. The five participants in the plan, among them the three name partners in the firm, took control of their individual accounts. "The participants believed that the partnership offered the optimal potential for appreciation in value of plan assets," Bielfeldt's attorneys explained in a Tax Court filing. In 1982, when Bielfeldt bought out his original partners' interest in the firm, the plan had done well, but not nearly as well as it would do over the next six years.

One of Bielfeldt's former partners, his brother-in-law James Lauritsen, told the Center that although he couldn't recall specific numbers, the company's pension plan was "medium sized" when he left the firm. He added that the amount of money in the pension plan had been "nowhere near the numbers" it rose to in the mid- to late 1980s. "That's when he made his big money," Lauritsen said.

Not everyone benefited from that big money. Bielfeldt's old partners certainly didn't, nor did the employees of Jefferson Bancorp, a Peoria-based financial institution that Bielfeldt came to control in 1986. They were covered by a plan somewhat less generous than Bielfeldt's. Their defined benefit plan guaranteed them a minimum increase of assets of 2 percent a year—a far cry from the massive growth of funds in the market wizard's personal retirement account. How he achieved that growth, and his failure to offer participation in the plan to Jefferson's employees, led the IRS to disqualify the plan— essentially, strip it of its tax-exempt status—in January 1996.

After auditing the plan, IRS agents concluded that the growth of Bielfeldt's retirement account was fueled only in part by the investments it made. The remainder of the growth came from profits of his trading firm, which were diverted to the pension fund, where they would escape taxation. Bielfeldt claimed that the large deposits made to his pension account each year were for interest it had earned; the

IRS disagreed, noting that there were no contemporaneous records to prove that. "Under such circumstances these payments cannot be considered payments of interest but rather excess annual employee additions to the plan," the Service concluded.

Bielfeldt had also put the assets of the plan at risk to cover his trading activities on several occasions. In March 1988, he took a huge position on Treasury futures, and, as was his habit, he used a significant amount of debt to finance the transaction. In this case, the market turned against Bielfeldt. After the October 1987 stock market crash, Bielfeldt went from bull to bear, betting that the economy would head south. It frustrated his expectations. Goldman Sachs, from whom he'd bought the futures contracts, needed more collateral to cover his positions as interest rates went against him. Bielfeldt authorized the firm to use the funds in his pension account to cover his trades. Had he not done so, he would have been unable to meet margin requirements, and Goldman Sachs would have been forced to sell off his contracts, at a considerable loss to Bielfeldt. With the retirement plan's assets backing the trade, it was also possible that a further upturn in the economy—against which Bielfeldt was betting—could have wiped out that account as well. The IRS argued that he "placed at risk for payment of partnership debts and liabilities" the millions in his nest egg.

Pension plans, of course, are not to be put at risk in the ordinary course of business. Section 401(a) is clear on this point, as the IRS noted in Bielfeldt's case. Assets in the plan, the Service stated, "cannot be diverted to purposes other than the exclusive benefit of plan participants"—that is, providing income for their golden years. The IRS discovered that not only was he risking the assets of the pension fund in his trading activities, he also allowed his firm, Bielfeldt & Company, to make use of them to buy the Learjet and the downtown real estate in Peoria that was never developed.

The IRS charged that Bielfeldt, his company, and the pension fund it maintained owed $48 million in back taxes and penalties. He and his lawyers fought back, insisting that the plan's tax exemption was wrongly revoked and that its funds had not been used for any improper purposes. One attorney noted in a pretrial hearing before Judge Laro that nearly every issue of tax and pension law was involved in the exceedingly complex case. The exhibits alone totaled thousands of pages and included documents stretching all the way back to 1973.

Bielfeldt never got his day in court. He didn't need it. The dispute was settled by mutual agreement between his attorneys and the IRS. Bielfeldt's pension retained its status as a qualifying, tax-exempt plan. For various irregularities in the operation of the plan, he had to pay a little over $500,000 in excise taxes, a tiny fraction of the $48 million the IRS had sought. Both the Service and Bielfeldt's attorneys declined to comment on the settlement reached in the case.

In 1991, a series of losses on the commodities markets finally forced Bielfeldt to cash out of his pension fund. He withdrew nearly $30 million to satisfy his creditors. When the IRS settled the case with Bielfeldt, the bulk of the money he had deposited in it was already gone. The victory for the market wizard was a hollow one.

Despite the taxes he's paid, he's still well off. He still lives in the comfortable home in Peoria Heights. He owns a vacation property in Wisconsin with an assessed value of $531,700. He still makes money on the commodities markets and enjoys a reputation as a local benefactor. In 1995, he faced an ethics investigation by the Commodity Futures Trading Commission, a federal regulatory agency, after he had used his wife's name to mask his own speculation in corn futures. The CFTC recommended fines of more than $5 million, but Administrative Law Judge George H. Painter, citing the "commendable record as philanthropists" of Bielfeldt and his wife, reduced the fine to $200,000. "Gary Bielfeldt has a clean record and positive reputation," Painter said in his decision. "This leads to the conclusion that the conduct under scrutiny here is not a good example of [his] usual practice."

Bielfeldt, who ended up paying more than $50 million in back taxes to the government after trying to get a refund for $81.8 million, insists that he is the victim of a corrupt federal taxation system. "I don't think that Tax Court judges are going to be objective. They're paid by the government," he told the Center. "I don't think you can beat the system.

"If someone could eliminate the IRS," he said, "more power to them."

9

Going, Going, Gone

Just inside the fabled Washington Beltway, at the far northwestern reaches of the stately, sprawling campus of the University of Maryland, at a business school whose students are counseled in everything from the promise of globalization to innovative e-business practices, is the Michael D. Dingman Center for Entrepreneurship. This independent unit of the Robert H. Smith School of Business provides networking opportunities, mentoring services, and access to funding sources for graduates intent on following in the footsteps of the center's eponymous founder and benefactor, himself an alumnus of Maryland's land-grant university.

Each year, the Dingman Center hosts lectures on everything from the promise of mergers and acquisitions to writing the "killer" business plan. In March 1997, however, the would-be MBAs were treated to a particularly special guest: Michael Dingman himself was on hand to deliver the keynote speech at the Conference of University Entrepreneurship Centers. The audience was treated to Dingman's gospel of wealth creation. "Successful entrepreneurs are people who break the rules," he told the crowd. "This willingness to break the rules, indeed the necessity, is really an American tradition. In fact, it's the essence of America and the wellspring of our economic strength."

For Dingman, this challenge was born of personal experience. After all, he broke rule after rule on his way to piecing together a *Fortune* 500 corporation from a motley group of troubled companies. His life story, in fact, is a cross between Horatio Alger and F. Scott Fitzgerald: young love left a well-born son destitute, but with hard work and a singular devotion to success, he overcame his early stumble.

Dingman's father was a vice chairman of AT&T, a top-tier executive with the sort of old-boy connections that would have given Dingman a leg up in the business world. But the son defied the father while he was still a student. "I gave in to the eagerness to get out into the world," Dingman explained in a 1997 speech. "I married in college. My father cut off my support and I dropped out."

Without a degree, Dingman swept factory floors in Newark, New Jersey, on the graveyard shift. "After I dropped out I got what I was looking for—a job and a taste of real life. It was an inauspicious beginning, but one thing led to another over the years."

In 1964, that circuitous path led the college dropout to a job with the staid Wall Street firm Burnham & Company. But he would not languish there: by applying the knowledge of manufacturing operations he'd gained at menial jobs, Dingman eventually worked his way up to general partner.

The Burnham firm was a predecessor to Drexel Burnham Lambert, Inc., the high-flying home of Michael Milken and the biggest insider trading scandals of the 1980s. Dingman had left the firm long before it made headlines with its hostile takeovers, its scandals and bankruptcy, but he likely would have felt at home among the corporate raiders. Like other successful entrepreneurs, Dingman forged a strategy that set him apart from his competitors. "Mine," he explained in that same speech, "was to take control of underperforming companies, usually parts of unwieldy large corporations, and manage them so they'd make money."

Dingman first put his theory into practice in the early 1970s, when he took over Equity Corporation as president and chief executive officer. Within a matter of years, through a dizzying array of spinoffs and acquisitions, the failing conglomerate emerged as Wheelabrator-Frye, an engineering company whose profits soared to $1.5 billion. Not satisfied with his success, however, Dingman then merged Wheelabrator with Signal Companies, which he in turn merged with the Allied Corporation to form AlliedSignal, a technology and manufacturing giant that has since ranked among the 500 largest corporations in America.

But Dingman still wasn't satisfied. He identified thirty-five underperforming subsidiaries of AlliedSignal and spun them off into the Henley Group, a company that Dingman promised to turn into another business powerhouse. This high-stakes gambit didn't impress the financial press, however, which dubbed the Henley Group "Dingman's dogs."

The brash college dropout was nonetheless undeterred, and went on to transform his stable of mutts into a fleet of greyhounds. When he finally took Henley public in 1986, the sale of stock raised $1.2 billion—at the time, the largest initial public offering that Wall Street had witnessed. *Fortune* magazine called him "the turnaround king investors love," in part because those shareholders who rolled the dice on the IPO enjoyed hefty returns on their investments.

Like those investors, Dingman also profited handsomely from his business acumen: by the late 1980s, his net worth was estimated to be around $100 million, according to *Fortune* magazine. To his way of thinking, Dingman represented all that America, with its wide-open financial system, has to offer—a place where any visionary with a great idea, guts, and determination can make a fortune. It's a message that Dingman, now retired and in his sixties, is fond of repeating. In fact, he has spent the last dozen years using his life story to champion American business ideals, and he has become an evangelist of the glories of American capitalism. In the Czech Republic, for example, Dingman sought to teach companies accustomed to government subsidies how to thrive in an American-style free market. In Russia, Dingman tried to help turn a banking firm into a Western-style venture capital powerhouse. And at the Dingman Center for Entrepreneurship at the University of Maryland, Dingman's would-be protégés are schooled in the fine art of breaking the rules. "The United States economy is the world's largest and strongest," he rhapsodized in the 1997 speech to those assembled at the entrepreneurial center he funded. "Our future is brighter than ever."

Dingman's choice of pronouns certainly was odd, given that he's no longer a citizen of the United States. In the mid-1990s, he sold his oceanfront estate in chichi La Jolla, California, packed up his family's belongings, and removed his many millions from the country. In fact, he took the ultimate step to avoid paying taxes: he renounced his U.S. citizenship, legally severing any and all bonds between himself and the country whose system of government had created the world's largest and strongest economy—the one that allowed a lowly janitor in a New Jersey factory to end up in the executive suite of a *Fortune* 500 company.

As much as Dingman may love his birthplace, though, he decided that the Bahamas were better: "We wanted a gentle, thoughtful, pleasant place to raise our three children," he told the *New York Times* in a 1995 interview. He denied that paying taxes prompted his decision to renounce his citizenship, but he also expressed strong feelings in the interview about the Internal Revenue Code. "I'm investing money in China and the Czech Republic now," he told the *Times*. "Why would I want to pay U.S. taxes on money if I invest in China? Other countries don't do that." To avoid paying those taxes, Dingman renounced his citizenship.

The Sixteenth Amendment to the Constitution, which was ratified in 1913, gave Congress the power to "lay and collect taxes on incomes, from whatever source derived." In 1921, the commissioner of internal revenue issued Treasury Regulation 62 to clarify the reach of the government. "Citizens of the United States," it read, with the sort of heavy-handedness expected of the Internal Revenue Service, "wherever resident, are liable to the tax. It makes no difference that they may own no assets within the United States and may receive no income from sources within the United States." In other words, an American citizen living and working abroad nonetheless owed income tax to the U.S. Treasury.

George W. Cook was such an individual—a U.S. citizen who lived in Mexico City and earned his livelihood there. In 1924, to fight a tax bill of $1,193 that the Bureau of Internal Revenue—as the Internal Revenue Service was then known—had sent him, Cook appealed his case all the way to the Supreme Court. In their brief to the High Court, Cook's lawyers labeled the relatively small tax bill ($11,600 in 1999 dollars, after adjusting for inflation) "a mere extortion under the guise of taxation."

Needless to say, attorneys representing the Bureau of Internal Revenue saw the matter differently. They noted that, even in Mexico, Cook enjoyed all the protections and privileges that U.S. citizenship confers on an individual. "How can the duty of the citizen to support the government that protects him depend upon his place of residence?" they asked. The Court agreed, deciding that "The government, by its very nature, benefits the citizen and his property wherever found." As a result, the court held, Cook and all other Americans living abroad were liable to pay taxes for the privilege.

The government's brief in the case went even further: it argued that paying taxes was one proof of citizenship. "The failure to pay such an income tax is, inter alia, of considerable weight in determining that the nonresident citizen has given up his allegiance to the United States," the brief noted. In order to remain a citizen in good standing, Cook had to pay his taxes.

Not everyone in his position has chosen to do so. State Department statistics show that an average of 781 U.S. citizens have expatriated—that is, foresworn their allegiance to the United States—each year since 1980. Some married citizens of other countries; others were immigrants who chose to retire to the country of their birth. But a handful of American millionaires—Michael Dingman, among them—have been motivated by issues related to taxation. Kenneth and Robert Dart, for example, who inherited Dart Container Corporation (the world's largest manufacturer of foam cups), both gave up their citizenship. So did Frederick Krieble, whose grandfather developed a glue that made the Loctite Corporation one of the world's most successful adhesive companies. Ditto an heir to Campbell Soup Company, John T. Dorrance III.

The State Department publishes a document that warns Americans who consider renouncing their citizenship that "severe hardship" could result, particularly if one is not a citizen of another nation. Such individuals become stateless, and can't depend on the protection of any government in case of trouble. What the State Department doesn't disclose is the ease with which an expatriate can acquire a passport in a new country—provided he can pay the tab.

Ireland, for example, has enjoyed an influx of immigrants from the United States, the Middle East, and Hong Kong, although the newcomers have hardly been the poor, huddled masses. In 1998, the government of the Emerald Isle finally abandoned its controversial economic-development scheme that gave any foreigner a passport in return for a $1.4 million investment in an industry that creates domestic jobs. John T. Dorrance III, the heir to the Campbell Soup fortune, who's worth an estimated $2 billion, became an Irish citizen in 1994. He donated $1.5 million to plant trees, and in return for his investment in the Irish economy, he received an Irish passport that enabled him to live and work in the European Union, and to enjoy the lush Irish countryside when he wasn't traveling. But more important, Dorrance could take advantage of the lower Irish tax rates. And unlike the United States, his adopted home Ireland does not levy a tax on a citizen's income from foreign sources.

The Campbell Soup heir wasn't the only rich American who bought an Irish passport. Kenneth and Robert Dart, heirs to the Dart Container Corporation fortune, became dual citizens of Ireland and Belize in 1993. (Belize has a similar cash-for-passport program, although the price is a mere $55,000.) Originally based in Michigan, the privately held company moved its headquarters to Sarasota, Florida, in the late 1980s, to capitalize on lower state tax rates. Although the foam cup manufacturer has estimated annual revenues of $1 billion, it is an unfamiliar name—and purposely so. The firm is so secretive, in fact, that Dart management—fearful of revealing the particulars of its cup-making process—won't allow salespeople into company plants.

While its company has maintained a low profile, the family's own internecine squabbles have made headlines over the last decade. A third brother, Thomas, sued his siblings and his father, claiming that he had been cheated out of the proceeds of a $350 million family trust established by his grandfather in the late 1970s. The clash between the three brothers eventually included allegations of firebombings, bribery, and drug abuse, with Thomas once even accusing Kenneth of planning to live on a heavily armored yacht to avoid the tax authorities of all nations. The case involving the family fortune was settled out of court in late 1998; the terms of the agreement were sealed.

Although details of that settlement remain elusive, it's certain that the brothers Dart were not left paupers. In 1994, for example, Kenneth moved to a $5.3 million resort in the Cayman Islands, a British colony an hour's plane ride from Miami. The Darts also opened an office in the Caribbean tax haven to manage their international investments. But Lamar Matthews, a Sarasota attorney and Dart family spokesman, adamantly denied rumors that the family was moving out of the country. "Nobody plans to move down there and live," Matthews told the Sarasota *Herald-Tribune*. "They like Sarasota a lot and have made a commitment to have a bit more profile in the community."

Apparently, Matthews had been misinformed. Within a few months, Kenneth Dart had secured his Belize citizenship and had moved to the Cayman Islands.

In its November 21, 1994, issue, *Forbes* published an article by Robert Lenzner and Philippe Mao called "The New Refugees." "You could practically fill a Boeing 747 with well-heeled U.S. citizens who have taken on foreign citizenship" to avoid their taxes, the piece declared. "The exodus may speed up under an administration that campaigned for office on a tax-the-rich platform."

President Bill Clinton, incensed by the article, decided to make the fleeing millionaires a centerpiece of his battles with the newly elected Republican Congress—a skirmish that proved to be one of the least important legislative fights in the history of the Internal Revenue Code. In 1995, Clinton proposed legislation that would have imposed a 55 percent tax on the assets of any millionaire who renounced his U.S. citizenship. Republicans opposed the measure. "While Democrats are fighting for $1.3 billion in funding for kids and education," Vice President Al Gore declared, "Republicans are fighting to allow 24 billionaires to escape $1.4 billion in taxes by renouncing their citizenship."

In 1995, Congress began working out the details of what was informally called "the expatriate tax debate." Senator Edward M. Kennedy, Democrat of Massachusetts, represented the view of many in his party: "The renunciation of one's citizenship is a right we respect," Kennedy proclaimed in debate on the Senate floor. But, he added, "the renunciation of citizenship by individuals so that they do not have to pay their fair share of taxes is unacceptable."

Members of Congress disagreed on how to discourage expatriation for tax avoidance purposes, without literally chaining citizens to U.S. soil. Those against harsh penalties argued that the group of rich Americans abandoning their citizenship was too small to justify massive action, but Kennedy, who was outspoken on the issue, insisted otherwise. He cited an estimate that wealthy expatriates would cost the country $1.5 billion over a five-year period—or $300 million a year. "That is a very substantial amount," the Massachusetts senator told his colleagues, "which, if not collected, will either add to the Federal deficit or deny us the opportunity to invest in our first order of priorities."

The legislative debate was contentious in both Houses of Congress. Democrats accused Republicans of coddling "Benedict Arnold billionaires." Republicans looked for a face-saving compromise to make the issue go away.

"I never thought I would see the day when Republicans would stand up on the floor of the House of Representatives and defend the rights of billionaires to give up their U.S. citizenship in order to avoid paying taxes. But that is exactly what they did," David Bonior, a Democrat from Michigan and the House minority whip, charged.

Bill Archer, a Republican from Texas and chairman of the House Ways and Means Committee, proposed his own version of the expatriation legislation: "The Archer amendment is far tougher, far stronger, and constitutional," he claimed. "It generates, as I said, $2.4 billion of revenue for the Treasury, whereas the [Democrats'] bill . . . generates only $800 million. It clearly is a pansy approach to this problem compared to the Archer amendment."

While partisans on both sides of the aisle hurled rhetoric at one another in 1995, eighty-four millionaires who hadn't fled the country filed tax returns on which they owed no income tax. Some 13,630 tax returns were filed by individuals who earned more than $200,000 but paid taxes at an effective rate of under 10 percent. And some 17 percent of the roughly 7,500 corporations with assets of over $250 million filed returns claiming they owed no income tax. But Congress was more concerned with posturing over expatriates.

In the midst of the legislative battle, one millionaire took matters into his own hands. Joseph Bogdanovich, son of the founder of the canned tuna maker Star-Kist Foods, Inc., a subsidiary of the H. J. Heinz Company, was preparing to renounce his citizenship when Congress began considering changes to the expatriation rules. According to the *Washington Post*, Bogdanovich's lawyers hired lobbyist Guy Vander Jagt, a former Republican representative from Michigan and member of the House Ways and Means Committee, to voice his concerns. The Star-Kist heir's interests wielded considerable clout. Not only was Bogdanovich a prominent contributor to the Republican Party, but Vander Jagt was a good friend and former law partner of Kenneth Kies, chief of staff of the Joint Committee on Taxation.

Congress continued its search for a legislative compromise, and in so doing shifted the effective date of the expatriation law several months forward. But when the media cried foul, lawmakers caved in and instead added over a year of retroactivity to the new legislation.

Then the *New York Times* weighed in with an inflammatory front-page article. The paper reported that an exception in the legislation—exempting any expatriate who became a citizen of a country where he, his spouse, or at least one parent was born—was designed specifically for Bogdanovich. Because his father was a native of Yugoslavia, the Star-Kist heir could have avoided the expatriates' tax if he became a citizen of one of that nation's successor states. (Bogdanovich's lawyers refused comment, so it's unclear whether he took advantage of this exemption. The eighty-seven-year-old tuna heir now reportedly lives in London, and recently relinquished his position as vice chairman of the board of directors of the H. J. Heinz Company.)

In the end, Congress agreed to implement new restrictions on expatriation, attaching an amendment to the Health Insurance Portability and Accountability Act of 1996, a popular measure that had broad bipartisan support. Gone was the 55 percent exit tax on all the assets of billionaires who renounced their citizenship; however, the burden that the Internal Revenue Service must meet in order to prove someone has expatriated to avoid paying taxes was lowered. According to the law, anyone who renounces his citizenship is presumed to have tax avoidance as his motivation if his average annual federal income tax liability for the past five years exceeded $100,000, or if the taxpayer's net worth is $500,000 or more. Certain categories of former citizens were exempted from this presumption, however, including those who at birth were citizens of the United States and another country and continue to be a citizen of the other country; those who become citizens of a country where they, their spouse, or either of their parents were born; and those who gave up their citizenship before reaching the age of eighteen years and six months. And expatriates were allowed to get out from under the presumption of tax avoidance—individuals who exceed the income thresholds, the law decreed, may submit requests for a ruling from the IRS that avoiding taxes was not their principal reason for renouncing their citizenship.

Congress also barred tax expatriates from reentering the United States—a sanction that placed them in select company. Former citizens, like all other foreigners, are allowed to visit the United States for 120 days per year—a provision that Kenneth and Robert Dart, John Dorrance, and Michael Dingman happily availed themselves of. But the new law gave the Immigration and Naturalization Service and the IRS broad discretion to bar them, and others like them, from entering the country at all. (As of early 1999, however, no one had been prohibited from entering the country because he had renounced his citizenship to avoid taxes.)

In the two years that followed passage of the restrictions on expatriates, Congress continued to tinker with the issue—even while being publicly castigated by critics of the measure. The law, according to a *Wall Street Journal* feature, "makes Americans who give up citizenship to escape taxes 'excludable.' That means banishment: Like terrorists and people with communicable diseases, renouncers can be barred from setting foot in the U.S. ever again."

A Seattle lawyer criticized later tax code revisions requiring all expatriates—even the nonmillionaires—to submit detailed financial information to the U.S. government. In a September 1998 letter to the IRS, attorney Henry Haugen wrote: "I had the occasion to become involved with these new procedures in connection with the submission of a ruling request by a former U.S. citizen who expatriated to a Western European country. Quite frankly, I find the new procedures contained in [IRS regulatory Notice] 98-34 to be an extraordinary example of bureaucratic arrogance that is far removed from our concepts of what is right and fair."

Restricted visits, shrinking loopholes, the possibility of being banned—given such hazards, why would anyone still consider expatriation? Because it's still pretty easy to get around the loopholes, according to Michael Pfeifer, a partner in the international tax division of Ernst & Young.

Pfeifer should know. He formerly worked for a London firm that handled international tax-planning issues, including expatriation, and his client list included John Dorrance III, Ireland's wealthiest citizen. While Pfeifer believes that expatriation is an indisputable right, he was troubled by the loopholes that Dingman and other expatriates exploited. As a result, he resigned his partnership in London and went to the IRS to help design more restrictive laws. "I did this because it struck me that there was a loophole for the wealthy," Pfeifer told the Center. "I was trying to level the playing field."

The resulting 1996 law did indeed make expatriation more difficult, and it also forced the IRS, the INS, and the State Department to increase their monitoring of those who decide to abandon their mother country. But some of the law's harshest limitations, such as the banning of tax expatriates, have never been enforced. Part of the problem, said Pfeifer, is that immigration and State Department officials feel the law banning U.S. visits is poorly written. "It's still on the books, but it's not being implemented," he said. "I doubt they're ever going to do anything with it."

There's also virtually no communication about private taxpayer information between the agencies involved, making enforcement close to impossible. According to Edward Betancourt, director of office policy review at the State Department's consular affairs office, the IRS and the State Department operate under very different assumptions. "U.S. citizenship [law] and tax law evolved in different directions," Betancourt said. "It's maybe not surprising that these two areas of law, to put it mildly, didn't work hand in hand."

Betancourt agreed that the expatriation law accomplished little. The restrictions "may have decreased the number of people leaving to some degree," he said. "The fact that it's in the books has had some effect." But Betancourt admitted that his colleagues still see a number of wealthy Americans renounce their citizenship every year. Citizens leaving because of family responsibilities abroad will often tell U.S. consul officers exactly why they have to leave. "People of considerable means tend to say nothing at all," he said. "We don't inquire or require them to disclose their motivation. We wouldn't have the means to determine whether they're telling us the truth."

While the 1996 act didn't much dent the ability of the wealthy to expatriate, there's no indication that Congress will again tinker with a law that, among other things, didn't affect those who had already renounced their U.S. citizenship. Dingman, for example, now lives in Lyford Cay, an exclusive enclave in the Bahamas—a member of the British Commonwealth with no income tax burden whatsoever. Dingman built a $10 million house there that overlooks the clear, blue waters of the Caribbean. His home is equipped with a satellite dish and other amenities to keep a modern-day financier in touch with events in the largest and strongest economy in the world. His neighbors have included actor Sean Connery and investment king John Templeton, also tax exiles. Dorrance, whose primary residence is a castle near Dublin, Ireland, owns a home near Dingman's as well. We traveled to the Bahamas to see where and how the expatriate billionaires live, and we attempted, without success, to interview both Dingman and Dorrance. Whether it is government tax authorities or persistent journalists, both men answer to no one, which is not unusual behind the gates of Lyford Cay. John Mosko, Dingman's builder in the Bahamas, told the Center, "Most of the people who live there are wealthy foreigners."

And chances are, more will be putting down roots there. That's because, congressional blather notwithstanding, the biggest loophole for the runaway millionaires wasn't closed. In fact, none of the proposed amendments even addressed it.

When Dingman and Dorrance expatriated—before Kennedy, Archer, or Bonior had taken up the issue—the Internal Revenue Code stipulated that anyone fleeing the country for tax-related reasons would have to continue to pay taxes on his U.S. income for another ten years. If he sold all his U.S. assets, the Code decreed, he'd have to pay capital gains taxes. Furthermore, if he died before ten years had passed, his estate would be subject to U.S. estate taxes. Those regulations have been on the books since 1966, when Congress first addressed the expatriation issue.

But there's one glaring loophole that has been ripe for exploitation: foreign corporations and individuals are taxed differently from their U.S. counterparts.

While an American who renounces his citizenship is still obligated to pay U.S. taxes for ten years, an offshore corporation he forms is treated by the IRS as a foreign corporation. And here's the kicker: not only are foreign corporations exempt from paying U.S. capital gains taxes, but they also pay far lower rates on investment income. It's a complicated bit of tax arcana—the sort of tax code end run that justifies the seemingly inflated fees of ingenious tax lawyers and accountants.

For the IRS, there are three types of corporations: domestic, foreign, and controlled foreign corporations. The first and second seem simple enough—Ford Motor Company is domestic, whereas Honda Motor Company is foreign. By contrast, a controlled foreign corporation is set up outside the United States but is at least half owned by U.S. citizens.

The distinction is crucial. Without it, any American could form an overseas corporation and conduct all his business in the United States without being subject to federal income taxes. Because of it, any American who owns at least 50 percent of a foreign corporation must report on his tax return the income derived from that business. But the regulations defining a foreign corporation contain none of the antiabuse regulations that apply to expatriates. In other words, someone who has just forsworn his allegiance to the United States may form a foreign corporation that is not subjected to the taxes that apply to a domestic or a controlled foreign corporation. Doing so requires a complicated transaction and the skill of a top-flight tax attorney, but the paperwork shuffle is amply rewarded: it permits an expatriate to transfer all of his wealth to the foreign corporation in a nontaxable transaction, thereby circumventing U.S. taxes entirely.

Frederick Krieble, another wealthy heir who fled the land of his birth, appears to have engineered just such a transaction. Krieble lives in the Turks and Caicos Islands, thirty miles southeast of the Bahamas. His grandfather invented a liquid resin that attaches metal to metal, solving such problems as how to permanently bond nuts and bolts. By the time Krieble was old enough to walk, his family was being touted as the Rockefellers of glue, and their Connecticut-based Loctite Corporation was selling its products internationally.

Frederick's father, Robert, retired from Loctite in 1986 and gained notoriety for his work with conservative groups like the Heritage Foundation. He also founded the Krieble Institute, which promoted democracy and free enterprise in Eastern Europe and the Soviet Union. When the cofounder of Loctite passed away in 1997, typical of the eulogies were the remarks of U.S. Representative Ralph M. Hall, Democrat of Texas: "As a scientist, entrepreneur, and supporter of freedom throughout the world, Bob Krieble influenced thousands of lives, helped make the world a better place in which to live, and helped change the course of history."

Krieble family members have allocated hefty sums to philanthropic projects. Robert's sister, Gladys, gave more than $20 million to cultural and educational groups before her death in 1991. Frederick's sister, Helen, has made a name for herself as a benefactor of Connecticut artists—a distinguished track record that includes a million-dollar donation to the University of Hartford's art school. And part of the Krieble fortune funds a Connecticut-based foundation named after the family patriarch, Vernon K. Krieble.

But Frederick hasn't followed in the footsteps of his philanthropic family members. His name is not associated with any notable gifts or contributions during the past ten years. Richard Rahn, former chief economist for the U.S. Chamber of Commerce and a longtime friend of Frederick's father, told the Center that Frederick has completely disconnected himself from his native country, and may no longer be investing in any U.S. endeavors, charitable or otherwise.

Like many wealthy Americans, Robert Krieble and his wife, Nancy, created trusts for their two children; they also gave them a controlling stake in Loctite. In 1996, the Kriebles sold large blocks of their shares back to the company as part of a deal to sell Loctite to Henkel KGaA, a German chemical manufacturer. The rest of the family went through a fairly standard process of selling their holdings, while Frederick devised a more complicated, and ultimately more lucrative, financial strategy. Long after he had renounced his U.S. citizenship, Frederick transferred his stock to Theta II Limited, his holding company in the Turks and Caicos that handled all of his business and investment interests. Filings with the Securities and Exchange Commission indicate that Frederick transferred 700,000 shares of Loctite stock to Theta, in exchange for Theta stock. Because that exchange produced no immediate profit for Krieble, he wasn't taxed on it. When Theta II sells those Loctite shares to Henkel, Krieble's Caribbean corporation will realize about $30 million in profits. But because it's a foreign corporation, it will not have to pay a dime in capital gains taxes. And because Krieble has expatriated, he's subject to taxes only on his U.S. income, not his income derived from foreign sources. So those profits derived from Theta will come tax free.

The continuing benefits of expatriation keep a cottage industry of entrepreneurs in business, offering advice to wealthy Americans interested in moving offshore. A search of the Internet will take the curious to Web sites selling books, magazines, and investment options for expatriates. One page claims to be "the Web site for anyone moving to another country," and targets clients including "escaping Americans, expatriates," and even "tax exiles." Another advertises a book that will help "free yourself from tax slavery forever," and at a bargain price of only $100.

Investment companies, tourist agencies, and even the countries themselves encourage investors to take advantage of offshore tax havens. Brochures from Re/Max realtors in the Turks and Caicos remind potential buyers that the islands are virtually tax free, enforcing no income taxes, property taxes, or capital gains taxes. A Web site calling itself The Official Site of the Bahamas celebrates the islands' favorable investment climate, which levies neither capital gains, nor income, sales, or inheritance taxes.

The enticing advertisements probably had little to do with Michael Dingman's decision to expatriate. Instead, he may have been influenced by those pesky lawsuits that disgruntled investors filed against him.

In 1986, just after Dingman formed Henley Group, a shareholder suit was filed against the company's chief and several of his executives. Among other things, the suit attempted to halt the company's stock purchase program, which would have allowed the brass to receive $100 million in loans from Henley to buy the company's stock. These loans were nothing like normal bank loans, however—they were considered "nonrecourse," which means that no action would have been taken against the executives if their loans were never repaid. The company, and the shareholders who owned it, would be left holding the bag.

Prominent class-action attorney William Lerach represented the shareholders in the case against Dingman. In his complaint, the San Diego–based lawyer accused Henley executives of "self-dealing, deception, and constructive fraud." At the time, Dingman seemed unflustered, and told *Business Week* that Lerach was going to wish he never heard of Henley's equity purchase program. But within months, Dingman and Henley Group agreed to settle out of court for $52 million.

The case of the equity purchase program wasn't unique. Dingman was also accused of paying for his family's relocation to San Diego with some $9 million from Henley's company account.

Upon moving to the Bahamas, Dingman continued to make money by taking advantage of his eye for unrecognized business opportunities. The companies involved weren't American, however, but were located in the newly formed Czech Republic, where privatization was in its infancy and the financial system was anything but transparent.

One of Dingman's neighbors in the Bahamas is Czech expatriate Viktor Kozeny, who earned his millionaire stripes by taking advantage of his country's emerging financial market. Kozeny formed Harvard

Capital & Consulting, which operated a mutual fund for Czech investors who had been granted shares in state-owned enterprises during the country's privatization program. Kozeny blitzed Czech media with a slick ad campaign that both touted his financial expertise and made an outlandish promise to potential investors: within a year and a day, he'd increase their money tenfold. For a time, Kozeny's mutual fund did in fact perform incredibly well, increasing its net asset value and, in the process, upping its assets to $1 billion. A former director of Harvard Capital estimated Kozeny personally made $45 million from the venture.

Flush with cash, Kozeny transferred ownership of Harvard Capital to a Netherlands Antilles corporation ostensibly owned by his mother. He got an Irish passport, and in 1994 moved to the Bahamas, where he met Dingman. Before long, the two joined forces and began acquiring Czech companies with the promise that they would transform them into American-style lean, mean profit machines.

The two investors were wholeheartedly welcomed into the country. After all, Harvard Capital & Consulting, one of the largest Czech investment funds, had indeed made money for its investors. And Dingman's promise to invest $140 million quieted many who doubted the pair's promises.

But by the end of 1995, there was mounting concern from individual Czech investors, who in some cases had emptied their savings accounts to invest in the companies that Dingman and Kozeny had taken control of. Most of the companies targeted by the two continued to flounder, even as Dingman applied his so-called insider knowledge. In July 1996, Kozeny's investment firm, which managed the two partners' holdings, was charged with siphoning off some $30 million of investors' cash on inflated fees. Investors panicked and sold out, and Kozeny was later ordered to pay a restitution fee of $6.8 million.

But, like Dingman, Kozeny ultimately did just fine. The partners gained control of a few Czech companies, one of which they unloaded for $35 million.

Dingman told *Fortune* magazine that it was "probably true" that he traded on his insider knowledge; he also proclaimed that he had little sympathy for the ordinary Czechs who lost their shirts. They "are saying 'We can't get enough information so we're going to sell, we're going to go home to bitch and complain.' That's the kind of meat I like to eat," he said.

The various funds and businesses that the pair of expatriates controlled are now owned by a corporation based in Cyprus, another tax haven. John Sununu, the White House chief of staff in the Bush administration, and astronaut Thomas P. Stafford are on the board of directors, along with Kozeny and Dingman. The company, in which many Czech citizens in theory still have shares, publishes no financial reports or disclosures of any kind. Which suits Dingman just fine.

"That's the way you do business in that part of the world," he told *Fortune.* "It's not the New York Stock Exchange."

10

Package Deal

The e-commerce revolution has changed the way companies do business: with a click of the mouse, they now order raw materials, components, and finished goods from one another, much the way consumers order books and compact discs. Surplus inventories, once the bane of factories, have largely been eliminated through sophisticated just-in-time manufacturing processes that perfectly match supply to demand with nothing left over.

While orders, payments, and shipping instructions can travel the wired world at incredible speeds, the actual products—the real, tangible things that are bought and sold in millions of electronic transactions each day—can't be conveniently attached to an e-mail. Packed in crates, pouches, or cardboard boxes, everything from medical instruments to microprocessors, from perfumes to personal computers, are shipped through the air by a handful of companies that have provided the link for a far-flung global network of producers and consumers.

The instantaneous orders and overnight deliveries are a far cry from the economic revolutions that swept the country, and the world, a century ago. Then, slow-moving surface ships transported bulk goods to the great harbors and docks of Boston, New York, Philadelphia,

Seattle, and San Francisco, which were then loaded onto equally ponderous rail cars for their journey to the interior. Today, the freight hubs of airborne shippers in cities like Memphis and Cincinnati have surpassed the old ports. Federal Express and United Parcel Service of America, Incorporated, dominate the domestic market for rapid delivery of freight by air. Internationally, however, they pale in comparison to DHL Worldwide Express.

DHL handles more than 40 percent of the world's airborne cargo trade. Its growth has gone hand in hand with the globalization of business. As multinationals have expanded their manufacturing operations to the four corners of the earth, DHL has followed right behind, expressing their documents and deliveries to more than 230 countries and territories. It has transported complete boxing rings, the luggage for the Queen of England (weighing a majestic 5,000 pounds), and absentee ballots from South Africa's first election in which the country's black majority was allowed to vote. The closely held firm, which celebrated its thirtieth anniversary in 1999, has 2,300 offices worldwide, connected to a global transport system by 222 aircraft.

Just as important as its offices and aircraft, its shipping hubs, and its white delivery vans emblazoned with the letters DHL in fire-engine red—not nearly as familiar to American eyes as the brown UPS truck or the FedEx logo—is the high-tech computer network that makes the company's packages run on time. DHL is a creature of the global economy it serves.

But DHL Worldwide Express isn't exactly a company. It's a trademark shared by a pair of companies: DHL Airways, Incorporated, which is as American as FedEx or UPS, and DHL International, Ltd., the far more profitable of the two, which is a corporate citizen without allegiance to any particular country. The latter entity took a page from the annals of those slow-moving merchant ships of yesteryear. It flew flags of convenience to shelter its income in tax havens like Hong Kong and the Netherlands Antilles. How much that name was worth to the two companies that shared it evolved into an accounting dispute with the Internal Revenue Service over hundreds of millions of dollars of unpaid taxes.

The letters *DHL* come from the names of the airfreight company's founders—Adrian Dalsey, Larry Hillblom, and Robert Lynn. In 1969, they got into the express shipping business with a simple idea: they flew bills of lading for ships to their destinations long before the vessels themselves arrived in port. Local customs and port officials could process all the paperwork in advance, so the ship could be unloaded immediately upon its arrival. Initially, their service was limited to the San Francisco–Honolulu route. Their first vehicle, a Plymouth Duster owned by Dalsey, plied the streets of San Francisco, making pickups and deliveries.

In 1970, they expanded their reach in the United States and brought in as an investor William A. Robinson, an army veteran with experience managing manufacturing operations. Robinson had $3,000 he'd inherited from his grandfather and a gas credit card for capital. The company consisted of a few Volkswagens, an answering service, and an apartment that doubled as a corporate headquarters. Robinson managed the Los Angeles–San Francisco traffic under a separate corporate entity; in 1972, it was merged into DHL Corporation.

The domestic expansion was sluggish compared with DHL's overseas ventures. In 1972, Dalsey and Hillblom (Lynn had already left the company) formed Document Handling Limited, International, a Hong Kong corporation. By 1973, the venture was overseeing deliveries to destinations in Australia, Guam, Hong Kong, Japan, New Zealand, the Philippines, and Thailand.

When DHL entered a new market, the company arranged for space at the local airport, made arrangements with local customs officials, set up an office location, acquired vehicles, and hired and trained local managers. In a prefiguring of the high-tech start-ups of the 1990s, DHL expanded to some locations by offering employees stock in lieu of salary. In 1972, Robinson, who already owned 7 percent of the company's stock, went to Sydney, Australia, and began the pickup-and-delivery service there. Robinson and his local contact, David Allen, who would go on to become chairman of the company's United Kingdom subsidiary and one of its major shareholders, formed Document Handling Limited, Australia. That company was shuffled around the globe until it eventually landed in the Netherlands Antilles in 1979, renamed Middlestown, N.V. The company came to own—and receive a portion of the revenue from—the local offices in DHL's foreign network.

DHL's expansion owed much to the autonomy it gave to its local offices. Managers and employees had flexibility and freedom to tailor their operations to local demands. The decentralized way the company did business was a reflection of Larry Hillblom, the only one of the three founders who took an active role in the company's affairs. An associate of Hillblom's once said he did all his business on the back of an envelope. His freewheeling style served the rapidly growing courier service well.

Hillblom was a law student at the University of California, Berkeley, in 1969 when he invested his student loans in the delivery venture with Dalsey and Lynn. Early on, Hillblom, with a suitcase loaded with lading bills, took commercial flights from San Francisco to Honolulu to deliver the documents personally. Hillblom bucked traditional corporate practices—he favored jeans and T-shirts over expensive suits, and never took a formal title with the company. He preferred to be known simply as a "shareholder." That informal style masked a keen business acumen. The bespectacled California native with a zest for profit soon dominated the company, which in turn came to dominate the international market for express delivery, although not before it hit a snag on the domestic front.

On April 11, 1972, DHL filed for authorization from the Civil Aeronautics Board to act as an international freight forwarder. The Civil Aeronautics Board was the government agency that, until the Airline Deregulation Act of 1978, oversaw passenger and freight air service. The company's competitors objected, citing the large stock holdings granted to the foreign managers. Federal regulations at the time prohibited granting U.S. shipping rights to any airline and airfreight company with foreign ownership of 25 percent or more. Hillblom and Dalsey got around the restriction by making a distinction between DHL and its foreign cousin, DHL International. The domestic corporation got its authorization from the Civil Aeronautics Board in December 1973. From that point forward, maintaining the separate status of the two was paramount in the thinking of Dalsey and his managers.

The companies coordinated their operations through a group of DHL shareholders and senior management called the Network Steering Committee, which established policies and strategies for the two companies. The committee served another purpose: it assured the company's international customers that DHL was indeed a single company, and that a package sent from Tokyo or Auckland or Seoul would have a seamless journey to New York, under the single umbrella of DHL Worldwide Express.

In 1973, Hillblom extended the company's reach to Europe. In 1977, DHL entered the Latin American market. In 1976, it began service to the Middle East. The wildly successful enterprise made Hillblom—and cofounder Dalsey—millionaires many times over. And then, abruptly, Hillblom, who was only in his mid-thirties, withdrew from the day-to-day operations of his company. He moved to Saipan, part of the Commonwealth of the Northern Mariana Islands, which has been a U.S. territorial possession since Japan ceded control of the islands after World War II.

Saipan, whose land area of forty-six and a half square miles is slightly smaller than the District of Columbia, is a tropical paradise that has long been a favored destination for Japanese tourists. The remote Pacific island is dominated by Mt. Tapotchau, which rises some 1,500 feet above sea level. Saipan was the site of a fierce battle during World War II, and even today, the island's shallow lagoon is filled with the wreckage of American and Japanese aircraft and boats. Hillblom got into the spirit of Saipan's wartime history; as a hobby, he piloted vintage World War II aircraft. He also built a spectacular home on the western shore of the island.

Hillblom became a legal resident of the island. He was president of the Bank of Saipan, the island's largest savings institution, from 1982 to 1986, and actively invested in cable television and cellular telephone enterprises there. In 1990, he even ran for political office. Supreme court justices of the Commonwealth are elected; in 1990, Hillblom won a seat on the court.

The move to the islands had other benefits for the DHL founder: residents of Saipan are subject to the island's tax laws, which, though modeled on the Internal Revenue Code, are much less exacting. The top tax rate for individuals is a mere 9 percent—a far cry from the current 39 percent rate levied by the United States. Hillblom didn't have to renounce his citizenship to become a tax expatriate.

Though the eccentric Hillblom withdrew from the day-to-day oversight of the international company he had created, he was still involved in its major decisions and still earned millions from the company's operations. Making even more, at the expense of tax authorities around the world, remained a priority.

In 1974, Hillblom hired attorney Peter J. Donnici to represent DHL in its dealings with the Civil Aeronautics Board. Donnici taught at the University of San Francisco School of Law; he served as a consultant to the mayor of San Francisco from 1967 to 1973, and, since 1983, he has served as the special counsel to the Commonwealth of the Northern Mariana Islands. Hillblom, who became quite friendly with Donnici, was so pleased with his services that he asked the attorney to form a law office to handle DHL's legal affairs.

Donnici introduced some of DHL's shareholders, including David Allen, to a tax attorney named Stephen J. Schwartz, an expert in international tax issues. Schwartz helped his new clients minimize their tax burdens by, among other means, establishing corporations in tax-haven countries.

In 1981, for example, Schwartz formed Management Resources International Ltd., which helped supervise the far-flung network of companies that operated under the DHL trademark. The new entity, incorporated in Hong Kong, provided information and advice on marketing, advertising, electronic data processing, insurance, accounting, and legal issues. But its main purpose was to avoid taxes.

Management Resources, paid by both DHL and DHL International for its services, was little more than an extension of the company. Most of its employees worked in the United States; they were even covered by DHL's benefits package. However, the money it was paid for providing all that advice wasn't taxed by the IRS, but rather by the government of Hong Kong, and at a much lower rate.

Meanwhile, DHL continued its expansion. In 1983, the company was the first international air express service to operate in the Eastern Bloc. It opened a massive hub—a central point from which it coordinated shipments—for its U.S. operations in Cincinnati, Ohio. In 1985, it opened an international hub in Brussels, Belgium, which was expanded four years later to keep up with the ever-increasing volume of international shipments. It formed a joint venture with the People's Republic of China in 1986 to bring air express delivery service to that country.

While its foreign business grew by leaps and bounds, the domestic operation suffered losses ranging from $5 million to $25 million a year from 1983 to 1988. DHL International formed a company in the Netherlands, Nirada Corporation, B.V., to forward capital to its U.S. sister. While the domestic deliveries failed to turn a profit, the U.S. presence was critical for the international company's transatlantic and transpacific trade. In 1986, DHL hired Bain & Company, a Boston-based management consulting firm, that recommended cost-cutting strategies. Bain's final report suggested that, rather than compete in the domestic market, it should merge with a competitor to ensure its access to the U.S. market.

UPS was the first suitor for DHL, but negotiations broke down in 1988 because the two companies failed to agree on a price for DHL's network. A group of foreign investors, including Japan Air Lines Company, Ltd., and the German carrier Deutsche Lufthansa A.G., came forward with an offer. Nissho Iwai Corporation, a large Japanese trading company that deals in everything from steel production and construction to food and textiles, was a third potential investor.

The negotiations were complex. All of the parties were advised by investment bankers, accountants, and attorneys specializing in mergers and acquisitions, corporate law, and, of course, taxes. Hillblom, roused from his idyllic life on the island of Saipan, took the lead in the negotiations for the DHL and DHL International shareholders. The eccentric millionaire insisted that he retain an interest in DHL's various entities, and rejected several offers from the three foreign suitors. The parties disagreed over how much the companies were worth.

Hillblom insisted on a valuation for DHL of $600 million if he were to surrender majority control of the company to the new investors; for a minority stake, he would agree on a valuation of $500 million. The negotiations caused friction among DHL's long-term shareholders, who were accustomed to deciding issues by a unanimous vote. David Allen worried that Hillblom was negotiating without the consent of the other shareholders.

At last, on December 7, 1990, the shareholders struck a deal with the foreign investors to sell 12.5 percent of DHL International and Middlestown N.V., based on a valuation of $450 million. All that remained to do was configure the agreement so that all the parties to the transaction would minimize the tax consequences of the transaction. Hillblom and Robinson, two of the four largest shareholders in the firm (the others, David Allen and Po Chung, were not U.S. citizens), stood to realize tens of millions of dollars in capital gains. With the consent of their foreign investors, they structured the timing and terms of the deal to pay as little in taxes as possible.

In 1992, DHL Airways, the U.S. company that was still required to have three-quarters of its stock held by American investors, again faced a challenge over its authorization to operate in the domestic market. Federal Express filed a complaint with the Transportation Department, citing the new foreign investors in the company as proof that DHL could no longer meet the requirement.

DHL's attorneys responded to the action in unequivocal terms. "The plain truth is that DHL is beyond question a 'citizen of the United States' within the meaning of the Federal Aviation Act," they argued. "None of the news reports, advertisements, speeches or bald speculation cobbled up by Federal [Express] cast the slightest doubt on this fact." They noted that DHL Airways was still incorporated in the United States, that its president and two-thirds of its board of directors were U.S. citizens, and, most important, that more than 75 percent of the American company's stock was held by U.S. citizens.

Federal Express claimed that its competitor's foreign and domestic operations constituted one company, operating under the name DHL Worldwide Express—a contention at which the attorneys for DHL scoffed. " 'DHL Worldwide Express' is not a company, it is a trade or service mark to identify a service," they argued. Who owned that trademark, and how much it was worth, became the central issue in a dispute between DHL, its shareholders, and the IRS for $581 million in back taxes.

The IRS audited DHL's returns from 1990, 1991, and 1992. The Service determined that the domestic company had extra income of more than $30 million that was attributed on its books to DHL International. It had additional income of $46 million from its network, money that again was attributed not to the corporate "citizen of the United States" but to its foreign operations. The Service disallowed deductions and credits the company claimed for research and development, charitable contributions, and net operating losses. And it charged that DHL had all but given away the rights to its trademark to its foreign counterpart as part of the effort to minimize the tax consequences of the sale.

The profits generated by what the IRS calls "intangibles"—a corporation's good name, or the name of its product—have long been shifted outside the United States. Marlboro and Camel cigarettes are among the world's most popular brand names, in part because of the money the Philip Morris Companies and RJR Nabisco Corporation spent promoting their brands in the United States. Determining how much royalty is owed for the use of those brand names by a tobacco company's foreign subsidiaries is a problem that the IRS and Congress have grappled with for years.

In the 1986 Tax Reform Act, Congress amended the transfer pricing regulations to include trademarks. Enforcement has proved difficult. In a 1999 report on transfer pricing, the IRS stressed the difficulty its international examiners—agents who specialize in the operations of multinational companies—had obtaining appropriate records for their audits. "These problems were especially difficult in the case of entities located in tax haven countries with which the United States had no provision for sharing of tax related information," the report stated. "In some cases, delays on the part of the taxpayer in providing information required international examiners to close transfer pricing audits with no adjustment."

DHL's attitude was little different. The company refused to provide the IRS with documents, and the company's personnel were contentious in their dealings with the Service. The audit process was protracted, with neither side backing down. The IRS contended that DHL postponed meetings, held back documents, and tried to mislead auditors on the relationship between the domestic and foreign companies. The IRS was forced to issue summonses, in some cases to DHL's foreign investors, to get the information it needed. It requested that DHL waive the statute of limitations for the tax years in question while it assembled information; DHL refused. In the end, the IRS was forced to issue the Notice of Deficiency without the benefit of all the records it had requested. It took a shot in the dark.

DHL pointed that out when it disputed the Notice of Deficiency in U.S. Tax Court. It noted that IRS agents "knew that the information and documents in [their] possession prior to issuance of the notice were not fully reviewed, evaluated or understood." It claimed that the large tax bill was a reflection only of the IRS's "incomplete review" of the facts in the case, and called the Notice of Deficiency "an abuse of discretion" by the IRS. DHL claimed that the "abuse" could seriously damage the company's reputation and its financial viability. And DHL insisted that it had accurately reported the amount it received for its trademark.

As part of the agreement with JAL, Lufthansa, and Nissho Iwai, DHL sold the ownership of its trademark, "DHL Worldwide Express." Determining a price for the name was almost as difficult as determining the value of the company. Credit Suisse First Boston Corporation, an investment banking firm that Lufthansa hired as an adviser during the negotiations with Hillblom and DHL, valued the name at a minimum of $100 million. London-based Robert Flemings & Company, Ltd., another investment banking firm involved in the negotiations, gave a high estimate of $195 million for the value of the name. DHL's own shareholders put the price tag for the name at $100 million.

There was just one problem with selling the name. The rights to the name "DHL Worldwide Express" were the property of DHL Airways, Inc., the U.S. company. Selling the name would require the company to report the capital gain on its income tax returns. DHL's shareholders were loath to do so, and came up with different schemes to get around the difficulty. They considered transferring the name to a Dutch corporation for $10 million, which in turn would sell it to the foreign investors. While JAL, Lufthansa, and Nissho Iwai's negotiators were sympathetic to the shareholders' desire to minimize their taxes, they didn't like the scheme, and vetoed the idea. Eventually, they all agreed on a formula that transferred the trademark from DHL Airways to DHL International in return for $20 million in cash and a fifteen-year agreement for the domestic company to continue using the trademark for free. That price was based on an estimate of the name's value prepared by Bain & Company, the financial advisers hired by DHL in 1986.

The IRS's auditors, deprived of all relevant documents, claimed in their Notice of Deficiency that the true value of the trademark was more than $600 million. By the time the Service presented its arguments in Tax Court, they reduced that figure to $300 million, providing expert testimony on the value of the name. DHL had its own experts as well; they held that the trademark was worth, at most, only $50 million. The trial proved to be just as contentious as the audit process that led to it, with dueling experts insisting the other side's position was groundless. Determining the tax consequences of the transaction was no easy process.

"We are convinced that there was a certain acquiescence on both sides of this transaction that was motivated by the desire to close the deal and save taxes," Tax Court Judge Joel Gerber wrote in his decision, issued on December 30, 1998. Gerber ruled that the true value of the name was $100 million—far less than the IRS said, but five times as much as the company had reported on its tax return. He also ruled that DHL had indeed understated its American income, and supported the millions in penalties that the IRS had assessed. He dismissed DHL's contention that no penalties should be assessed because the company had relied on the advice of tax experts. "As this trial has again demonstrated," he wrote, "parties can find experts who will advance and support values that favor the position of the person or entity that hired them."

DHL was ordered to pay $400 million in back taxes, and another $150 million in penalties. The company has appealed the decision.

The IRS sent the Notices of Deficiency to DHL on September 14, 1995. Four months earlier, its millionaire founder, Larry Hillblom, died while flying in one of his vintage World War II aircraft off the coast of Saipan. The twin-engine plane, and the bodies of his pilot and another passenger, were recovered the day after the crash. His body was lost at sea.

Two years earlier, Hillblom had been involved in another plane accident. In that episode, the front of the aircraft ran into a tree stump embedded in the ground, forcing its engine into Hillblom. He was badly disfigured in the wreck; he lost an eye, and surgeons at the Davies Medical Center in San Francisco had to reconstruct his face using metal plates.

At the time of his death at age fifty-two, Hillblom had amassed a fortune of over $600 million. The bulk of it was from his investments in DHL, the rest was from ventures like the cable and cellular communications businesses he'd bought into on Saipan and his ownership stake in Air Micronesia, an airline that served the Commonwealth of the Northern Mariana Islands. The largest holder in Air Micronesia was Continental Airlines; when Continental declared bankruptcy in 1992, Hillblom was one of the investors who helped bail out the company.

Hillblom, who never married, left the bulk of his estate to a charitable trust for the benefit of five teaching hospitals that are part of the University of California, including Davies Medical Center. Peter J. Donnici, the attorney Hillblom hired in the 1970s to represent DHL before the Civil Aeronautics Board, was named as the trustee of the charitable trust. The Bank of Saipan was listed as the executor of the estate, responsible for distributing its assets to the rightful beneficiaries. But first it had to contend with DHL. Under the terms of a 1982 agreement, in the event of the death of a shareholder, his stock would be transferred to the surviving DHL shareholders in return for appropriate compensation to the estate. Hillblom's old partners set about making sure that happened.

Donnici was not only an attorney for DHL, but he was also Hillblom's personal friend, his primary legal adviser, and a partner in some of his business dealings. Over the years, DHL had paid the rent for the law office Donnici had set up at Hillblom's request, as well as the salaries for the attorneys working there. In the early 1980s, Donnici became a shareholder in the company. In the weeks following the death of his friend and client, Donnici set up a shell company owned by DHL insiders that orchestrated a takeover of the Bank of Saipan. With the executor of the estate under their control, the shareholders could rest assured that their interests were protected.

Unfortunately for Donnici, his old friend's eccentric proclivities led to the unraveling of the scheme. A number of young women came forward with a similar tale about Hillblom: the scruffy mainlander in the T-shirt and jeans had propositioned them. For a few weeks, Hillblom treated each young woman—some of them just teenagers—like a girlfriend, taking her to dinner, buying her gifts, and romancing her. Then he dumped her, but not before he had fathered a child by her. Some eight putative offspring from Hillblom's liaisons with young Asian women came forward, each claiming a piece of the DHL founder's fortune.

Saipan law gives standing to illegitimate children to pursue claims against a late father's estate, unless the father has explicitly excluded them in his will. Hillblom's last testament contained no exclusion, and there began a legal battle royale that cost, by one estimate, $110 million in legal fees. The state attorney general's office in California got involved to protect the interests of the teaching hospitals, and tried to prevent the heirs from suing. Donnici and the DHL investors sought to protect their interests, and extricate the company from the legal wrangling. Some forty lawsuits were filed against the estate in eleven separate jurisdictions, including one by a Saudi Arabian prince who claimed that Hillblom owed him $282 million from a deal the two had made in the mid-1980s.

In 1996, Judge Alexandro Castro, the Saipan judge overseeing the case, ordered an investigation into the estate's executor, the Bank of Saipan. The inquiry exposed the influence of the DHL insiders over the bank. The shareholders themselves had millions of dollars in claims against the estate; the court charged that Donnici created a serious conflict of interest through his takeover of the bank. The attorney denied any wrongdoing, but the court removed the bank as executor of the estate.

After losing his commanding position in the estate's affairs, Donnici appealed to the office of the California attorney general to enter the case on behalf of the medical schools that stood to benefit from the charitable trust that Hillblom's will authorized. The state entered the case and aggressively fought any attempt by the heirs to secure a legacy from Hillblom's millions. Donnici, who remained trustee of the charitable trust, used the state to try to retain control of all of Hillblom's fortune.

In late 1995, Saipan's legislature passed a law that in effect disinherited every illegitimate child on the island; dubbed the "Hillblom Law," it contained retroactive provisions setting high legal burdens of proof on the potential heirs. Hillblom's body had never been recovered, so DNA testing could not be done.

In May 1999, nearly four years after his plane went down, a settlement was reached. Four of the potential heirs had proved they were related to Hillblom; they had paid his mother $1 million for a sample of her blood, and used that to establish paternity. The four received $34 million in cash and a share of the tycoon's hotels, real estate holdings, golf courses, and other assets scattered around the globe. The charitable trust, which the IRS granted tax-exempt status under Section 501(c)(3) of the Internal Revenue Code, got roughly $133 million. Because of its nonprofit status, the trust will pay no federal estate taxes on its share of the proceeds. Hillblom's children got no such exemption.

11

Sweet Charity

 In 1995, tax attorneys for Verner, Liipfert, Bernhard, McPherson and Hand—the Washington, D.C.–based law and lobbying powerhouse whose members include the likes of Bob Dole and former treasury secretary Lloyd Bentsen—prepared a thirty-page confidential report for a client in search of a new home. The attorneys surveyed the tax and legal consequences of relocating in forty-nine states (only Hawaii was excluded), then recommended a single location to their client: the Cheyenne River Sioux Reservation in South Dakota, some fifty miles northwest of the state's capital of Pierre.

The reservation, established in 1889 by an act of Congress, is home to more than 12,000 native Americans of the Teton Lakota (Sioux), including the Minneconjou, Itazipco, and other bands. It sits on land roughly the size of Connecticut—some 2.8 million acres of empty, rolling prairie that's crisscrossed by rivers and creeks. Summertime temperatures soar as high as 110 degrees, and droughts are common. Hot winds stir up "black blizzards," as the fine topsoil is blown across the land. And winter is equally unforgiving: frequent blizzards heap deep snow in the coulees—the depressions that pockmark the gently rolling plains.

Mobile homes, trailers, and cinder-block buildings topped with corrugated steel roofs dot the mostly empty land. The reservation has an unemployment rate of nearly 60 percent; the poverty rate is staggering; simple amenities are nearly nonexistent. In short, the economy has more in common with the Third World than with the instant-wealth 1990s of the Internet and the ferocious bull market.

But none of that mattered to Verner, Liipfert's client, which wasn't looking for cheap labor, abundant land, or big skies. The appeal, it turns out, was otherwise: the reservation has government-to-government relations with the United States. It has its own legislature, courts, and executive branch. It enjoys a large measure of autonomy from the federal government in conducting its affairs. And finally, this nation within a nation could, potentially, exempt Verner, Liipfert's client from paying federal taxes—a luxury to which it had long since become accustomed.

The Bishop Estate, a charitable organization set up in the nineteenth century to educate Hawaii's native children, is that state's largest private landowner. The nonprofit's vast endowment had always been exempt from federal taxes, but in 1995, the charity's five-member board of trustees considered taking the drastic step of moving the estate's legal domicile thousands of miles away from the beneficiaries it was meant to serve. The reason had nothing to do with schooling the poor, nor with dispensing some of its largesse on the impoverished Sioux reservation. Instead, former attorney general Margery Bronster told the Center, "Their main motivation was to avoid oversight from the state attorney general and the IRS."

And they certainly had every reason to fear such scrutiny. Bronster's investigation of the estate's trustees uncovered a pattern of self-dealing, abuse, cronyism, and corruption—a series of egregious missteps that risked the estate's status as a tax-exempt organization—all while neglecting their duty to the children of Hawaii. Bronster's inquiry revealed that trustees or their employees have, in recent years:

- given themselves significant pay raises, even while programs at the school were being cut;
- moved profits from the estate's taxable subsidiaries back into the estate to lessen the subsidiaries' tax burdens;
- invested in questionable ventures recommended by a trustee's personal acquaintances, including an Internet directory of would-be adult-film actors and casting agents;
- frequented adult entertainment clubs and casinos using money from the charitable trust's coffers, reportedly inviting state legislators on such trips; and
- lobbied Congress to defeat or alter legislation designed to give the IRS more authority to penalize their multimillion-dollar compensation packages.

Not surprisingly, none of these actions promoted the services that the Bishop Estate and its sister organization, the Kamehameha Schools, were meant to provide. When Princess Bernice Pauahi Bishop died in 1884, the last surviving descendant of Hawaiian King Kamehameha the Great, her estate—today consisting primarily of more than 365,000 acres, or nearly 11 percent of Hawaii's total land area—was entrusted to five men, the first trustees of the Bishop Estate.

Kamehameha I had united the five islands of Hawaii under his rule, and attempted to preserve native Polynesian culture while allowing European missionaries to live on the island kingdom. As the European business community's zeal to harvest Hawaii's massive sugar crop grew, sugar planters were able to obtain favorable American tariffs, and eventually, in 1898, annexation by the United States. By the time Hawaii finally became a state in 1959, its tourism industry and pineapple crop provided increased economic stability, and the Bishop Estate was one beneficiary of this growth.

The goal of the estate and its schools, according to the princess's will, was to provide quality education to children of Hawaiian ancestry. And for nearly a century, that is exactly what estate trustees sought to do.

Because the estate never had much in liquid assets, it leased much of its land to individuals and businesses for income. During the 1980s, however, the Hawaii Supreme Court ruled that the estate had to sell the land outright to the leaseholders—a ruling that provided a windfall of nearly $1 billion. With that much capital, the estate could have augmented and expanded its charitable giving. It didn't quite work out that way, however. "This tremendous influx of money was a relevant factor in the Estate's eventual corruption," University of Hawaii law professor Randall Roth told the Center.

The wealth of the Bishop Estate is hardly an anomaly. Groups granted tax-exempt status by the IRS control a staggering amount of wealth. In 1999, more than 1.5 million nonprofits, including approximately 350,000 religious organizations, controlled assets of $1.3 trillion— nearly one and a half times the amount of government debt held in the Social Security trust fund. But whereas the Social Security trust fund holds government bonds, many nonprofits engage in businesses with potentially much higher rates of return. In 1998, for example, the American Association of Retired Persons derived 60 percent of its $541 million in revenue from its business activities. These included investment income, advertising revenue from its magazine, *Modern Maturity*, which is mailed to all of its members, sales of health insurance, and royalties and revenue from joint ventures with companies such as Scudder Kemper, an investment firm, and First USA Bank, a credit card provider. The same year, the Red Cross, known for its blood drives, raised 59 percent of its revenues by selling, among other things, donated blood and blood products to hospitals. Nonprofits have long engaged in business—four decades ago, the International Basic Economy Corporation, an arm of the Rockefeller Foundation, set up and operated American-style supermarkets in Italy and in South America.

Such nonprofit endeavors may on their face have little to do with "religious, charitable, scientific, literary or educational purposes" (the

IRS's definition for 501[c][3] nonprofit activities), but the precedent for using the cover of benefiting mankind to avoid taxes has a long, rich tradition. Consider, for example, the Tariff Act of 1913. The federal law, which established the modern income tax system, exempted such groups from paying their fair share—a loophole through which many of the nation's financial elite unabashedly moved much of their wealth over the years. Howard Hughes, for example, set up the Howard Hughes Medical Institute, which owned the stock of his aircraft manufacturing corporation. The nonprofit medical institute gave hardly any money to charity during his lifetime, unless one considers bankrolling the reclusive lifestyle of millionaire Hughes a charitable purpose. It did provide millions of dollars in deductions over the years to Hughes's principal asset—the Hughes Tool Company, a closely held manufacturer of oil field machinery. The scam allowed Hughes to use the charitable provisions of the Internal Revenue Code to save himself millions in taxes.

Over the years, lawmakers concerned about such abuses have tinkered with the rules governing nonprofits. One prolonged inquiry unfolded throughout the 1950s and 1960s, when the great foundations created by the robber barons in the early part of the nineteenth century came under congressional scrutiny. In 1954, Chauncey Belknap, the legal counsel to the Rockefeller Foundation, defended nonprofits: "The basic motive for these tax favors," he wrote, "has been a wish to encourage activities that were recognized as inherently meritorious and conducive to the general welfare. In some cases it was also true that the exempted organizations performed activities that government would otherwise be forced to undertake. . . ." Belknap went on to say that saving the government money was not necessarily the decisive factor in the government's decision to grant nonprofit status to various groups.

Among its many tax-exempt endeavors, for example, the AARP runs a Web site and unleashes a regular flood of mass mailings suggesting that the current Social Security system requires only minor adjustments, if any. The Cato Institute, another nonprofit group, spends some of its money disseminating commentaries, sponsoring symposia, and maintaining a Web site to argue that Social Security is a vast, government-operated pyramid scheme, and that without the radical reform of privatization the inevitably bankrupt system will leave baby boomers and their progeny hopelessly impoverished. The National Council of Churches paid for the grandmothers of Elián Gonzalez—the young boy whose mother drowned while they and others were fleeing Cuba—to visit Elián in Miami and lobby lawmakers to return him to his father in Cuba. Brothers to the Rescue and the Cuban American National Foundation sent their spokesmen to the airwaves and organized demonstrations to advocate that the boy not be returned to a country under the heel of communist oppression. All three groups are nonprofits.

Greenpeace, Ozone Action, the Sierra Club, and dozens of other organizations publicize various studies on the effect of chemicals, auto emissions, and pesticides on the environment. By contrast, the Foundation for Clean Air Progress, since its founding in 1995, has rebuked the media bias that air quality has suffered nationwide over the years.

Clean Air Progress was originally an educational organization, but at the end of 1999 changed its exempt status to that of an advocacy group that promotes a specific agenda. The change was appropriate. Clean Air Progress, headquartered in the offices of the public relations giant Burson-Marsteller, has a roster of employees that reveals just whose perspective the foundation promotes. Its treasurer is a vice president at the American Petroleum Institute, whose members include ExxonMobil and Chevron. Its secretary is a vice president of the American Trucking Associations, which promises its members "powerful representation on Capitol Hill." Its president, William D. Fay, is also president of the American Highway Users Alliance, which cites the Foundation for Clean Air Progress as a nonpartisan organization "dedicated to educating the public about the great strides that have been made in improving air quality."

Fay admitted that there is cooperation between his foundation and Burson-Marsteller, but called it a "client relationship." In fact, he added, all of the foundation's previous educational campaigns had been administered by the well-known PR firm.

Several other foundation members have attempted to pass off Clean Air Progress's studies as impartial, unbiased evidence when contesting claims by groups such as Greenpeace, which assert that industry is not doing enough to improve air quality. By using the Foundation for Clean Air Progress as a source for scientific studies that happen to support their views, Burson-Marsteller's clients are getting maximum spin value for their money. And any wealthy corporations that give money to Clean Air Progress can write off the expense as high-minded philanthropy: in 1998, the foundation received $421,000 in donations.

The practice of creating a tax-exempt think tank to promote the views of clients is nothing new to public relations firms working in the nation's capital. Author John Stauber, who has studied the PR industry, said it is uncertain how many tax-exempt groups had been established by advertising or public relations firms as part of their efforts to bolster their clients' public profile.

"I would guess that most of the Washington, D.C.–based nonprofit organizations are industry fronts and tax exempt arms of lobby operations," Stauber said. "People hear 'nonprofit' and they think 'white hat public interest,' but all it really means is a tax designation. Most Washington nonprofits are either industry fronts or rely on industry money and good will."

This has not gone unnoticed by Congress, which has tried to tighten the rules governing nonprofits. Foundations must give away a certain percentage of their assets, for example; what's more, they must disclose to the public, when asked, the amount of income they receive and how they spend it. Yet the same basic rules enacted in 1913 still govern nonprofits today: "In order to qualify for tax-exempt status, an organization's purpose must be to serve the public good, as opposed to a private interest," an IRS publication said.

Some groups that qualify as providing a public good include title-holding companies, teachers' retirement funds, trusts set up to pay coal miners suffering from black lung disease, chambers of commerce, credit unions, nonprofit cemetery operators, and mutual insurance companies. Each group has its own special exemption in the Internal Revenue Code: black lung trusts are exempt under section 501(c)(21), and teachers' retirement funds under section 501(c)(11). Some sections cover groups one wouldn't normally associate with the adjective nonprofit—section 501(c)(6), for instance, which exempts chambers of commerce, business leagues, and certain real estate boards, also exempts the National Football League. Charitable organizations—everything from the American Association of University Professors to the Zoroastrian Society of Washington State—are classified under section 501(c)(3).

So are the Kansas City Royals, a professional baseball team that's in the business of providing entertainment for a profit.

When the team's owner, Ewing M. Kauffman, died in 1993, two of the charitable trusts he had set up to benefit the citizens of his hometown—the Greater Kansas City Community Foundation and the Ewing M. Kauffman Foundation—gained full control of many of his assets. Including the Royals.

Upon his death, Kauffman planned to have the Greater Kansas City Community Foundation sustain the team until a new owner, who would keep the struggling franchise in Kansas City, could be approved by the owners of Major League Baseball teams. With a net worth of $122 million, the Royals franchise could hardly be considered large by today's standards. But for the Greater Kansas City Community Foundation, which had net assets of $338 million in 1997, including the Royals, this was a significant acquisition.

On July 1, 1995, two months after the IRS ruled in favor of Kauffman's plan, $53 million worth of Royals stock and more than $47.6 million in cash was "gifted" from Kauffman's estate trust to the Community Foundation. The team would continue to play games and sell seats, and the Community Foundation would receive all the income. There was only one problem: the Royals were perennial

money losers. Even *Forbes* magazine, which annually riles sports owners by reporting that many teams cry poverty while actually making
money hand over fist, listed the Royals as an unprofitable franchise.
Thus, the Greater Kansas City Community Foundation, dedicated to
serving the underprivileged of Kauffman's hometown, would be saddled with a money loser until the team could be sold.

The IRS approval of the transition kept the team in Kansas City. It
also saved Kauffman's heirs millions in estate taxes that would have
been levied if the Royals were simply regarded as another asset in
Kauffman's massive portfolio. By donating the team to charity rather
than selling it, Kauffman's heirs were able to avoid millions in estate
taxes.

Kauffman was not alone in using the Greater Kansas City Community Foundation to lower his tax burden. Richard A. Bloch, who made
millions as cofounder of the nation's largest tax preparation service,
H&R Block, has been one of the foundation's largest financial supporters in recent years. He has also used the nonprofit group to do
some tax maneuvering of his own.

Richard Bloch partnered with his brother, Henry, not long after
Henry launched a small bookkeeping firm in 1946. From a modest,
single office building in Kansas City, the firm now boasts more than
10,000 tax preparation centers in the United States, Canada, the
United Kingdom, and Australia. H&R Block specialists prepare over
18 million tax returns worldwide each year; some 81 percent of the
company's $1.5 billion in 1999 revenues came from helping average
taxpayers deal with the complexities of filling out tax forms.

Richard Bloch has profited handsomely from providing the service,
and his lifestyle reflects his success. His vacation residence in Rancho
Mirage, California, had a market value of more than $500,000 in 1997,
and a condominium he sold in Fort Lauderdale in May 1998 fetched
another $275,000. He also owns a home in Kansas City worth another
$600,000.

In 1978, Bloch was told that he was dying of lung cancer. But, with
the aid of a second opinion and chemotherapy, Bloch beat the disease.

Since then, the cofounder of H&R Block, who today serves only as an emeritus board member of the corporation, has donated millions of dollars both to cancer research and to building "cancer survivor parks" around the country. What's more, from 1992 to 1995, Bloch gave more than $11 million to the Greater Kansas City Community Foundation. His generosity made him the Community Foundation's third-largest contributor.

The Community Foundation returned the favor to Bloch: in 1996 and 1997 alone, Bloch's R. A. Bloch Cancer Foundation received more than $9 million from the Greater Kansas City Community Foundation. In essence, Bloch gave money to one charity that in turn gave much of it back to his own charity.

This back-and-forth flow of funds was particularly advantageous for Bloch. He could deduct more of the donation made to the public community foundation than had he given the money to his own private foundation under IRS regulations.

Bloch denied that he donated to the Community Foundation to gain any tax advantages, and told the Center simply that "it's a good organization." Although he said he knew Kauffman, Bloch insisted that he had no other connection to the Greater Kansas City Community Foundation. In truth, his brother and former business partner, Henry, sits on the board of the Community Foundation as its vice chairman.

Saving a few million dollars in taxes or swapping contributions with another charity is small potatoes compared to the con game John G. Bennett Jr. ran in Philadelphia. Bennett founded the Foundation for New Era Philanthropy in 1989; a few years later, he said his organization would help fellow nonprofit groups prosper through the donations of "anonymous benefactors," with the promise of doubling within six months any amount a group sent to him. A charity that paid Bennett's group $1 million would soon be paid $2 million, thanks to Bennett's roster of wealthy donors who wished to make their gifts in secret.

For a time, Bennett was the toast of his city, drawing accolades from the local press for his charitable works. The *Philadelphia Inquirer* ran a gushing article about Bennett, noting that in 1995, New Era Philanthropy would give away more money than the Carnegie, Mellon, or Rockefeller Foundations. Prior to that article's publication, Bennett's foundation helped underwrite the costs of a report commissioned by the newspaper's editorial board.

While he was praised for bringing a religious fervor to his fund-raising, Bennett was actually running an elaborate pyramid scheme. He told the charities he suckered that New Era had a board of directors, and that their contributions were being held in a "quasi-escrow" account at Prudential Securities. In fact, Bennett was the sole director of New Era, and the donations were being used to secure a loan Prudential made to him. As for the wealthy philanthropists who wished to remain anonymous—the *Inquirer* reported that Bennett kept the names of all 125 of them locked in a safe-deposit box—there were none. Just as in the original Ponzi scheme, Bennett made good on his promises to his earliest "investors" by paying them off with money he raised from the newcomers. In the end, his foundation bilked $135 million out of more than 500 charitable groups.

Among the groups that lost their initial investment was the Nature Conservancy, a Virginia-based charitable group that buys land in an effort to preserve habitats that species need for survival. From November 1994 to March 1995, the Nature Conservancy invested $2 million in New Era's New Concepts in Philanthropy Fund, with the understanding that its investment would double within six months.

"We conducted a thorough investigation of New Era and their philanthropic programs," the Nature Conservancy said in a statement. "The information we received in the subsequent inquiry indicated that New Era was a legitimate and highly regarded enterprise."

Nothing could have been further from the truth. When New Era filed for bankruptcy protection in May 1995, it reported only $80 million in assets and more than $550 million in debts owed to the various charitable groups that had given it their money. While Bennett was in court facing multiple federal charges, the court-appointed bankruptcy trustee for New Era reached a settlement with the defrauded charities to repay a portion of their lost contributions. Prudential also settled before the charities could bring a suit, agreeing to pay $18 million for its role in the scandal.

In 1996, Bennett was indicted on charges of mail, bank, and wire fraud; money laundering; tax evasion; and making false statements to the government. Federal investigators charged that Bennett had diverted hundreds of millions of dollars from charities to his personal businesses rather than depositing the money in escrow accounts or investing it in low-risk government securities, as he had promised to do. His attorneys said Bennett acted under an "unchecked religious fervor" that convinced him he was on a mission from God, but, after a judge refused to allow that argument as a defense, he pleaded no contest and was sentenced to twelve years in federal prison.

Bennett's case may be extreme, but it's by no means the only example of an individual spending money destined for the public good on his own private interests. While most tax-exempt groups follow the rules and exist for charitable or educational purposes, the IRS recognizes that nonprofit abuse is an emerging issue. "The large amount of money involved in employee plan trust funds and tax-exempt organizations provides both a temptation and an opportunity for fraud," the Service noted in a 1999 publication.

This revelation notwithstanding, the IRS rarely revokes the tax-exempt status of groups that abuse the privilege. In fact, a February 1995 study of certain nonprofit sectors (not including 501[c][3] groups) by the U.S. General Accounting Office found that of the tens of thousands of nonprofit organizations operating from 1992 to 1994, only sixty-seven had their tax-exempt status revoked. Since 1997, only seventy-five social welfare groups have had their tax-exempt status revoked. In addition, taxes and penalties assessed against exempt organizations—levied to curb illegal or inappropriate behavior without withdrawing a group's tax status—exceeded $159 million in 1994.

One reason many tax-exempt groups are able to avoid scrutiny, the

GAO report noted, was that the IRS did not release the reasons for withdrawal of exemption status. Instead, the Service only revealed the names of the groups whose status was revoked, limiting the amount of media and public attention these organizations receive once the IRS has made its decision.

Although few tax-exempt organizations are ever threatened with revocation of that status, such a threat against the Bishop Estate was a significant factor in creating reforms at the estate in early 1999.

University of Hawaii law professor Randall Roth said the IRS's oversight authority made the estate's trustees more accountable than they would have been if the estate only had to report to state governmental or judicial authorities.

"I see the IRS as being a very important mechanism of accountability," Roth said. "Because the estate is tax exempt, the IRS came in and took a close look and determined that things weren't the way they should be."

Indeed. In 1988, annual compensation for a trustee of the fund dedicated to educating the native children of Hawaii was a generous $648,094; a decade later, the trustees increased their annual pay to more than $1 million. (A subsequent IRS audit determined that the trustees should have paid themselves $60,000 to $160,000 a year, based on the practices of comparable nonprofits.) The trustees disputed all claims that they were overpaid, citing a study which concluded that their salaries were in line with comparable jobs in the nonprofit and private sectors. Call it coincidence, but these same cash-strapped trustees had commissioned the study.

While the trustees paid themselves handsomely, in 1995 they cited financial concerns when deciding not to pursue a community outreach program that would have benefited 32,000 residents at a cost of $6 million, according to former Hawaii attorney general Margery Bronster. "The organization seemed far more concerned with building a financial empire than with the people they were supposed to educate," she said. The trustees cut programs that helped children learn to read and helped adults earn high school equivalency diplomas. Teachers at Kamehameha Schools didn't get raises some years, and students couldn't participate in track meets because they lacked facilities.

Even as the schools' situation worsened, the financial health of the estate flourished. The trustees had accumulated nearly $350 million in income—five times a single year's operating budget—but failed to spend more than a token sum on the schools. After the Hawaii supreme court ordered the trustees to sell off the land that had for years formed the basis of the charity's wealth, the trustees looked for ways to make that billion-dollar windfall into a multibillion-dollar bonanza. To that end, the estate became a player on Wall Street, purchasing 10 percent of the Goldman Sachs investment firm in 1992 and 1994 for more than $513 million. In 1996 alone, the estate's share of Goldman Sachs's profits was $200 million, Henry Peters, a trustee, told the *Honolulu Star-Bulletin*. When Goldman Sachs went public in May 1999, the estate reaped an additional $477 million in profits.

The investment in Goldman Sachs—a firm with a long track record of success on Wall Street—certainly proved to be prescient, but the trustees didn't always choose companies with such long pedigrees of financial success. In fact, they sometimes preferred the advice of acquaintances over the advice of professionals. Trustee Lokelani Lindsey, for example, suggested that the estate invest in KDP Technologies, the marketer of an Internet database of would-be porn-film actors called Starbook. Lindsey took an interest in the company after discussing it with a former business partner, according to the Hawaii attorney general's office.

Lindsey said her contact with the KDP executive occurred during litigation about a gold investment that also included individuals from Switzerland and Australia. "None of us knew each other," she told the Center in an interview. "We just gave our money. It was a very good investment."

Not everyone was so enthusiastic. KDP was "managed by principals with no proven business track records . . . and the soft-porn nature of the investment was not suitable for a charitable educational trust," a court filing by the attorney general's office said.

Employees of the estate were just as uncomfortable with the investment in KDP Technologies. But on July 2, 1997, against the advice of an internal staff report, $500,000 of estate money was wired to the porn-catalog vendor. The investment would eventually be increased to $1.3 million.

In fact, the trust continued to supply KDP with loans until the company's treasurer—who had also been Lindsey's attorney—was indicted for mail fraud and money laundering, a charge for which he was later convicted. KDP Technologies has continued to have "serious financial and managerial problems" and repaid none of the loans made by the trust set up to finance it, according to the attorney general's report.

Debacles of this sort did not go unnoticed within the community. On August 9, 1997, the *Honolulu Star-Bulletin* published a commentary titled "Broken Trust," authored by five prominent Hawaiians, including Roth and District Court Judge Samuel King. The piece criticized the excessive compensation of the trustees, the selection process that chose them, and the conflicts of interest that were rife among the trustees. They noted several occasions in which the personal interests of the trustees were opposed to those of the estate's beneficiaries, the native children of Hawaii.

"In [one] transaction," the authors wrote, "this one involving a golf course, trustee Henry Peters actually found himself negotiating a multimillion-dollar deal in which the Bishop Estate was the other party. One can only wonder if he gave any thought to the obvious ethical and serious legal implications of someone with a fiduciary duty moving from one side of the table to the other."

The article set off a firestorm. The attorney general's office launched an investigation. Charges and countercharges were leveled by the trustees at one another and at those accusing them of mismanagement. A lawsuit was filed by two of the trustees, Oswald Stender (singled out for praise by the authors of "Broken Trust") and Gerard

Jervis, to have Lindsey removed from the estate for financial mismanagement and intimidating the faculty and administration of the
schools. All the while, auditors from the IRS were quietly auditing the
estate's books.

The IRS audit of the Bishop Estate, which began in 1995, is still
sealed by the First Circuit Court of Hawaii. Hawaii deputy attorney
general Hugh R. Jones, who has seen the audit, told the Center there is
evidence that the estate was shifting its capital loss investments to its
for-profit subsidiaries and keeping the good investments at the trust
level for tax advantages. The Bishop Estate, records show, has a majority interest in thirteen for-profit subsidiaries meant to create new capital for the estate itself, including several investment and venture capital
groups and two real estate investment firms that managed more than
$3.4 billion in assets in 1998. By reducing the income of its taxpaying,
for-profit subsidiaries, the estate may have avoided some $165 million
in taxes, according to the IRS.

As state and federal investigators began poring through the estate's
books, they uncovered a pattern of cronyism, corruption, and self-
dealing that shocked Hawaiians. The trustees of the Bishop Estate did
not limit their largesse to themselves, but also placed friends in key
positions. They hired Milton Holt, a friend of Henry Peters who
served with him for several years in the state legislature. Holt worked
for the estate from 1987 until August 1999; his last title was "special
projects officer." Holt, according to the attorney general's petition, was
paid as a full-time estate employee, even though he did not work full-
time. The petition went on to note: "From 1992 to early 1998, Holt
repeatedly used a credit card issued to the [estate] Trust for charges at
Honolulu adult entertainment nightclubs and to obtain cash advances
at Nevada casinos."

Holt, who plea-bargained his way out of unrelated charges of alleg-
edly laundering $9,940 in campaign funds to himself, had been arrested
several times, including once for a misdemeanor spousal abuse charge
to which he pleaded guilty in 1992. To offset a portion of Holt's credit
card bills—before the other trustees even knew about them—Trustee

Richard Wong and Peters issued him a retroactive pay raise of $12,325 in 1994. The credit card bills exceeded $23,000, according to IRS documents cited in the *Star-Bulletin*, and were also reportedly used to entertain state legislators. Holt did not return phone calls from the Center.

The retroactive pay raise was not the only subterfuge the estate employed or considered to keep auditors off their trail. There was, for example, the idea of changing the nonprofit into a for-profit corporation, to be headquartered on the Cheyenne River Sioux Indian Reservation in South Dakota—a move that might have allowed the trustees to circumvent both federal and state oversight and, in the bargain, earn them lucrative tax breaks.

Verner, Liipfert, Bernhard, McPherson and Hand, the Washington, D.C.–based law firm that explored this never-consummated scheme, had a cozy relationship with the Bishop Estate. The estate had relied on the services of Verner, Liipfert in 1995, when the law firm lobbied to kill a provision of the Taxpayer Bill of Rights 2. The bill contained language, known as the Intermediate Sanctions Act, that would have imposed an excise tax on "insiders" at nonprofit organizations who partake in "excessive benefit transactions"—exactly the sort of transactions that Bishop Estate trustees were involved in for years. The trustees spent $900,000 of estate money to lobby against the Intermediate Sanctions Act. They later compromised and sought only changes in certain provisions of the legislation, which President Clinton signed on July 30, 1996.

Among those enlisted by the Bishop Estate was former Hawaii governor John Waihee, who after leaving the gubernatorial mansion joined Verner, Liipfert. Waihee met with Clinton's then deputy chief of staff, Erskine Bowles, in late 1995 to discuss the bill; he and his wife have also spent the night at the White House as a guest of the president. Waihee's partner at Verner, Liipfert, former Senate majority leader George Mitchell, also contacted Clinton's then chief of staff, Leon Panetta, about the bill. Waihee did not return phone calls from the Center; trustee Lokelani Lindsey denied knowing whether Waihee did any lobbying for the estate.

Marcus Owens, the former IRS Exempt Organizations Division director, said he is not convinced that the law will make any difference. "The Intermediate Sanctions law reaches only a narrow class of issues," Owens told the Center. "Revocation can affect a number of issues that this legislation wouldn't touch."

Lindsey claimed she fought for passage of the legislation, since it would provide a penalty other than revocation of tax-exempt status "in case anything were to happen." She preferred the bill's more measured approach to nonprofits. "Prior to Intermediate Sanctions, you could just be done away with," she said.

Owens fears charitable groups that are run like oligarchies—such as the Bishop Estate—would simply exploit this weakness in the law, pay the fines, and continue their illegal behavior. "If you have a situation where a charity is dominated by a single individual, and it pays the excessive benefit penalty as the cost of doing business, I doubt that this law will be as strong of a deterrent," he said.

It certainly didn't deter the trustees of the Bishop Estate, some of whom seemed to go out of their way to harm the schools they were supposed to oversee. Lindsey released a report in December 1997 blasting the performance of the schools, claiming that only 48 percent of the most recent graduates met the minimum standard for admission to the University of Hawaii. Lindsey, who at the time was the lead trustee for education, and responsible for maintaining a high standard of instruction at the schools, blamed the sorry state of affairs entirely on Michael Chun, the top administrator of the Kamehameha Schools. Shortly after Lindsey's attack on Chun, the Western Association of Schools and Colleges, an independent group that accredits educational institutions, confirmed the dire straits at the schools, but cited a different problem. While they gave high marks to the faculty, the curriculum, and the students, they found fault with what they characterized as the "dysfunctional management" of the trustees.

For trustees Oswald Stender and Gerard Jervis, Lindsey's public criticisms of the schools were the last straw. On December 28, 1997, the pair filed a lawsuit in the Circuit Court of Hawaii that sought her permanent removal from the estate. Nine months later, in September 1998, the state attorney general's office filed a motion to have the whole board of trustees removed.

In the months that followed, not a week went by without some revelation of mismanagement by the trustees. Lokelani Lindsey had not only swung the deal with KDP Technologies, she also owed some $230,000 in back taxes, according to the IRS, which placed liens on all her property in Hawaii. Richard Wong was accused of participating in a kickback scheme with Jeffrey Stone, a local land developer; in December 1999, Wong was indicted for perjuring himself before the grand jury investigating the charges. Henry Peters was indicted for participating in another kickback scheme with the same developer, but the charge was later dismissed. Wong, Peters, and Stone have all vigorously maintained their innocence. As of this writing, Wong still faces charges of perjury.

On May 6, 1999, Circuit Court Judge Bambi Weil permanently removed Lindsey from the board; a day later, Probate Court Judge Kevin Chang, ruling on the attorney general's motion to remove the trustees, accepted Stender's resignation and suspended the remaining members of the board indefinitely. On August 24, 1999, the IRS reached agreement with the Bishop Estate over its tax bill, although with one unusual stipulation: "In the event that any removal action of the incumbent trustees . . . is set aside on appeal or by collateral attack and one or more of the incumbent trustees is reinstated . . . this closing agreement shall be null and void." In other words, should Lindsey, Wong, Peters, Jervis, or Stender ever return to the estate, the IRS would strip it of its nonprofit status. (Such a move could have cost the estate as much as $750 million in taxes, an audit by Arthur Andersen found.) Under this additional pressure, the remaining trustees one by one agreed to resign. In return for the permanent removal of the trustees, the IRS sought only $9 million in penalties, plus interest—a far cry from the $65.4 million, plus interest, that the Bishop Estate was eligible to suffer in penalties had the conditions of the Service not been met.

"The IRS is not trying to put the estate out of business," Jones told the Center. "It is a charity that educates children. What they want to do is make sure that something like this never happens again." He added, "It seems that the $9 million is more of a token payment than anything, at least for this trust."

Five interim trustees were appointed by the Hawaiian probate court to oversee the Bishop Estate while the outgoing trustees were dealt with. They have taken measures to create more accountability at the estate. They also capped their current income at $180,000 a year per trustee—less than one-fifth of what the former trustees were paid. More recently, a state judge reduced that figure to $120,000 for the trustees' chairman, $90,000 for the other trustees.

Although her participation in the corruption of the Bishop Estate's honorable intentions cost her an extremely lucrative position, Lindsey said the IRS's "abuse of power" was the main reason she and her colleagues are no longer at the estate.

"I don't think they're in the business of managing nonprofits," she said. "The only thing that has to do with the IRS was that we were a 501(c)(3). Otherwise, there would be no way they could touch us."

For that, the children that the Bishop Estate was meant to serve can be thankful.

12

Hide-and-Seek

Joseph and Pamella Ross, like many others in this book, have enjoyed a lifestyle that most Americans only dream of. If the Rosses wanted a yacht, or an airplane, or a ranch in South America, they pulled out their checkbooks. If the weather in Acapulco turned a bit hot, they flew off to Geneva. If they tired of the endless round of high-society parties among Vancouver's elite, they hopped down to Belize and started a world-class resort in the remote Mopan River Valley. They've traveled to China, Malaysia, Australia, New Zealand—even Thailand, where they tarried long enough for Pamella to take a course in the fine art of native cooking.

The Rosses didn't always trot around the globe, however. For most of his life, Joseph Ross called Oklahoma home. He ran an aviation company that trained pilots, and, like many wealthy men, Ross put his time and expertise at the service of his government. A subsidiary of his aviation operation, which schooled both commercial and military fliers, had a contract with the Nuclear Regulatory Commission to transport radioactive materials—including components used to build atomic weapons—to research facilities around New Mexico. He was a consultant to the U.S. Army and the U.S. Air Force, the Federal

Bureau of Investigation, and the U.S. Postal Service. By his own estimate, Ross landed more than 100 government contracts during the three decades that he ran his aviation company, and for a time, he claimed, his vital role earned him a top-secret clearance.

Ross—a spry, ruddy-faced septuagenarian who oozes folksy, Oklahoma charm—was also prominent in his local community. In 1970, he was elected director of the Tulsa Community Bank and Trust Company; by 1985, he owned 34 percent of the stock of the bank's holding company and 10 percent of another savings institution, the Bank of Glenpool. He had friendly relationships with several Oklahoma politicians, including Finis Smith, who served in the Oklahoma state senate. For a brief time he retained an attorney named Frank Keating, who would later become governor of the state.

In 1986, at age sixty-two, Ross took an early retirement of sorts. He left behind Oklahoma politics, the banking business, and even aviation (he had already sold his company). He and his new wife, some thirty-two years his junior, traveled from one exotic locale to another via their yacht or private plane. Ross still worked after a fashion—he called himself a bond trader, and bought and sold Eurobonds on the international exchanges. A decade and a half later, he's still involved in one form or another with a dozen companies scattered around the globe. His wife has remained active as well: she worked for the government of Belize, and now runs a publication that promotes that country's trade and tourism. But the new careers the couple took up did not interfere with their enjoyment of their life as retirees. And the fact that Joseph Ross is a fugitive from justice in the United States, with an outstanding federal arrest warrant, hasn't troubled their golden years either.

Ross didn't cheat on his government contracts or violate the laws that govern the shipment of nuclear material; instead, he is wanted on five counts of income tax evasion. During those years when he raked in millions from federal contracts, he stashed sizable amounts of that money in foreign bank accounts without reporting it on his income tax returns. Ross purposely broke the laws of his country to evade his taxes. And despite the best efforts of federal prosecutors, the State

Department, the Internal Revenue Service, and a particularly dogged agent, Ross hasn't paid any penalty whatsoever.

The Internal Revenue Code is littered with loopholes that allow the savvy millionaire to pay proportionally far less in taxes than middle-class, two-earner parents struggling to pay mortgages, save for their children's education, and put a little aside for retirement. George Kaiser used net operating losses, Mario Kassar had his offshore trusts, and Aron and Phyllis Katz made use of real estate shelters. All of them substantially reduced or eliminated their federal tax burdens thanks to the porousness of the code. But it requires some work for the wealthy to legally avoid their taxes. Even Frederick Krieble, who took the extreme step of renouncing his American citizenship, had to engineer a complicated transaction, swapping shares of his Caribbean holding company for shares of the family's business, to make sure he was in the clear.

For Ross, all that was too much trouble. He didn't bother with the niceties of offshore trusts or foreign corporations. He didn't scour bankruptcy courts for companies with net operating losses, nor did he shop around for real estate shelters. He simply hauled cash in his private plane to Mexico, deposited it in a secret account, and used the money to invest overseas. And when the IRS caught up with him in December 1985 and issued a subpoena for him to appear before a grand jury in Oklahoma, he didn't spend a small fortune fighting his case in court. Ross and his wife, Pamella, took their money and ran. And, as they've proven time and again, there's almost nothing that the federal government can do to catch them.

"I analyzed the pros and cons and came to the conclusion that maybe one person out of a thousand could make [fleeing] work, and that was me," Ross wrote in 1994 in a nine-page letter describing his 1986 decision to take it on the lam. "I had all the ingredients—that is, money, travel, knowledge and a great wife to make it all worthwhile."

A man with the highest national security clearances, with a record of achievement and entrepreneurial success in his community, a pillar of the establishment who had created hundreds of jobs in Tulsa, a sixty-two-year-old man who had never gotten in trouble with authorities (including the IRS) anywhere, anytime, decided to abandon not only his relatives, his friends, and his country, but also his good name. It was a huge decision, but his only alternative to flight was a cell in a federal penitentiary—a fate that he had seen befall a friend and close associate.

In August 1984, a federal grand jury indicted former Oklahoma state senator Finis Smith and his wife, Doris, for tax evasion, mail fraud, and concealment of foreign bank accounts. Smith had served as chairman of the board of Tulsa Community Bank and Trust Company, of which Ross owned 34 percent. The Smiths were involved in a kickback scheme that skimmed fees owed to the state of Oklahoma from the sale of license plates. Doris ran the tag service; Finis transferred the money from Tulsa Community Bank to a bank in Texas and finally to a foreign bank account at a branch of Bancomer, S.A., in Tampico, Mexico.

In November 1985, they were convicted on seventeen counts, which carried a maximum penalty of seventy-three years in jail and over $2 million in fines. Many of Smith's former colleagues in the Oklahoma legislature wrote to the judge requesting leniency, and the pair were sentenced to six years in prison and fined slightly more than $90,000. But the former state senator and his wife, who cheated taxpayers while cheating on their taxes, served just one year and were released in the spring of 1987.

During their investigation of the Smiths, IRS agents discovered a similar route of transfers that funneled Ross's money to the Tampico branch of Bancomer. Ross had even relied on the same Mexican attorney—Gilberto Solbes Picon—to set up his foreign bank account.

Former IRS special agent John Thomas, who worked for twenty-five years in the Service's Criminal Investigation Division—the elite group of agents perhaps best known for sending Al Capone to jail for tax evasion—headed the Ross investigation. "We ended up subpoenaing bank records from the Mexican government," Thomas said. "We got his records and we were able to find quite a substantial sum that had been socked away down there and then also traced the transfers when he took it out. But we never seized a dollar from him. Not a dime."

Ross maintained accounts at Bancomer from at least 1978 to 1983—like the Smiths, transferring money there from Tulsa Community Bank—but he moved his bankroll out of Mexico when he realized that the IRS was after him. "He had a lot of money in Mexico," Thomas said. "As a matter of fact, he transferred most of the funds that he later turned into his traveling fortune out of Mexico." Thomas discovered that Ross moved some $500,000 from Bancomer to an offshore account in the Jersey Islands, one of the preferred international tax havens. "That was his grub stake to begin his international flight."

Although the IRS sleuths uncovered evidence of wire transfers, Thomas maintains that Ross's preferred method of evasion was to fill suitcases with cash and fly it to Mexico, thus leaving no paper trail. "He's a pilot and he had a cattle ranch down there, so he flew back and forth without any customs inspections or anything," Thomas said. But neither he nor the IRS got the chance to prove it in court.

With the evidence in hand, and with the knowledge that Ross had withheld details of his secret Mexican accounts on his tax return, federal prosecutors convened a grand jury in November 1985 and subpoenaed Ross as a witness. He knew the game was up. He had seen one of his closest friends go to prison for a similar transgression, and Ross wasn't about to let the same fate befall him. It was decision time.

Ross decided to run, and the slow wheels of justice—coupled with a masterful stall—facilitated his escape. December 13, 1985: Ross agreed to meet with an IRS agent. December 14: The IRS agent was told that Ross was called away unexpectedly on business. December 17: Former U.S. attorney Frank Keating, whose office opened the case that eventually put Finis Smith behind bars, told prosecutors he was representing Ross and would advise him to cooperate—a statement that bought Ross almost two months. January 31, 1986: Keating said he no longer represented Ross. February 5: A subpoena was served for Ross's foreign bank records. February 17: Thomas got word Ross had flown the coop.

Federal authorities made no attempt to arrest Ross while the investigation was ongoing, as he hardly fit the profile of a man bent on a run for the border. Prominent attorneys represented him, he had substantial property and assets, and he had long enjoyed a relationship with the federal government. Too late, Thomas discovered the kind of man he was dealing with. "We had an agent contact him [in Aspen] and tell him that we had a subpoena for him to appear here in Tulsa," the IRS investigator recalled. "He agreed to meet the agent, and then in the ensuing twenty-four hours decided it was time to get his hat and go." Thomas believes that fleeing had always been Ross's intention. "Joe never wanted to join the ranks of the taxpayers," he said. "He was a small-town farm boy who made good by making bad."

Ross and his wife headed for sunny Acapulco, where they lived for a time under assumed names, beyond the reach of subpoenas and federal investigators. They then flew to Europe, where they found trouble: while there, they learned that one of Ross's relatives had testified about his business affairs to the grand jury. "It was after this conversation that I knew my goose was cooked and that I would be indicted," Ross later wrote in his 1994 letter describing his life as a fugitive. "Anyway, when you know you are guilty why would someone want to stay around and arm wrestle with the long arm of the government when there is no doubt that you are going to lose."

Ross had no intention of losing. He and Pamella drove to Geneva to make a bank withdrawal. "I left Pam in the car and told her that I either was going to come out of the bank with over a million dollars in bonds or I would come out in handcuffs," Ross wrote.

He needn't have worried. The innocuous fugitive, who can even blend into a market crowd in a remote Central American village, waltzed into the bank, signed for his bearer bonds, and returned to his waiting wife. Even if the Swiss authorities had arrested him, Ross had the edge: while Switzerland has an extradition treaty with the United States, tax evasion isn't covered by it. Couple this with the nation's bank secrecy laws, its numbered accounts, and its historic role as a tax haven, and Switzerland has long been a favored destination of fugitives from the IRS.

Gerald Rogers, for example, who also went by such colorful names as Claude de Blue and Ambrose I. Goldsmith, fled to Switzerland while on trial for thirty counts of securities-law and tax violations. Rogers defrauded investors out of millions while running a phony tax shelter scheme that purported to sell interests in gold mines. Swiss police arrested Rogers in 1990 and agreed to return him to the United States, but only on the condition that federal prosecutors drop their tax evasion charges. The Justice Department complied, although it did manage to ultimately convict Rogers on some of the remaining charges.

"If that's the only offense, it's very difficult to get other countries to extradite," Edward Federico, deputy assistant director of the IRS's Criminal Investigation Division, said of tax evasion. Even when there are other charges against a suspect, he added, it's difficult for the federal government to return that fugitive to the country. "Many individuals commit other violations such as narcotics violations, or money laundering, but [extraditing them] is a very time-consuming, laborious process."

Ross and his wife decided that Switzerland, safe as it was, wasn't for them, so they headed elsewhere. "We proceeded to drive across France to another country where we rented a safe deposit box and stashed our loot," Ross wrote in his letter. "All during the drive, I had a grin on my face that was, as they say back in Oklahoma, like I had butchered a fat hog. Which I had."

Ross had plenty to grin about. The federal grand jury that had been investigating him issued a five-count indictment for tax evasion in June 1986. The indictment specified only $34,000 worth of unpaid taxes— small change for both a man like Ross and the federal government. How much more in taxes Ross evaded is a matter of conjecture. The IRS believes he moved hundreds of thousands of dollars out of the

United States to avoid taxation; his eventual debt to the Service could have been ten times what the initial indictment sought. Ross never appeared before the grand jury or turned over the records of his foreign bank accounts—as the law obligated him to do—so the exact amount he owes might never be determined. Because Ross fled, he avoided all that unpleasantness.

But he didn't avoid a place on the IRS's list of fugitives. Like the FBI, whose "Ten Most Wanted" list and posters of suspects have become part of the popular culture, the IRS maintains a list of people wanted for tax evasion. In many cases, other government agencies also have an interest in those fugitives. Some are drug dealers, money launderers, mobsters, and thieves. Some are millionaires who made their fortunes through dubious means. Marc Rich, an international commodities trader who evaded $48 million in taxes on an illegal sale of embargoed Iranian oil, is on the list. So is his onetime business partner, Pincus Green. Both of them live quite openly in Switzerland.

Unlike Rich and Green, however, Ross made his millions through entirely legitimate means. His résumé is long with strange twists here and there, but one thing remains constant: his biggest customer over the years was the federal government.

Ross was born on an Indian reservation in 1923. His mother was seven-eighths Choctaw Indian; his father, a farmer, was Anglo. Ross developed an early interest in aviation. He skipped college and went to work for Pan Am, making planes for World War II. In 1945, in Tulsa, Oklahoma, he leased an airplane for $3 a day, hired a flight instructor, and began Ross Aviation, Inc. From those modest beginnings the company would go on to win dozens of federal contracts. Ross Aviation trained helicopter pilots for the U.S. Army at Fort Rucker, Alabama. By 1965, at the height of the Vietnam War, Ross boasted that his company trained 95 percent of the pilots on active duty there.

Thomas, the IRS agent who investigated Ross, had served in Vietnam before joining the agency. "Joe's history and the way he made his money always infuriated me," he said. "The fact he stung the government the way he did and then his arrogance as a fugitive. Joe was originally made rich by government contracts, which adds insult to injury."

Ross became a wealthy man. He owned a yacht and a private plane. Then, at age fifty-two, he was diagnosed with lymphoma, a form of cancer that attacks the body's immune system. Ross was given only a 20 percent chance of survival, but extensive chemotherapy and radiation helped him beat the disease.

The fifty-six-year-old cancer survivor was retired, living in high bachelor style in an 8,000-square-foot home on an Aspen, Colorado, hilltop adjacent to a ski resort. Ross had been divorced twice, and, as he tells the story, life changed with a classified ad placed by a woman who wanted to be a pilot. When Ross met twenty-four-year-old Pamella Denham, he instantly fell in love. The two were married within a year. And they were fugitives within six years, fleeing Aspen—Ross's last-known residence in the United States—to jet around the world, securing his overseas fortune and possessions while fabricating new identities. After picking up the Eurobonds, they drove across France to Costa Brava, the magnificent Mediterranean resort area on the east coast of Spain. Then it was off to a wonderful apartment at a quaint ski village in the eastern Alps. Greece was next on the itinerary, where they set sail for Yugoslavia in Ross's yacht, *Blue Dragon*, which was soon renamed *Joy Ging* ("good-bye" in Chinese). From the deck of their yacht, Ross and his wife videotaped a Christmas message for their family that described their travels—although without providing any clues that could lead to their capture. "He was careful not to reveal any of the details of it in case it fell into our hands," Thomas said of the videotape, adding dryly, "which it did." The couple finally left Europe and flew to South America, where Ross arranged for a new identity and a new citizenship. He remarried Pam, which entitled her to take his new name. "We continued for the next several years flying between our home in South America and our apartment in Europe," he wrote.

Despite his globe-trotting, his lavish spending, and the messages he sent back to America, the trail on Ross grew cold. When the fugitive's mother died, Thomas attended the funeral. He also attended funerals for Ross's brother and sister. "Just in case. That's what I thought. I should have known better. I don't think Joe really cared," Thomas said. "I was at all the funerals. But he wasn't.

"We never had any solid leads on him. Once in a while we'd see a credit card receipt. He traveled around a lot." Thomas feared that Ross's boast had come true—that his wealth, arrogance, and strength of will had made him the one in a thousand who could outrun the tax-man. As far as the IRS could tell, Ross had vanished into thin air. In 1989, a shadowy Liechtenstein-based company called Dordogne D.A. Anstalt purchased a luxury apartment on the seventeenth floor of the prestigious Tudor Manor in Vancouver, British Columbia, for $705,000. The condo came complete with a spectacular view of English Bay, a concierge, and high-security underground parking. A short time later, Gilberto Picon and his wife moved in.

The Picons lived the high life among the elite of Vancouver society. They attended black-tie charity balls. They were active in the Vancouver Opera Society and other cultural organizations. They attended the "best" parties. They were conspicuously wealthy—they vacationed at their French apartment with a view of Mont Blanc, and they spent summers cruising the coast of British Columbia in their new yacht, which they christened *No Refund$*.

Robert Gray, a neighbor of the Picons, said they maintained a high profile at charity events, but at home they kept the blinds closed, blocking out the view that is the prime attraction of the heavily secured building. Gray remembered that no matter what the topic of conversation, the Picons always stuck to "one sort of canned speech"—a recitation of how Gilberto, a South America native, lived in Greece for twenty years, and how the couple met when she came to work aboard his yacht.

"I found them both to be charming," Randall Ward, a Vancouver attorney, said of the Picons. "I saw them all the time. I was quite amazed at how quickly they integrated into Vancouver society." Picon spared Ward the tales of hailing from South America. And it was just as well, because Ward, a native of Kansas, wouldn't have been fooled: "He was from Oklahoma," he said, "because the accent was from there."

Of course, Gilberto Picon was the Mexican lawyer who set up the foreign bank accounts of Finis Smith and Joseph Ross. But his namesake in British Columbia was none other than Ross, who had resurfaced in Canada with a new identity. He was no longer the Oklahoma farm boy who made good by making bad, but Gilberto "Jay" Picon.

In the Vancouver circles in which the couple moved, Jay Picon was a bond trader and his wife, Pamella, was the consul of Belize, a position that entitled her to diplomatic immunity. Among the perks she enjoyed were consular license plates, which granted her the freedom to park her maroon Cadillac limousine anywhere without getting a ticket. According to her neighbors, she often took advantage of the privilege.

The tiny Caribbean nation of Belize, the only country in Central America in which English is an official language, has a population of approximately 200,000. The Belize government had only one consulate in North America before Pam opened the office in Vancouver. "She was an honorary consul," Ward said. "Most are appointed by a country and the duties aren't onerous. It's a question of who's willing to do it, who's willing to entertain and make the social appearances. There are 100 countries represented here and there's a party for one of them almost every day."

In their new identities, Pamella Picon and her husband, Jay, were both citizens of Belize. Anyone can be—anyone, that is, with $55,000 and access to the Internet, where a few dozen companies peddle Belize passports and citizenship. Even pricier diplomatic passports, which aren't advertised quite so openly, are available for purchase. Countries are rarely specified, but the price is always spelled out: Offshore Secrets, Inc., for example, offers United Nations special counselor passports for $75,000. If that's not prestigious enough, the firm also sells honorary consul passports from undisclosed foreign governments for $130,000 and European Union special counselor passports for $195,000.

The Rosses, who had forged new identities and secured their worldwide fortune, also enjoyed diplomatic immunity a mere five years after they fled the United States. Back home, the federal warrant for Ross's arrest gathered dust.

Thomas never gave up on the case, even though the government deemed Ross small potatoes. "These kinds of things fall way down on the list of priorities with terrorists and drug smugglers and all manner of ne'er-do-wells out there," Thomas said. Even among the IRS's own list of fugitives, other criminals drew more attention. "He's not at the top of that list," Thomas conceded in an interview with the *Tulsa World* in 1996. "But he's at the top of mine because he's the only fugitive I have and these crimes are serious."

For Thomas and Ross, 1996 was a pivotal year. That January, someone notified the IRS that Belize's consul in Vancouver was married to Joseph Ross. "We got an anonymous tip that identified his exact address and the name he was using: Gilberto Picon," Thomas said. The IRS agent, nearing retirement, was closing in on the man who for years had reveled in his status as a fugitive tax cheat. "I was overjoyed. I knew we finally had a chance to nab him.

"We got the information earlier in the year and it took nearly the whole year to arrange through the Department of Justice and through the help we were getting from the Canadian authorities," Thomas continued. "It took that long to establish that he was there and we could do something about it. Even though it took a long time, we worked as hard as we could to do it and it all came together right at the end of the year." Finally, on December 20, 1996, nearly a decade after Ross first fled the United States, the Royal Canadian Mounted Police arrested him outside the Belize consul general's office.

Among the documents obtained by the Center from the IRS's files on Ross is a "wanted" poster, complete with a photo of the fugitive, his vital statistics, and a description of the charges for which he's wanted. Someone at the IRS celebrated Ross's capture by writing on the poster, in thick Magic Marker, "GOTCHA!" followed by that fateful December date.

But the celebration was premature. The millionaire fugitive hired Randall Ward, his Vancouver society acquaintance, to represent him at a bail hearing. Ward told Canadian judge Deborah Satanove that he had known Ross for years (albeit under the assumed name of Jay Picon). He insisted that his client wanted to settle his troubles with the IRS, and that his financial support of four local charities proved he wasn't a flight risk. Satanove released Ross—over the protest of Canadian prosecutors—sparing him even a night in jail. She also ordered him to post $50,000 cash bail, relinquish his Belize passport, and report to a bail supervisor once a week until his extradition hearing in January.

Ross dutifully showed up for the first four meetings, but he was a no-show on January 22. Canadian police called off their short-lived search after being informed by Pamella Picon that her husband had left a note indicating he was leaving the country. Joe Ross had successfully fled from another government.

"It's no secret to me now why all the draft evaders during the 1960s went there," Thomas said of Canada. "It's nearly impossible to extradite someone from there. You basically have to try them and present all the evidence, and their bail system there and the court system tends to err on the side of letting someone out pretty quickly." Thomas never believed that Ross had any intention of returning to America to address the charges against him. "He simply didn't want to stay around and waste his time arguing with a bunch of lawyers when he had the means and opportunity to live a wonderful life on his yacht or wherever he wanted to go."

By the end of January, Belize had rescinded Pamella Ross's diplomatic credentials and the Canadian government was threatening to deport her. So she followed her husband south. Randall Ward, the Rosses' attorney, was sorry to see her go. "She would have been the next dean of the consular corps here," he said. "It's funny how you can know people and not really know that much about their life stories."

Before fleeing Canada, Pamella Picon cleaned out her apartment and relegated the couple's furniture to storage (Canadian authorities, who apparently weren't interested in the armoire, seized Pam's limousine and a Mazda sports car). A Vancouver real estate broker, hired by an unnamed law firm, listed the condo for sale. Price tag: $675,000.

Pamella headed to Belize, where she joined her husband. Joseph Ross bragged that, despite his arrest, he was still the one in a thousand who could make his life as a fugitive a success. "He wrote several letters that we got a hold of talking about how he fooled everyone, that his capture in Canada was due to bad luck, and investigative work was not a factor," Thomas said. Noting that they only found Ross through an anonymous tip, he added, "Maybe he's right. He's still a free man."

That was as close as Thomas got to Ross. "This was all happening about thirty days before I retired," Thomas said of the Vancouver arrest and Ross's subsequent escape. "If I thought we could have kept him, I would have stayed on." While Thomas still carries a grudge against the one who got away, Ross has carved out quite a comfortable living in the tropical climate of Belize, a tax haven country that knows how to keep a secret about someone's bank accounts. The U.S. State Department made some effort to get authorities in Belize to return Ross, but got no results. "As it turned out, Joe's connection with the government in Belize was not just incidental, it was quite strong," Thomas said. "The Belizean lawyer who assisted in getting him out of there also happens to be the minister of justice and had a couple of other titles," he added, referring to Dean Barrows. In 1997, Barrows was the country's deputy prime minister, attorney general, minister of foreign affairs, minister of national security responsible for police and the Belize defense force, minister of immigration, and minister of information. In his spare time Barrows also practiced law, and he wisely put Ross's assets into a Belize trust to protect them from U.S. authorities. "He and Joe were business partners," Thomas said.

Newspaper accounts in February 1997 noted that Barrows was also helping the Rosses acquire property in Belize. The land they eventually purchased is in a mountainous region, just north of the Guatemalan border. It is from here that Ross and his wife operate their latest endeavor—a luxury resort in the wilds of Belize.

From the capital of Belize City, it's a two-hour drive to the tiny town of Benque Viejo. There, the traveler must wait for a ferry that will carry him across the Mopan River to the Rosses' new hideaway. The resort's brochure refers to the strange sensation of feeling incommunicado, with no phone in your room, no stores nearby, and no newspapers within reach. "Because the resort is accessible only by our private ferry or boat, it has an atmosphere of remoteness," the brochure boasts.

The so-called jungle lodges of the Cayo District are a relatively recent phenomenon in Belize. Francis Ford Coppola has a resort in the area called Biancaneux Lodge, but Mopan River Lodge is the newest. Designed by the Rosses, it sits on ten lush acres and abuts hundreds of miles of Guatemalan jungle. Belize's "first all-inclusive luxury resort," which opened in November 1999, features orange, fig, mango, banana, and other tropical trees on perfectly manicured grounds, with twelve thatched-roof, river-view cabanas and private, shaded verandas. Atop the hill, overlooking both the town and the resort's grounds, is the large, beautiful house that Joe and Pamella Ross now call home.

The 5,000-square-foot residence, with its high ceilings and striking, orange-tiled roof, is one of the most impressive in the country. All the building materials had to be transported across the Mopan River, adding considerably to the cost of construction. The remoteness of the resort hasn't prevented the Rosses from keeping up with world events, however. Their four-foot satellite dish brings them Direct TV, with 150 or so stations. They watch CNN daily. Ross reads the *Wall Street Journal, Time,* and *Newsweek.* Despite their estrangement from their native country, they are quite aware of news developments from the United States and around the world.

But most of their time is taken up with running their resort. Pamella sees to most of the details, including planning the three gourmet meals served each day. Ross himself, known to his guests as "Jay," is affable and warm, full of folksy, Oklahoma charm and ever the host. He conducts tours to nearby points of interest. Xunantunich is a 1,000-year-old Mayan ruin with a 120-foot-high pyramid offering a spectacular view of Guatemala. Ross climbs every step with his guests—not bad for a seventy-six-year-old man. None has a clue that he is an international fugitive.

In December 1999, the Center visited Ross at his Belizean lodge. "Hello, I'm Gilberto Picon," he said, his hand outstretched. "I must be pretty damn important for you to travel halfway around the world to come see me," he added with a twinkle in his eye and a smile. Nonetheless, he declined to sit for a formal interview. "I won, so why do I need to talk to anyone?" he asked. "There's no use in gloating."

And indeed, it's clear that Ross has won. With a beautiful wife by his side, twenty-five cheap workers he hires and fires, and a spectacular home and resort, he is the master of his own universe. The Third World ambiance, with its intrinsic difficulties, is still a reality he can substantially dominate. The poverty around him is not his poverty; Ross believes that he is helping some of the Belizeans—and he is.

He and Pamella advertise their resort on the Internet; Frommer's, the travel book publisher, visited the Mopan River Lodge in its first month of operation in preparation for a feature in a forthcoming guidebook. Pamella is the editor and publisher of an annual tourist booklet called *Belize Report*. The compilation of outstanding Belizean restaurants, hotels, resorts, and diving expeditions is even on the Internet, complete with links to tourist sites, offshore banking advisers, and articles explaining how to become a citizen of the small country. Naturally, you can send them e-mail.

Thomas, who retired in January 1997, just after Ross slipped through his fingers for the second time, takes some comfort in the failed Vancouver attempt to bring the millionaire to justice. "It brought me some satisfaction that we interrupted his Canadian sunset there at the end," he said.

"I regret I never got to meet him face-to-face. I'm thinking about sending him an e-mail and telling him it's not over until it's over. I doubt he'll be much frightened by that, but then again, I don't think he ever expected to be found and arrested in Canada either.

"He still got away and he's still got his money."

13

What You Can Do

Frustrated that the wealthy can find ways to avoid paying their fair share? That movie moguls move profits offshore, *Forbes* 400 members play the code like a fiddle to lower their taxable income to zero, and that one tax evader, a former government contractor, lives the good life in Belize without a care in the world? Does it seem like only the rich can avoid their taxes, and why can't someone in the middle class ever get away with it?

That may sound like a pitch for the latest book or Internet site touting dubious tax avoidance methods, but there's a good reason not to try them yourself. Just ask the Skalas.

For more than a dozen years, Christopher Skala and his wife, Nuris, ran a video production firm in Charlotte, North Carolina, called Television Innovation Company, Incorporated, that produced instructional videos. Skala also served as a producer for a number of British sitcoms—most notably *Brighton Belles,* which tried to export the geriatric charm of *Golden Girls* to the British Isles. The couple had built his company into a lucrative venture. From 1994 to 1995, according to the Internal Revenue Service, the Skalas' company had increased its revenues from more than $300,000 to slightly less than $1 million.

During that time, they moved much of their profits—more than $531,000 in the two-year span—into a pair of trusts, which, they had been promised, would substantially reduce their taxable income.

A trust is a legal arrangement that allows an owner, the grantor, in legal parlance, to transfer the title of his assets to an independent entity. A trustee manages the assets for the trust's beneficiary, who is chosen by the grantor. The trustee has a fiduciary duty to ensure that the beneficiary's interests are protected. Under the Internal Revenue Code, a trust owes taxes in much the same way a regular taxpayer does.

If it earns income, it must pay taxes.

In 1994, the Skalas heard about a series of seminars offered by National Trust Services, a Missouri-based firm that promised to protect their assets from lawsuits and provide a tax benefit. The firm claimed on its Internet site that "Trusts are taxable entities but many taxes can be deferred by the ability to distribute cash and assets between the trusts." After attending a seminar, the couple hired National Trust and paid it $10,000 to set up their two trusts.

The Skalas frequently called National Trust Services representatives for help with their two trusts. They found out how to transfer income from their business, how they could deduct all their personal expenses from the trusts' income. At tax time, they used a National Trust accountant to prepare their returns. In 1994, the Skalas filed a return claiming $37,331 in income. The next year, their return showed they had lost $1,984. Their National Trust–recommended accountant claimed the Earned Income Tax Credit, intended to help the working poor, for their two children. The Skalas were satisfied that the low taxes they paid were "legal and acceptable."

The IRS disagreed. When the Service audited their 1994 and 1995 returns, the Skalas turned again to National Trust Services for advice. They were referred to Frank Kowalik, who they were told was an expert in dealing with the IRS. He's an expert of sorts; in 1984, he told the Center, he was jailed for refusing to file a tax return. Kowalik is a tax protestor, and a relatively famous one at that. Like the self-proclaimed offshore tax haven guru Jerome Schneider, he's written a book

254   THE CHEATING OF AMERICA

on his area of expertise, called *IRS Humbug: Weapons of Enslavement*, that can be purchased from a few dozen sites on the Internet. He claims that the Sixteenth Amendment, interpreted literally, applies only to federal workers. "If you're not a federal government employee and you file a 1040 form, the federal government accepts your money as a gift," he said.

When contacted by the Center, Kowalik emphatically denied having anything to do with either National Trust Services or the Skalas. Twice. "I never advised anybody to do anything," he said. Eventually he admitted that the Skalas contacted him directly. "They got us into the act to help with what they were doing; they needed somebody to help them make a response to the IRS," he said.

Kowalik told them to make no response at all. He advised them to refuse to sign for certified mail from the IRS, or answer letters or phone calls from auditors. If agents did manage to reach them, he told them to answer any questions with a series of their own questions. The Skalas took the advice. Then, in July 1998, the Service slapped them with a Notice of Deficiency for taxes and penalties for more than $991,000.

"There were criminal fraud charges brought against us," Nuris Skala said, "but they were all dropped." That's because the Skalas hired a tax attorney, one not connected with National Trust Services, who filed a petition in U.S. Tax Court claiming the couple had been victimized. "The Skalas were victims of an elaborate and sophisticated 'tax protestor' organization, and did not commit fraud or negligence in reporting their income or expenses. . . . [T]he Skalas have reasonable cause for the deficiency, and should not be charged any negligence, fraud, or other penalties."

Abraham R. Brown, who represented the Skalas, said, "The IRS just asks the taxpayer to redo the returns." The Skalas, who in all their years of paying taxes had never had a problem with the IRS prior to hiring National Trust Services, refiled their returns, and paid what they owed.

Abusive trust and shelter schemes have proliferated in the last few years, and both the IRS civil and criminal divisions have tried to crack down on promoters of illegitimate schemes that promise tax-free living but instead provide tax nightmares for the people who buy into them. There are certain warning signs—the Service calls them "red flags"— that should alert any potential taxpayer that a tax planner's services are too good to be true. Promises that an individual can deduct the cost of his residence or his children's education expenses are sure signs something's amiss. There are also advertising slogans that should make a taxpayer wary, including the ever-popular line, "The IRS doesn't want you to know about this."

The IRS maintains a hotline for individuals to check the claims of tax shelter promoters, and report abusive operators. The Service encourages individuals who've just been told something that sounds too good to be true—a lifetime of living without paying taxes—to run the scheme by them. They can tell you whether or not a scheme will get you charged, as the Skalas were, with criminal fraud.

But beyond ensuring that your own return is "true, correct, and complete," as the bottom of Form 1040 makes you avow, under penalty of perjury, when you sign it, there is not a great deal you can do to limit tax avoidance and evasion. You can refuse to pay cash for services. If an auto mechanic or a plumber or an accountant who does bookkeeping for you in his spare time asks to be paid in cash, it's quite possible he might not report some or all of the amount you paid on his tax return. It may seem penny-ante, but collectively, what the IRS calls, "informal suppliers" and a closely related group, sole proprietors, who have businesses in which they are paid partially or primarily in cash cheat the government out of some $29.2 billion a year.

Payments by check or credit card both leave paper trails; cash, by contrast, can be used without detection by the IRS. Someone who doesn't deposit the fees he earns in a bank account can spend it without fear of the Service discovering it. By insisting on writing a check or using a credit card, you can ensure that the people you do business with will be more likely to report their earnings accurately to the IRS.

More and more Americans own stock, and if you happen to be one of them, you are entitled to receive copies of each corporation's Form 10K, the annual report it files with the Securities and Exchange Commission. Unlike the glossy annual reports that tout the company's achievements in the past year, Forms 10K—which are generally printed on cheap paper in small type—include information on the taxes the company expects to pay. The figures in the Form 10K don't necessarily accurately reflect what the company will pay, but rather represent the company's good faith estimate of the amount of taxes it will owe from its operations. Buried in the notes at the end of the report, the company will explain whether it paid taxes at the federal statutory rate and, if not, why not.

As a shareholder, of course, you have a vested interest in the company's performance, but not everything that helps its bottom line helps yours. As the percentage of the tax burden paid by corporations has dropped dramatically in the last half century, individuals have had to pick up more and more of the tab. Think of it this way: the taxes that a company you own doesn't pay come out of your pocket.

Corporations don't always have the best interests of their shareholders first and foremost in their minds, but that shouldn't prevent you from writing the company to express your displeasure. You might be told that the company had in fact paid more in taxes than it claimed in its 10K, or it might convince you that all the deductions it took were proper. But as an investor, if you have any doubt that the company you own a piece of is paying its fair share of taxes, you can always take your money elsewhere.

Of course, that would be easier to determine if corporations, like charities and some nonprofit groups, were obligated to make their tax returns public. Any number of commentators have argued that the strength of American companies and financial institutions relative to other nations is a result of the transparency—the amount of information corporations, banks, and the like must make public. If corporate tax returns were public, investors would have another tool to determine whether the glowing earnings statements companies like to release had any basis in reality. For the truth of the matter is that many profitable companies tell the public one thing and the IRS something else entirely. Corporations might be less willing to engage in elaborate tax shelters if they had to reconcile the bottom lines they report to the public with the ones they report confidentially to the government.

While these few modest suggestions might help a little, the fact remains that tax avoidance and evasion costs the government more than $195 billion a year, and if the past if any prologue, that number will continue to grow.

Conclusion

 Taxes are as old as recorded time. Indeed, as Charles Adams wrote in *For Good and Evil*, "the three roots of modern civilization—ancient Greece, Rome, and Israel—involved histories filled with drama centered on taxation." Not only have many of the great upheavals of history been tax related, but the American independence movement was founded when colonists began meeting with one another to protest the Stamp Act taxes.

There can be no taxes, of course, without something of value to assess. From the first days that *Homo sapiens* walked the planet, they have accumulated wealth, in the broadest sense. And the accumulation and concentration of wealth has always occurred alongside the relative absence of it. The perpetual challenge of public governance is how to achieve fairness and consensus between the wealthiest and the poorest of society. The extent to which that difficult equilibrium actually exists can sometimes be gauged by who really pays the taxes, and how much.

As we have shown in *The Cheating of America*, many of the nation's wealthiest individuals and its largest corporations are *not* paying their fair share of taxes today. Beyond that disturbing fact, it is no secret that the United States now has the widest gap between rich and poor of any industrialized country. One percent of the population controls 40 percent of America's assets. More billionaires have been created in the last fifteen years than during any other time in U.S. history. At mid-year 2000, the economy was growing at a sizzling rate of 5.8 percent a year, generating $1.5 billion worth of new wealth each day. That is enough to create sixty-two new millionaires every hour.

At the same time, the number of "full-time, year-round workers" living in poverty shot up 459,000 in 1998 to 2.8 million, the biggest such increase in U.S. history. Between 1995 and 1998, mean net worth dropped for the lowest income group and increased for all other income groups, with the largest gain for families with incomes of $100,000 and above. One American child in five today lives in poverty. And the number of bankruptcy cases has increased almost 70 percent since 1995.

Generally, the least-advantaged Americans are also our least-enfranchised citizens politically, neither substantially contributing to political campaigns nor voting. Ordinary citizens are in no position financially to hire Washington lobbyists to attempt to influence U.S. tax policy or urge greater enforcement of the current tax laws. Poor and middle-class taxpayers are not organized en masse as an interest group. They do not have a telegenic spokesperson omnipresent in national news media coverage. They possess neither the carefully marshaled information nor the access to influence policymakers.

Against this stark dichotomy today, to what extent are our federal government officials maintaining the equilibrium between the wealthiest and the poorest segments of society?

Well, the United States does have a progressive tax system, in which the wealthiest citizens pay a higher percentage of their annual income in taxes, and, as we have noted, more than a million Americans making $200,000 or more do in fact pay their taxes. But at the same time, *thousands* of the most affluent individuals and corporations routinely avoid and evade paying billions of dollars in taxes each year. And the level of unabashed greed seems to be increasing. Everyone from the principals of the largest accounting, law, and brokerage firms to the sleaziest, fly-by-night Internet shysters are promoting offshore, cyberspace, and other avoidance schemes, and many of the most respected corporations and individuals are heeding their advice. There is no more audacious example of today's tax-shirking shenanigans that we could have cited than ex-con Jerome Schneider, author of *The Complete Guide to Offshore Money Havens*, who wrote, "It helps to realize that the [IRS] audit process is not so much an investigation as it is a negotiation. Your tax return was like your first offer to the IRS."

If you have a team of paid accountants and lawyers, Schneider is unfortunately correct. Most Americans, of course, can't afford such high-priced talent, and are practically terrified at the prospect of being audited. But hundreds of the best tax minds in the nation, including former commissioners and other ex-IRS officials, reap millions of dollars annually by helping the largest corporations and wealthiest citizens avoid paying their fair share of taxes. They overwhelm and wear down the IRS staff, dragging tax cases out literally sometimes for ten to twenty years, typically settling with the government in the end for pennies on the dollar of what they actually owe. Recall the disconcerting words of an IRS lawyer who told us, "When there are ten thousand documents, some of which are bank statements containing thousands of transactions, and the opposition argues over the significance of every single item, the process becomes extraordinarily difficult." The attorney, who requested anonymity for obvious reasons, added, *"Why do you think we go after the little guys? They can't fight back."*

In other words, it is well known, both inside and outside of government, that the Internal Revenue Service cannot stop this annual hemorrhage of major potential income to the U.S. Treasury, due to tax avoidance and evasion by the nation's most powerful and privileged interests. The IRS commissioner acknowledges that nearly $200 billion a year in taxable income is not being paid; the actual number is likely much higher.

Given the extent of this problem, then, perhaps the most surprising finding of *The Cheating of America* is the lackadaisical nonresponse by federal officials, from Congress to the White House, from the Office of

Management and Budget to the Justice Department to the Internal Revenue Service. Instead of increasing the number of revenue agents and auditors, instead of increasing examinations of individual tax returns, instead of finding ways to prosecute more tax cheats, exactly the *opposite* is occurring.

From fiscal year 1989 to 1999, while the total number of individual tax returns filed jumped 14 percent (from 107 million to 122 million), the number of permanent IRS employees dropped 26 percent (from 111,980 to 82,563). The president and Congress also cut the number of IRS Office of Examination staff, including revenue agents and tax auditors, by 34 percent, from 31,315 to 20,736. Not surprisingly, the percentage of audits of Americans keeps declining each year. Worse, under political pressure, the IRS is auditing poor people more often than well-heeled taxpayers. And tax-related prosecutions are half what they were nearly twenty years ago.

Why, in the face of garish flouting of the nation's tax laws, would our public officials reduce the resources available to enforce those laws? Why would they sharply reduce the number of revenue agents, auditors, and, over time, taxpayer audits? Why would they reduce by half the number of tax-related criminal prosecutions?

To try to get some answers, we requested an on-the-record interview with Charles O. Rossotti, the commissioner of internal revenue. But he declined to talk with us.

Is it entirely coincidental that as presidential and congressional campaign costs have skyrocketed into the billions of dollars—political careers brought to you by the wealthiest 4 percent of America—the tax enforcement dogs have been called off of the wealthiest individuals and corporations? Is it remotely possible that the political parties and their top politicians who control Washington have been told repeatedly by their powerful patrons that they don't particularly appreciate being pestered by persistent revenue agents, auditors, and prosecutors?

We don't know how to explain this intriguing confluence of circumstances, and our public officials would no doubt be shocked at *any* suggestion that they do not fully favor enforcing the nation's tax laws. But how else would they explain these odd, but compelling, facts? Getting a straight, dead-honest answer to any inconvenient political question these days is nearly impossible, certainly, but that does not mean that we should stop asking them. These curious facts confound easy, pat, ideological dogma. Conservatives, for example, have never seen a government agency voluntarily slash thousands of its own employees from the public payroll—and no one is suggesting the IRS is different from any other bureaucracy in that regard. And liberals, not known for being "tough on crime," have watched the Justice Department nearly double in size in the past decade and probably cannot fathom why the level of any type of tax-related federal prosecutions has declined.

So we have a series of questions that no one in Washington is particularly able or anxious to answer. The first prescriptive remedy toward even attempting to achieve the above-described equilibrium between the wealthiest and the poorest segments of society when it comes to taxes is very simple: demand that our elected representatives answer our questions. Why have tax return examinations and enforcement efforts decreased at the IRS in recent years? How serious are our federal officials in both parties, at both ends of Pennsylvania Avenue, about upholding the current tax laws today for all Americans? Politicians should be asked bluntly whether or not they favor increased enforcement of the existing tax laws. Do they think the poor should be audited more often than the rich? Should billionaires be able to renounce their U.S. citizenship in order to avoid taxes, and still be able to return home for months on end because the law barring their reentry is rarely, if ever, enforced?

Expect considerable squirming, hemming, and hawing. They're not used to getting such direct questions, whether from the public or the news media. But not until there is a serious, honest dialogue in this country about the thousands of wealthy individuals and corporations who don't pay their fair share of taxes will the cold winter of silence, obfuscation, and denial begin to thaw. It's great to conduct public hearings in Washington featuring tearful anecdotes about how ordinary taxpayers have been harshly treated by IRS officials, and it's great that new legislation was enacted increasing taxpayers' rights to redress wrongs committed against them. Who is against that? But how about a traditional congressional investigation into the issues raised here? Why, when it comes to paying taxes and being audited or prosecuted, do certain members of our society lead charmed lives?

Even if you assume the absolute worst in answering these questions, and thus succeed in elevating your blood pressure, the entire tax fairness subject is further complicated by our own deep personal ambivalence. On the most basic level, it is counterintuitive—indeed, almost heretical—to yearn for better enforcement of the tax laws, even in the name of fairness. Let's face it—no one particularly enjoys paying his or her taxes. And the tax collector consistently has earned the contempt of citizens of all societies for centuries.

Throughout the ages, raising revenue frequently has been a brutally repressive and corrupt means of controlling the populace and maintaining power. And citizens have sometimes fled their country in protest, or vented their intense anger directly at the tax collector. Weeks before the 1989 Tiananmen Square massacre in China, for instance, the official government newspaper, the *People's Daily*, reported that tax evasion was widespread. Over the preceding two years, thirteen income tax agents had been murdered, and over 7,000 had been injured by rebelling taxpayers.

Over the years, this intense, universal anger about taxes and those people with the unenviable job of collecting them has produced at times a somewhat perverse, corollary effect—admiration for the tax evader. In his 1776 classic, *The Wealth of Nations*, Adam Smith did not regard tax evasion as a crime. Indeed, he believed the tax evader is:

> in every respect, an excellent citizen, had not the laws of his country made that a crime which nature never meant to be so. In those corrupted governments where there is at least a general suspicion of much unnecessary expense, and great misapplica-

tion of the public revenue, the laws which guard it are little respected.

One of the reasons we have conflicted feelings about tax evasion is, frankly, because so many people at all levels subtly cheat on their taxes, from dubious deductions to underreporting cash earnings to . . . you name it. Beloved humorist Will Rogers once said, "the income tax has made more liars out of the American people than golf has." No improvement of the U.S. tax laws and their enforcement, of course, will ever completely eliminate human greed and fraud. And as citizens, because of our historic ambivalence about taxes, tax collectors, and the power of the state, it is difficult to muster great enthusiasm for increasing the number and resources for government auditors and prosecutors. That is certainly understandable, and this natural reticence of the populace partly explains why no one is really protesting the tepid enforcement of tax laws for certain individuals and corporations.

The central issue of *The Cheating of America*, and the subject a majority of Americans are frustrated about today, is tax fairness. Does our tax system and the Internal Revenue Service's enforcement of tax laws today maintain the equilibrium between the wealthiest and the poorest segments of society? Clearly not. Two-thirds of Americans already viscerally recognize this. They're convinced that upper-income taxpayers do not pay their fair share, and the information presented in this book affirms that sense.

Unfortunately, the opportunities for avoidance and evasion by our most fortunate citizens and corporations are increasing exponentially, because of the forces of technology and globalization.

On the most basic geopolitical and economic levels, the balance of power between governments and corporations clearly has shifted. As Hans-Peter Martin and Harald Schumann wrote in the international bestseller *The Global Trap*, today democratically elected governments can no longer dictate the level of taxes. Instead, "the people who direct the flow of capital and goods themselves establish what contribution they wish to make to state expenditure." For example, in April 1996, at a dinner with Bundestag deputies, Jurgen Schrempp, the chairman of Daimler-Benz A.G., announced that his company would no longer be paying to Germany any taxes on profits. "You won't be getting any more from us," he told the members of the German parliament.

Similarly, because of the exploding technologies and their inability to regulate cyberspace, governments today find themselves impotent to tax trillions of dollars in potential new revenue from electronic commerce. As one aptly titled book, *The Sovereign Individual*, put it, "anyone with a portable computer and a satellite link will be able to conduct almost any information business anywhere, and that includes almost the whole of the world's multi-trillion-dollar financial transactions. This means that you will no longer be obliged to live in a high-tax jurisdiction in order to earn high income. . . . Cyberspace is the ultimate offshore jurisdiction. An economy with no taxes. Bermuda in the sky with diamonds."

So besides corporations and individuals tax shopping around the world and utilizing creative bookkeeping—which they have been doing increasingly for decades—the new technologies further enable those who are hell-bent on outright criminal evasion to achieve it. Not only is cyberspace the final frontier of finance, it is also a growing safe haven for secrecy. With the emerging encryption technologies, financial transactions are becoming virtually impossible to track by the authorities. Since foreign income is often undetectable, people now more than ever—without leaving home—can choose where to officially "domicile" their business activities and the extent to which they choose to pay income tax.

And the combination of offshore banks and cyberspace is the ultimate elixir to tax evaders and others. Today, there are more than 3 million corporations operating worldwide with no identifiable owner. Virtually untaxable, offshore bank deposits (not just from U.S. citizens) are now estimated at $3 trillion, and rising. The offshore destination of choice is the Cayman Islands, with 585 banks and $700 billion in deposits. Meanwhile, the British Virgin Islands has over 370,000 "anonymous" corporations. The IRS estimates there are sixty to ninety jurisdictions today offering "offshore services."

But consider the haunting case of the now defunct European Union Bank of Antigua, which billed itself "the world's first Internet bank." Owned by Russians with ties to organized crime, the bank was chartered by the corrupt government of Antigua. It had two purposes: to serve as a "cutout" to conceal the origin and destination of funds coming from the former Soviet Union, and to solicit deposits on the Web. Most of the depositors were Americans evading U.S. taxes.

As it turned out, the computer server was in Washington, D.C. The man operating the "bank"—and the personal computer he relied on—were in Montreal, Canada. And depositors were strewn all over the world. The bank collapsed when money was "loaned" to a mysterious Bahamian shell company, and then disappeared. Depositors lost $15 million.

Former Senate investigator and Washington lawyer Jack Blum, who is a consultant on bank secrecy and financial havens to the United Nations and the IRS, testified before Congress about the EUB affair. "Who has jurisdiction in cases like the European Union Bank? Where was the crime committed? Which country should pay for the investigation and where should the offenders be prosecuted and imprisoned? These jurisdictional problems are reaching crisis proportions," he said in his testimony. Years earlier, in the late 1980s, Blum was instrumental in uncovering the notorious Bank of Credit and Commerce International (BCCI) fraud in twenty-six countries. He told the Center that now, because of the virtual nature of money, and the amazing speed with which offshore cybercriminals can operate and disappear, government-to-government, international cooperation is ineffectual and outmoded.

"Traditional law enforcement tools simply don't work," he said in an interview. "We need an entirely new international system. . . . This is *the* issue of the future."

Most of the anecdotes in *The Cheating of America* involve "good old-fashioned" tax avoidance and evasion, gleaned from thousands of pages of U.S. Tax Court records filed over the past decade. And those traditional tax avoidance schemes and crimes, as we have discussed, are frankly beyond the current competence and budget of the Internal Revenue Service. The full dimension of the tax fairness crisis becomes much clearer when viewed in the context of globalization and the new technologies. Money today has no real home, and those with the most money will be the most aggressive and proficient at hiding it from government authorities. The rest of us, not inclined or able to afford access to offshore havens or cybertax avoidance schemes, will continue paying our taxes, in full.

All of which means that, unless something is done very soon, we may lose even the pretense of maintaining the equilibrium between the wealthiest and the poorest segments of American society. Cynicism about the United States as a government *of the people, by the people and for the people* will rise inexorably.

In August 1864, in the closing months of the Civil War, the first U.S. president to implement an income tax, Abraham Lincoln, said: "It is fair that each man shall pay taxes in exact proportion to the value of his property; but if we should wait before collecting a tax to adjust the taxes upon each man in exact proportion with every other man, we should never collect any tax at all."

Then and today, the government muddles forward, year after year, collecting taxes in an inexact manner. We, as a people—call us "the little people"—complain and correctly perceive that this imprecision favors wealthier folks over us. The rich and the large corporations are more able to exploit the loopholes than we are. In fact, their lawyers and lobbyists wrote those loopholes. When wealthier folks do more than exploit those loopholes, and actually cross the line from avoiding to evading taxes, chances are nobody will be going to prison.

But despite the fundamental unfairness of it all, despite our simmering outrage, we also intuitively know that no civilization and no government can exist without taxes. And so we keep on paying them, because whether or not we want to admit it, despite the many imperfections, we like living in the United States of America. As nation-states go, and probably as long as nation-states exist, this is still the best show on Earth.

And taxes are the price of admission.

Acknowledgments

Back in 1996, we first began exploring the unbridled greed of some of America's most famous, affluent citizens, and how it had driven them to shortchange their fellow citizens. Daniel Suleiman, an enormously talented Center researcher from Harvard, was assigned that summer to do "reconnaissance research" into this subject. Within days, via the Internet, we were intrigued and amused at how easily he could become a citizen of Belize—for a fee, of course.

Our literary agent, Esther Newberg, of International Creative Management, really liked the book proposal to "investigate, identify, and confront some of the nation's wealthiest individuals and corporations for dodging taxes that nearly everyone else pays." So did three major New York publishers, none more than HarperCollins. For two and a half years, a Center investigative team ultimately comprising about a dozen people analyzed thousands of pages of U.S. Tax Court records—a task not for the faint of heart. We also studied other federal government documents; we sifted through thousands of news stories from around the nation, including some in terrific—but little-known—places such as *Tax Notes*; and we interviewed hundreds of government officials, lawyers, accountants, and others. What's more, we immersed ourselves in the most insightful, mass-market, tax-related books of the past thirty years, including the late Phil Stern's 1972 bestseller *The Rape of the Taxpayer*; Donald L. Barlett and James B. Steele's *America: Who Really Pays the Taxes?*; and Charles Adams's *For Good and Evil: The Impact of Taxes on the Course of Civilization.*

As systematically as possible, tethered substantially to U.S. Tax Court filings, we compiled a list of perhaps the thirty most interesting individuals or corporations to have crossed the IRS enforcement radar screen. We discussed the merits of our findings in formal meetings virtually every Monday morning. Case studies that had been written about too extensively, or too long ago, or with little supporting court documentation, were dismissed as not interesting to us. After much deliberation, the list was culled further. Finally, some people and companies became the subjects of full chapter profiles, while others were profiled in sections or paragraphs in chapters.

Subsequently, we traveled far and wide to better understand our profile subjects, from Beverly Hills to Peoria, from the jungle of Belize to the gated community of Lyford Cay in the Bahamas.

Many of those profiled in *The Cheating of America* unfortunately declined our requests to be interviewed, which was not exactly surprising. Given our organization's name and past work, those on the receiving end of our calls or letters generally understand that we are not seeking an interview for a breezy magazine feature. Indeed, to the people we contacted for this book, the act of paying taxes itself was probably a more appealing prospect than sitting down and answering our pesky, inconvenient questions.

We have conducted more than sixty investigations at the Center for Public Integrity since 1990, and *The Cheating of America* is our eighth commercially published book since 1995. The Center has become an unprecedented incubator of ambitious, investigative books, and the entire staff, led by managing director Peter Eisner, helped in innumerable ways to enable our work. But when it comes to acknowledging the fine work of specific people, let us not forget a fundamental reality:

because of the astonishingly dense thicket that the subject of taxes presents to any investigator or writer, this book posed the most formidable challenge to us to date.

No one contributed more than project manager Bill Allison. Without him and his fearless curiosity, acute intelligence, and dogged perseverance, we might still be mired in the peculiarities of the tax laws and the seemingly impenetrable maze of arcane court cases. But his significant contribution to this project was hardly surprising, given his years at the *Philadelphia Inquirer*, working with two-time Pulitzer Prize–winning investigative journalists Donald Barlett and James Steele, and his great reporting and writing for *The Buying of the Congress* and *The Buying of the President 2000*.

Four writers accompanying Bill and me into the heart of darkness were Paul Cuadros, Erin Bartels, Melanie Strong, and Derrick Wetherell. Melanie and Derrick worked steadfastly on *The Cheating of America* as indefatigable, intrepid investigators and chroniclers for nearly the duration of the entire endeavor, and thus composed the heart of the day-to-day team, along with Bill. At different stages, we got exceptional research assistance from Adrianne Hari, Arfa Mahmoud, Myra Marcaurelle, Ann Parker, Daniel Suleiman, and Vicki Velasquez.

For the reasons stated earlier, this project required more editing attention than most. *The Cheating of America* benefited along the way from two editors—former director of investigative projects Bill Hogan and, in the crucial final months, veteran journalist Alan Green. Alan had just won the Investigative Reporters and Editors book award for his 1999 Center exposé *Animal Underworld*, and he moved seamlessly into this difficult assignment and brought it home with aplomb.

In a book with thousands of facts, we are especially indebted to our fact-checkers, who had a lonely, overwhelming task. No one does it better, anywhere, than Center research editor Peter Newbatt Smith. For this book, he was assisted by Neil Gordon and Amy Zader.

Special thanks to Washington lawyer and IRS consultant Jack

Blum, who for years has been wonderfully supportive of the idea and the reality of the Center for Public Integrity. Jack is a well-known, internationally respected expert on offshore tax havens, money laundering, and global financial crime. The idea for this book arose following a memorable lunch conversation with this former Senate investigator and rare man of conscience. I also want to thank local reporters Karla Heusner in Belize City and Deborah Nash in the Bahamas for their magnificent on-the-ground assistance during my research there.

I want to thank our legendary agent, Esther Newberg—this is our first book together. And we are grateful to our thoughtful, unflinching attorney, Marc Miller, of McLeod, Watkinson & Miller, who has scrutinized every word to come out of the Center since the first report in December 1990.

Center development director Barbara Schecter and development associate Megan Vaughan felt like they were trying to bleed a turnip—more than usual—when it came to seeking support for this investigative project. The Center does not accept contributions from governments, corporations, labor unions, or advocacy organizations, nor does it accept revenue from advertising. We could hardly find a foundation or an individual with any remote interest in the broad subject of tax fairness, which meant the Center's general funds were required to foot more than $200,000 in expenses beyond the publisher's advance. Without our general support contributors, this book would not have been possible; the Center's major donors are listed on the Web site, at *www.publicintegrity.org.*

We are extremely grateful to the lonely, courageous folks who *did* help defray our research costs for *The Cheating of America.* Special thanks to Mike Lapham, the Daniel Solomon Tzedakah Fund of the Shefa Fund, and David Stern and Tracey Hughes of the Stern Family Fund. I well remember reading *The Rape of the Taxpayer* when Philip Stern wrote it back in the 1970s, and being inspired by its informed populism. Life takes interesting turns. In 1988, while at *60 Minutes* on an investigative political story, I had the great privilege of meeting him.

Few people in this country have been more dedicated supporters of investigative reporting than Phil Stern, who helped to start the Fund for Investigative Journalism (on whose board I proudly serve today), and who also served on the board of the Center for Investigative Reporting. During the two years before his untimely death in 1992, the support of the Stern Family Fund helped get the Center for Public Integrity through its leanest, start-up years.

Phil Stern told me at the time that he believed he was helping to create an important new institution. So imagine the delicious, uncanny symmetry that I have since had the great pleasure of getting to know Phil's remarkable public-interest lawyer son, David, and David's wife, Tracey. And when we could not find anyone to support this important investigative reporting, they and the Stern Family Fund stepped forward, as gutsy, generous contributors.

Beyond all of these wonderful people, as always, I want to express my sincere gratitude to the Center's outstanding board of directors and advisory board for their encouragement and insight over the years.

Last, and most important, all of us on the *The Cheating of America* adventure would like to thank our families and close friends for their remarkable patience and understanding. For me, once again my mother, Dorothy Lewis, my wife, Pamela Gilbert, and my daughter, Cassandra Lewis, continued their spectacular, unstinting support for this odd work I do. All of our loved ones countenanced our babbling about obscure tax provisions and the latest tax evasion and avoidance anecdotes, not to mention our long nights and weekends away from them.

Charles Lewis
June 1, 2000
Washington, D.C.

Source Notes

PROLOGUE

Leona Helmsley's tax evasion trial and conviction were well documented in the popular press. In particular, we relied on reports from the *Washington Times, Chicago Tribune, The Record* (Hackensack, N.J.), *St. Louis Post-Dispatch*, and the *Washington Post* during the latter part of 1989.

INTRODUCTION

The continued fascination with the television show *Dallas* and the Southfork Ranch have been captured in numerous articles over the years. Information about the Southfork Ranch and its parent company, Forever Resorts, came largely from press reports and the organizations' respective Web sites, *www.southforkranch.com* and *www.foreverresorts. com*. Especially helpful were Sheryl Smith-Rodgers's July 5, 1998, article in the *Houston Chronicle* and Diana Scott's March 10, 1996, *Sunday Telegram* (Worcester, Mass.) article.

For background on Rex Maughan and his company, Forever Living Products International, we consulted numerous magazine and newspaper sources, including Duncan Maxwell Anderson's interview with Maughan in *Success*, September 1995, and Christopher Palmeri's August 14, 1995, *Forbes* article, as well as Forever Living Products' Web site, *www.foreverlivingproducts.com*.

Information on Rex Maughan and his company's tax struggles with the Internal Revenue Service comes from several cases filed in U.S. Tax Court: *Rex G. Maughan and Ruth G. Maughan v. Commissioner,* Docket No. 23130-94; *Selective Art, Inc. & Subsidiary, Deco Container Print, Inc., formerly Forever Living Products, Inc. & Subsidiary, Deco Container Print, Inc. v. Commissioner*, Docket No. 23129-94; and *Selective Art, Inc. v. Commissioner*, Docket No. 26338-96.

We relied on several books, articles, and Internet sources in documenting the history of tax evasion in the United States. Robert M. Willan's *Income Taxes: Concise History and Primer* (Claitor's Publishing Division, 1993) was extremely helpful in documenting the numerous changes in the tax code. Donald L. Barlett and James B. Steele's *America: Who Really Pays the Taxes?* (Simon & Schuster, 1994) provided much valuable information on the changes in the income tax system, as well as several anecdotes of evasion. We are also grateful to Tax Analysts Online (*www.tax.org*) for its very thorough and often in-depth discussion of tax history in its Tax History Project. Also helpful in writing this section were Charles Adams's *For Good and Evil* (Madison Books, 1993), Ron Chernow's *The House of Morgan* (Touchstone, 1990), and the Department of Treasury's (*www.ustreas.gov*) Learning Vault.

In discussing corporate tax rates, we cited the Department of Treasury's white paper "The Problem of Corporate Tax Shelters: Discussion, Analysis and Legislative Proposals," issued in July 1999, as well as William Greider's *One World, Ready or Not: The Manic Logic of Global Capitalism* (Simon & Schuster, 1997). We also cited data and processed numbers from the 1995 Corporate Income Tax Returns annual, published by the IRS's Statistics of Income Division. David Cay Johnston published several articles in the *New York Times* that were helpful in the sections on corporate income tax and individual audit rates. We used data from the 1995 Individual Income Tax Returns annual, published by the IRS's Statistics of Income Division, and audit rate analysis from an April 1996 General Accounting Office report, "Tax Administration: Audit Trends and Results for Individual Taxpayers." Also cited in the introduction were Jerome Schneider's *The Complete Guide to Offshore Money Havens: How to Make Millions, Protect Your Privacy, and Legally Avoid Taxes*, revised and updated 3rd ed. (Prima Publishing, 2000) and James Dale Davidson and Lord William Rees-Mogg's *The Sovereign Individual* (Simon & Schuster, 1997).

1: NO MORE THAN A LIVING

The information about Jane Morgan came from a small Tax Court case (those involving disputed amounts of $50,000 or less). Like many other average Americans the Center interviewed in the more than two years spent researching this book, Ms. Morgan preferred that we not use her real name. Some cited fear of future IRS retaliation when they declined to speak to us, others feared that their friends, coworkers, and neighbors would think that they had done something unethical or illegal, and still others did not want details of their personal finances revealed in a commercially published book. In all cases, the Center respected the wishes of those ordinary, private citizens who preferred not to have their tax returns scrutinized a second time, in a far more public way.

For historical information on the tax code, Robert M. Willan's 1994 book *Income Taxes: A Concise History and Primer* (Claitor's Publishing Division, 1993) proved invaluable. Tax Analysts, a nonprofit organization based in Alexandria, Virginia, was also an amazing source of information on the history of the Internal Revenue Code. Its Tax History Project, an archive of documents from the twentieth century ranging from presidential speeches to analyses by Treasury Department bureaucrats, sheds valuable light on an all-too-neglected subject. Its work is available on the Internet at *http://taxhistory.tax.org*.

Statistics came from a wide range of sources, including the Internal Revenue Service, the Bureau of Economic Analysis, the Economic Report of the President, the Census Bureau, and the Bureau of Labor Statistics. The calculations on the relative tax burdens from 1956 and 1996 are the authors' own.

The information on Roy M. Speer comes primarily from the briefs, transcripts, and exhibits in *Roy M. and Lynnda L. Speer v. Commissioner,* Docket No. 6627-94, filed in U.S. Tax Court.

2: HAVEN'S GATE

We quoted liberally from Jerome Schneider's book *The Complete Guide to Offshore Money Havens: How to Make Millions, Protect Your Privacy, and Legally Avoid Taxes,* revised and updated 3rd ed. (Prima Publishing, 2000). Far more illuminating were a number of stories published in *Business Week,* the British paper *Mail on Sunday,* and in particular a profile of Schneider written by Douglas Frantz for the *Los Angeles Times,* "Island Bank King Profits as Industry Faces Scrutiny," published on April 16, 1989. Finally, John Shockey, a former official in the Comptroller of the Currency office, was kind enough to share his views of Schneider with us.

Statistics on the use of various deductions by the wealthy came from the Internal Revenue Service.

The information on the Katz family was gleaned from a few dozen cases filed in U.S. Tax Court, notably, *Aron B. Katz and Phyllis A. Katz v. Commissioner,* Docket No. 21043-94, and *Aron B. Katz and Phyllis A. Katz v. Commissioner,* Docket No. 181-98. We also relied on public records from several sources, most notably the Colorado secretary of state's office.

Information on the Pritzker family came from the Tax Court case *Estate of A. N. Pritzker, deceased, Jay A. Pritzker, Executor, v. Commissioner,* Docket No. 16867-90. We also relied on Donald L. Barlett and James B. Steele's 1994 book, *America: Who Really Pays the Taxes,* and various media accounts, most notably Paul Merrion's August 3, 1992, piece, "Pritzker Tax Showdown," in *Crain's Chicago Business.*

Details on Saul Zaentz and the tax shelters associated with the film *One Flew Over the Cuckoo's Nest* came from the Tax Court cases *Saul Zaentz and Linda Zaentz v. Commissioner,* Docket No. 3273-86; *Roger S. Baskes and Julie Baskes v. Commissioner,* Docket No. 26624-93; and *Calvin Eisenberg and Lana Eisenberg v. Commissioner,* Docket No. 16051-94.

Tony Schwartz's *New York Times* article "Cablevision's Brash Maverick," which appeared on August 3, 1981, provided much of the background on Charles Dolan and his company's unique corporate structure. The information on his dispute with the IRS came from *Charles F. Dolan and Helen A. Dolan v. Commissioner,* Docket No. 27550-92, filed in U.S. Tax Court.

Background information on Burton Kanter came from several sources, including many of the cases in which he's been involved, either as a petitioner or as an adviser to others disputing assessments made by the IRS. Alan Block's book *Masters of Paradise* (Transaction Publishing, 1990), a thorough account of Operation Tradewinds, also was invaluable for the history of Castle Bank.

Kanter's only significant loss to date, the 1999 decision that went against him, is massively chronicled in the consolidated Tax Court case *Investment Research Associates Ltd., et al. v. Commissioner,* Docket Nos. 43966-85, 712-86, 45273-86, 1350-87, 31301-87,

33557-87, 3456-88, 30830-88, 32103-88, 27444-89, 16421-90, 25875-90, 26251-90, 20211-91, 20219-91, 21555-91, 21616-91, 23178-91, 24002-91, 1984-92, 16164-92, 19314-92, 23743-92, 26918-92, 7557-93, 22884-93, 25976-93, 25981-93.

We are also grateful to a few dedicated IRS officials who spoke to us at length, off the record, about their frustrations and difficulties collecting taxes owed from sophisticated taxpayers.

3: GIMME SHELTER

Details on the Merrill Lynch tax shelter scheme were derived primarily from briefs, court rulings, transcripts, and exhibits in the following cases filed in U.S. Tax Court: *ACM Partnership, Southampton-Hamilton Company, Tax Matters Partner v. Commissioner*, Docket No. 10472-93; *ASA Investerings Partnership, AlliedSignal Inc., Tax Matters Partner v. Commissioner*, Docket No. 27320-96; and *Saba Partnership, Brunswick Corporation, Tax Matters Partner v. Commissioner*, Docket No. 1470-97.

The information on corporate income taxes and effective corporate tax rates are the authors' calculations based on data from the Internal Revenue Service's Statistics of Income Bulletin, various years; the Economic Report of the President, various years; and the Survey of Current Business, various years, published by the Bureau of Economic Analysis of the Department of Commerce. For the history of various provisions of the corporate income tax, we relied heavily on Robert M. Willan's book *Income Taxes: Concise History and Primer* (Claitor's Publishing Division, 1993).

We used the annual reports filed with the Securities and Exchange Commission to calculate the tax burden of individual companies and the thirty companies that make up the Dow Jones Industrial Index, unless otherwise noted.

Information on Apple Computer Incorporated's offshore subsidiaries and transfer pricing practices came from the Tax Court case *Apple Computer Inc. and Consolidated Subsidiaries v. Commissioner*, Docket No. 5496-93, while details on the company's use of offshore tax havens were taken from the Tax Court case *Halliburton Company and Subsidiaries v. Commissioner*, Docket No. 7838-96.

The history of Chrysler was downloaded from the company's old Internet site, *http://www.chrysler.com*. John Loffredo's testimony before the House Ways and Means Committee took place on June 30, 1999. Details on Chrysler's dispute with the IRS came from *Chrysler Corporation v. Commissioner*, Docket No. 22148-97, filed in U.S. Tax Court. The information on Daimler-Benz's tax dispute came from the Tax Court case *Daimler-Benz of North America Holding Company, Incorporated and Subsidiaries v. Commissioner*, Docket No. 8851-94.

As always, the work of several commentators in *Tax Notes Today* was helpful, notably that of Joseph A. Bankman and contributing editor Lee Sheppard.

4: SPECIAL EFFECTS

The rise and fall of Carolco Pictures and Mario F. Kassar, their wooing of stars and big-spending ways, was chronicled by several entertainment and business reporters. Stories from the *Los Angeles Times, Newsweek, Time, Forbes, Fortune, American Lawyer*, and the entertainment-industry trade journal *Variety* all provided valuable insights into the movie business that Kassar, his partner, Andrew Vajna, and their tax adviser, Peter Hoffman, for a time seemed to dominate. We made several efforts to interview both Kassar and Vajna, and traveled twice to Los Angeles with that purpose in mind, but both of them declined to speak with us. Citing attorney-client privilege, Peter Hoffman also declined to answer our questions.

Financial information about the company came from filings with the Securities and Exchange Commission. The details of the company's former cochairmen's disputes with the IRS came from *Mario F. Kassar v. Commissioner*, Docket No. 5195-96, and *Andrew G. Vajna and Cecilia M. Vajna v. Commissioner*, Docket No. 5038-96, both filed in U.S. Tax Court.

5: WELL-TO-DO

The boom and bust cycles of Oklahoma's economy, and the failure of many of the state's banking institutions, are well documented in numerous articles in the *Tulsa World* and the *Daily Oklahoman*. We also relied on a pair of thorough reports on the banking crisis of the late 1980s prepared by the Federal Deposit Insurance Corporation, *Managing the Crisis: The FDIC and the RTC Experience, 1980–1994*, and *History of the Eighties: Lessons for the Future*. The office of State Representative Russ Roach, along with Oklahoma's Department of Commerce and the State Finance Office, provided invaluable historical and current economic statistics on the state's last great boom and bust.

We relied on numerous sources for biographical information on George B. Kaiser, including interviews with fellow oilmen in Tulsa, William P. Barrett's March 4, 1991, article in *Forbes*, "Shrewd Sooner," and Jim Killacky's profile, "Quick-witted Tulsan Leads with One Eye," in the *Daily Oklahoman*, April 18, 1999.

We found Robin Robinson's daily reporting in the *Tulsa World* on the sale and recovery of the Bank of Oklahoma particularly helpful. We also sifted through dozens of documents the bank's holding company filed with the Securities and Exchange Commission regarding the bank's sale and subsequent financial performance.

The information on George B. Kaiser's tax situation comes from *George B. Kaiser and Betty E. Kaiser v. Commissioner*, Docket no. 10755-97, and *GBK Corporation and Subsidiaries v. Commissioner*, Docket no. 10756-97, both filed in the U.S. Tax Court.

The suits filed against Kaiser-Francis Oil Company by royalty owners in Oklahoma include *Galen Bridenstine, for himself and all others similarly situated v. Kaiser-Francis Oil Company et al.*, Docket no. CJ-95-54, filed in the District Court of Beaver County, Oklahoma, and *Murlene Mayo et al. v. Kaiser Francis Oil Co. et al.*, filed in the District Court of Grady County, Oklahoma.

Finally, we are indebted to the dozens of Oklahomans who told us their experiences living through the boom and the bust, which greatly broadened our understanding of the 1980s economic collapse that some, including George Kaiser himself, have said was statistically worse than the Dustbowl Depression of the 1930s.

6: SHORE LEAVE

The primary sources for this chapter are the filings, exhibits, and transcripts from *Seagate Technology, Inc., and Consolidated Subsidiaries v. Commissioner*, Docket No. 11660-

90, filed in U.S. Tax Court. We also relied on the corporate history the company posted on its Internet site (*http://www.seagate.com*), its proxies and annual reports filed with the Securities and Exchange Commission, trade adjustment assistance petitions it filed with the Employment and Training Administration of the Department of Labor, and interviews with current and former Seagate workers.

The decisions involving Compaq that we cited stemmed from a single Tax Court case, *Compaq Computer Corporation and Subsidiaries v. Commissioner*, Docket No. 24238-96. We were also aided by a fine analysis of the decision written by Burgess J. W. Raby and William L. Raby for *Tax Notes Today*, titled "Economic Substance Needed for Foreign Tax Credit," which appeared in the journal's October 6, 1999, edition.

The information on Compaq's accumulated offshore earnings, as well as those of Citigroup, the corporate parent of Citibank NA, MBNA Corporation, Apple Computer, Incorporated, CSX Corporation, and United Technologies, Incorporated, came from annual reports filed with the Securities and Exchange Commission.

7: TRICKS OF THE TRADE

Much of the information about Joe Conforte's business and the Mustang Ranch was compiled from *Nevada: True Tales from the Neon Wilderness*, by Jim Sloan (University of Utah Press, 1993). His suit against the IRS (and that of his ex-wife, Sally) was documented in the Tax Court cases *Sally Conforte v. Commissioner*, No. 8217-78; and *Joseph Conforte v. Commissioner*, No. 8218-78.

Accounts of the IRS's attempts to either sell or close the Mustang Ranch came from several news sources, including *The Columbian* (Vancouver, Wash.), the *Las Vegas Review-Journal*, the *Reno Gazette-Journal*, *Los Angeles Times*, the *National Law Journal*, and *The Independent* (London). We are grateful to CBS News for permission to reproduce portions of an interview of Joseph Conforte by *60 Minutes* anchor Mike Wallace, originally aired on November 2, 1971, under the title "House in Storey County."

Information about A.G.E. Corporation, which came to own Mustang Ranch for Conforte at one point, was from its voluntary petition to declare Chapter 11 bankruptcy, filed in September 1998 in U.S. Bankruptcy Court in Nevada. We relied on Nevada secretary of state filings for information about former sheriff Robert DelCarlo's involvement with A.G.E.

IRS Publication 15-A, *Employer's Supplemental Tax Guide*, revised in January 2000, provided a helpful explanation of the tax status of independent contractors versus employees. We also used court filings from David Burgess's case contending the prostitutes he employs are independent contractors filed in U.S. District Court in Reno, Nevada (*David Burgess, d.b.a. Old Bridge Ranch v. United States of America*, Case No. CV-N-93-713-HD). IRS data on self-employed individuals paying their taxes was cited in the February 1999 report by the U.S. General Accounting Office, *Tax Administration: Billions in Self-Employment Taxes Are Owed*.

8: THE MARKET WIZARD

The bulk of the information on Gary Bielfeldt and his battles with the Internal Revenue Service is derived from testimony and documents from the U.S. Tax Court case *Gary K.*

Bielfeldt et ux. v. Commissioner, Docket No. 5936-96. Several other cases proved helpful in documenting the pension plan aspects of the case, including *Bielfeldt & Company v. Commissioner,* Docket No. 116-96, 120-96, 6080-96, and 6081-96. Gary Bielfeldt also sued the IRS to contest the Service's denial of development costs for a downtown Peoria commercial center (see *Gary K. and Carlotta L. Bielfeldt v. Commissioner*, Docket No. 7264-96). Bielfeldt's son and business partner, David, sued the IRS in connection with his income tax returns (see *David and Julie Bielfeldt v. Commissioner*, Docket No 6155-96). His daughter, also a partner in Bielfeldt & Co., sued the IRS in *Linda S. Bielfeldt v. Commissioner*, Docket No. 6154-96.

We collected other valuable information about Bielfeldt, his business dealings, and his Tax Court cases in several telephone interviews, including with Gary Bielfeldt himself. Bielfeldt's former accountant, Jack A. Williams, and his former business partner, James E. Lauritsen, also provided particularly useful information. Commodities and Futures Trading Commission case information was obtained from the CFTC Internet site, *www.cftc.gov.*

Several sources about Bielfeldt's philanthropic activities included news articles in the *Chicago Tribune*. Bielfeldt's early business dealings and the growth of his company were well chronicled in *Market Wizards: Interviews with Top Traders*, by Jack D. Schwager (HarperBusiness, 1993). We are also grateful to the Foundation Center for providing financial information regarding the Bielfeldt Foundation.

9: GOING, GOING, GONE

Information about the Michael D. Dingman Center for Entrepreneurship at the University of Maryland was obtained from *www.rhsmith.umd.edu/dingman*, including financing information about the Dingman Center and speeches given by its founder. Transcripts of other speeches given at the Dingman Center, specifically on March 23 and 24, 1997, were obtained from the Ewing M. Kauffman Foundation (*www.emfk.org*), which sponsored the event.

Details of Dingman's success with Henley Group were well chronicled in several *Fortune* articles, including Brian Dumaine's January 1987 article "Michael Dingman: The Turnaround King Investors Love" and Alan Deutschman's July 1990 article "Reconstructing Plays for the 1990s." We also consulted press reports from *Crain's Chicago Business* and *Business Week*. For information on his investments in the Czech Republic, we referenced the *Prague Post,* the *New York Times*, and the *Rocky Mountain News* (Denver, Colo.).

Details about Dingman's La Jolla, California, residence came from an interview with real estate agent Edward Mracek, as well as from reports by the *San Diego Union-Tribune* and *Forbes*.

The 1924 *Cook v. Tait* decision, in which the Supreme Court found citizens living overseas to be responsible for U.S. taxes on their income, was retrieved from the Supreme Law Library, *www.supremelaw.com.*

Details of the Dart family's feud over citizenship and inheritance of the family's multibillion-dollar cup company were well told in Norman Sinclair's October 1998 *Detroit News* article "Dart Family Feud Comes to an End," as well as in the *St. Petersburg Times* and the *Wall Street Journal*. The stories of other expatriate billionaires, including Campbell Soup heir John Dorrance III, were told in Robert Lenzner and Philippe Mao's article "The New Refugees" published in *Forbes* in November 1994. Ireland's passport for cash program was detailed in an April 1998 article by Agency France Presse, as well as in *The Guardian* of London.

Dart Container Corporation's suit against the IRS was documented by Jerry Moskal of Gannett News Service in his article "Dart Container Fights IRS," published in June 1999. Other material about enforcement of the tax expatriate law came from the testimony of tax attorney William K. Norman before the House Ways and Means Oversight Subcommittee on March 27, 1995. Also see the 1995 *Congressional Record* for Senator Edward Kennedy's speech about legislation to increase enforcement against tax expatriates.

10: PACKAGE DEAL

The bulk of the information regarding DHL's case against the IRS is from the U.S. Tax Court case *DHL Corp. et al. v. Commissioner*, Docket No. 26103-95. We relied heavily on Tax Court Judge Joel Gerber's opinion in the case, as well as the testimony of DHL president William A. Robinson and letters between the company's shareholders and attorneys. Federal Express's complaint about DHL's level of international ownership and the company's reply, also included in this case file, were helpful as well.

Information about the culture, geography, and politics of Saipan and the U.S. Commonwealth of the Northern Mariana Islands was culled from many sources, most notably *www.saipan.com*.

Descriptions of DHL cofounder Larry Hillblom's life at the University of California, Berkeley, as well as on Saipan, were derived from a May 23, 1995, DHL press release. Details of the paternity suits brought against his estate were well chronicled in Krysten Crawford's *American Lawyer* article "Misplaced Trust," published on October 26, 1999.

11: SWEET CHARITY

Much of the information about the Bishop Estate and its trustees came from documents filed with the Hawaii Circuit Court, particularly the Hawaii attorney general's petition to have the trustees removed, filed on October 23, 1998, and the closing agreement between the Bishop Estate and the Internal Revenue Service, filed on August 24, 1999. We also found articles from the *Honolulu Star-Bulletin* helpful, particularly those written by Rick Daysog. Information about the Bishop Estate's finances was gleaned from its Form 990, filed with the IRS in 1997, and from supporting documents found on the Bishop Estate's Web site, *www.ksbe.edu*. We interviewed several public officials who dealt with the Bishop Estate matter, including Hawaii deputy attorney general Hugh Jones, former attorney general Margery Bronster, and Hawaii state bar association president Randall Roth, as well as Bishop Estate trustee Lokelani Lindsey. We are grateful to the Center for Responsive Politics for providing valuable lobbying information.

We gathered financial data for the American Association of Retired Persons from its 1998 annual report, and for the American Red Cross from its 1997 financial report. The

Social Security Administration's Web site (*www.ssa.gov*) provided data on the Social Security Trust Fund.

We used the Foundation for Clean Air Progress's 1998 IRS Form 990 to gain financial and executive information about the organization. We also relied on the Web sites of the American Highway Users Alliance, the American Trucking Associations, and the American Petroleum Institute.

In researching the Greater Kansas City Community Foundation, we found the organization's 1996 and 1997 IRS Form 990s particularly helpful, as well as an interview with foundation donor Richard A. Bloch.

Information about the Foundation for New Era Philanthropy came from Securities and Exchange Commissions filings, at *www.sec.gov*, press reports in *Christianity Today* and the *Philadelphia Inquirer*, as well as statements from Prudential Securities, filed on November 15, 1996, and the Nature Conservancy, in November 1998.

Finally, statistics on tax-exempt organizations came from a number of sources, including the 1999 IRS Organization Blueprint, a February 1995 report by the U.S. General Accounting Office (*www.gao.gov*), a report in the 1998–99 IRS Winter Statistics of Income Bulletin, and *IRS Handbook 9.5*, Section 3.3.2., focusing on exempt-organization fraud. We are also indebted to former IRS Exempt Organizations director Marcus Owens for his help in understanding this often complex tax designation.

12: HIDE-AND-SEEK

We are particularly grateful to former IRS special agent John Thomas, who gave us a great deal of insight into Joseph Ross's tax evasion scheme, his flight from justice, and the IRS's long pursuit of him. We made extensive use of the public portion of the IRS case file on Ross, which included the original indictment against him and supplemented charges added later as Thomas continued to doggedly pursue him. The file also contained information on his life as a fugitive and the somewhat poignant "wanted" poster. For background, we also relied on various news accounts, including stories from the *Tulsa World*, the *Daily Oklahoman*, and the *Vancouver Sun*.

We tracked Ross down through the Internet site his wife maintains, *www.belizereport.com*. Apparently, being a fugitive from the IRS doesn't require maintaining a low profile. We traveled as far as Ross's resort in Belize to try to secure an on-the-record interview with him, but he declined to speak for the record.

13: WHAT YOU CAN DO

The information on the Skalas came from *Christopher A. and Nuris Skala v. Commissioner*, Docket No. 16559-98. Information on abusive trusts, and contacting the IRS about them, can be found on the IRS's Internet site at *www.irs.gov/ind_info/abuse/index.html*.

CONCLUSION

Although the conclusion was largely a review and analysis of the preceding chapters, there were several key sources used in its writing. Charles Adams's *For Good and Evil* (Madison Books, 1993) once again provided valuable historical perspective. We again consulted

James Dale Davidson and Lord William Rees-Mogg's *The Sovereign Individual* (Simon & Schuster, 1997), as well as Hans-Peter Martin and Harald Schumann's *The Global Trap: Globalization and the Assault on Prosperity and Democracy* (Zed Books Ltd., 1997).

The Transactional Records Clearinghouse at Syracuse University (*http://trac.syr.edu*) proved to be a useful resource for IRS statistics. We relied heavily on the respected publication *Tax Notes* as a source of congressional hearings, GAO reports, news stories, and analysis.

We are indebted to Jack Blum for his insights on financial havens and the cyberspace explosion.

The ending quote from Abraham Lincoln can be found in *Lincoln: Speeches and Writings 1859–1865* (Library of America, 1989), in his "Speech to the 164th Ohio Regiment."

About the Center for Public Integrity

The Center for Public Integrity began operation in May 1990. It is a nonprofit, nonpartisan research organization founded so that important national issues can be investigated and analyzed without the normal time or space limitations. Described as a "watchdog in the corridors of power" by *National Journal*, the Center has investigated and disseminated a wide array of information in more than sixty published Center reports since its inception. More than 5,000 news media stories have referenced the Center's findings or perspectives about public service and ethics-related issues. Since 1996, Center reports have won awards for excellence given by the Society of Professional Journalists and Investigative Reporters and Editors. The Center's books and studies are resources for journalists, academics, and the general public, with databases, backup files of government documents, and other information available as well.

As with its previous books and reports, the views expressed herein do not necessarily reflect the views of individual members of the Center for Public Integrity's board of directors or advisory board. Besides revenue from the sale of publications and consulting contracts with news organizations, the Center is supported by contributions from philanthropic foundations and individuals. Major donors and IRS 990 reports for the past three years are listed on the Center's Web site. We do not accept money from corporations, labor unions, governments, advocacy organizations, or advertisers. To access the most recent findings of the Center, including additional or updated information and photographs of some of the people featured in *The Cheating of America*, you can visit the Center's Web site at *www.publicintegrity.org*, or subscribe to *The Public i*, the Center's award-winning investigative report, on-line at *www.public-i.org*.

For more information, to buy books and other publications, or to become a member of the Center, contact the Center for Public Integrity:

The Center for Public Integrity
910 Seventeenth Street, N.W.
Seventh Floor
Washington, DC 20006

E-mail: *contact @publicintegrity.org*
Internet: *www.publicintegrity.org*
On-line investigative report: *http://www.public-i.org*
Telephone: (202) 466-1300
Facsimile: (202) 466-1101

Index